IMAGES
*of America*

# TARRYTOWN AND SLEEPY HOLLOW IN THE 20TH CENTURY

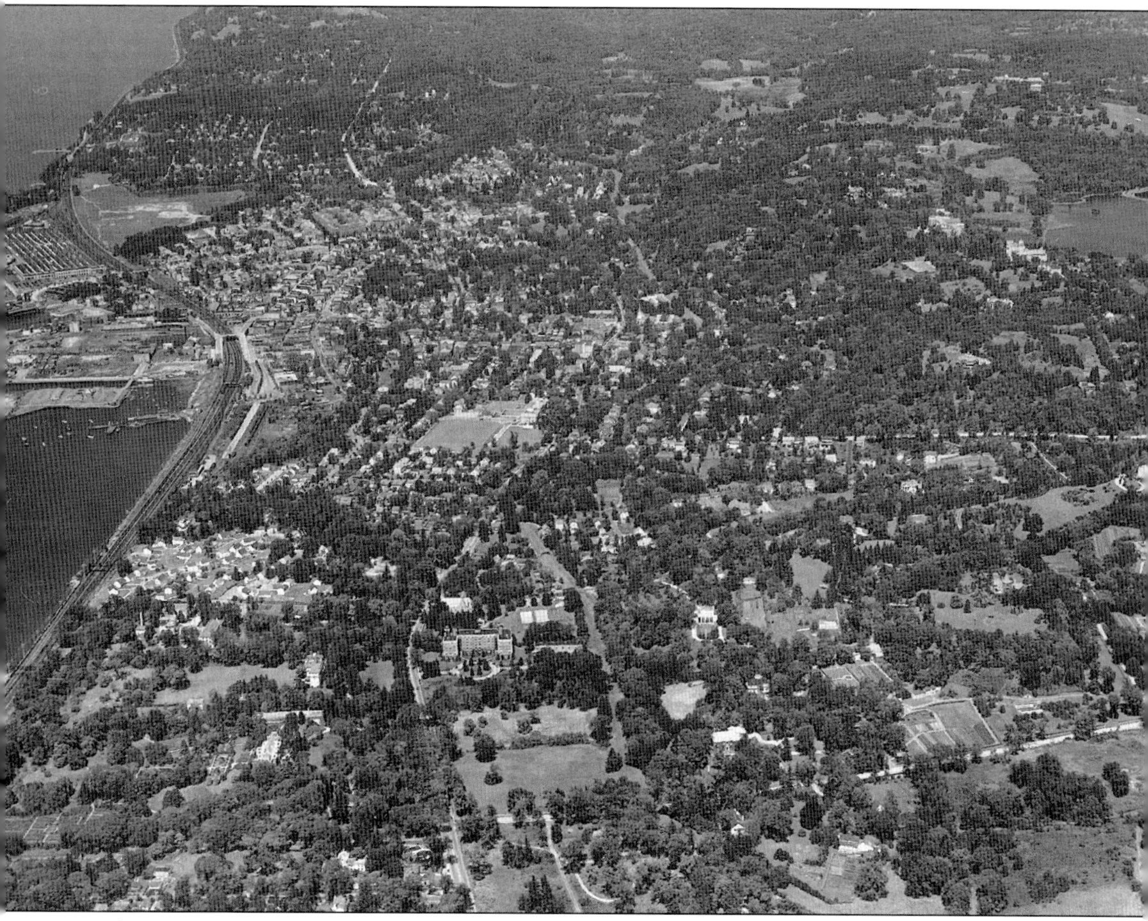

This is an aerial view of Tarrytown and Sleepy Hollow during the mid-20th century. (Courtesy of the Historical Society, Inc., serving Sleepy Hollow and Tarrytown.)

**On the Cover:** Girl Scouts and Brownies march in the Memorial Day parade on May 30, 1952. Hundreds of spectators lined Broadway to watch the parade as it made its way through both villages. (Courtesy of the Historical Society, Inc., serving Sleepy Hollow and Tarrytown.)

IMAGES
*of America*

# Tarrytown and Sleepy Hollow in the 20th Century

MaryAnn Marshall and Sara Mascia

ARCADIA
PUBLISHING

ISBN 978-0-7385-7373-1

Published by Arcadia Publishing
Charleston, South Carolina

Printed in the United States of America

Library of Congress Control Number: 2010925885

For all general information, please contact Arcadia Publishing:
Telephone 843-853-2070
Fax 843-853-0044
E-mail sales@arcadiapublishing.com
For customer service and orders:
Toll-Free 1-888-313-2665

Visit us on the Internet at www.arcadiapublishing.com

# Contents

# ACKNOWLEDGMENTS

We would like to thank the countless historians, archivists, and volunteers who meticulously recorded information over the years about the photograph collection for the files at the Historical Society, Inc., serving Sleepy Hollow and Tarrytown. We were fortunate to have the vast archives of the Historical Society, Inc., to utilize while researching this book. Also essential was the information contained in the *History of the Tarrytowns* by Jeff Canning and Wally Buxton, *The Centennial History of North Tarrytown* by Lucille and Theodore Hutchinson, and GM *Tarrytown: An Autobiography* by Jared C. McDade.

We are grateful to Elizabeth Laite and Tara Van Tassell for their generous support, research expertise, and editorial assistance. Heartfelt thanks are offered to Tara for her many hours scanning these incredible photographs.

Special thanks are extended to Beverly Jansen, Leonard Abraham, the Community Opportunity Center, and Eileen Pilla. We would also like to acknowledge the current village historians—Henry Steiner from Sleepy Hollow and Richard Miller from Tarrytown, who continue to document local history for the archives of the society. Finally, we are particularly appreciative to the residents of Tarrytown and Sleepy Hollow who continue to donate their photographs to our collection. All images are from the collection of the Historical Society, Inc.

# INTRODUCTION

Tarrytown and Sleepy Hollow (formerly North Tarrytown) are neighboring Hudson River villages steeped in tradition and literary legends. Connected by a public school system, a shared local library, and a historical society that represents both villages, residents collectively experienced the economic, social, political, and cultural changes that occurred during the 20th century. This volume is not meant to present a complete detailed history of that period; instead, chapter themes were chosen by the subject matter of the photographs donated by residents to the archives at the Historical Society, Inc., serving Sleepy Hollow and Tarrytown.

Several wonderful local photographers chronicled the history of the villages during the 20th century. Included in the society's collection and this book are images by Leonard Abraham, Leslie V. Case, Edward Coles, Joseph V. De Michele, Catherine McCaul, Fred Peters, and Alfred Trevillian, along with many pictures from unidentified photographers who captured moments in history.

To illustrate this period of time, this book includes a sampling of images of local personalities, the changing business landscape, the growth and consolidation of the public schools, residential development, the participation of the local population in various business and social organizations, and a selection of appealing photographs that show the changes in fashion over the years. Also chronicled is the construction of the Tappan Zee Bridge, which provided easy access between Westchester and Rockland Counties. This important link across the Hudson River enabled increased commerce, commuter access to the railroad, and visitors to this historical region. The impact of this massive public project continues to resonate in the villages to this day. The Hudson River played a vital role in the changing 20th-century landscape, as the villages first industrialized and later reclaimed the riverfront for residential purposes. For residents, the majesty of the river was a continued inspiration through all the highs and lows of the century.

# *One*

# Celebrations

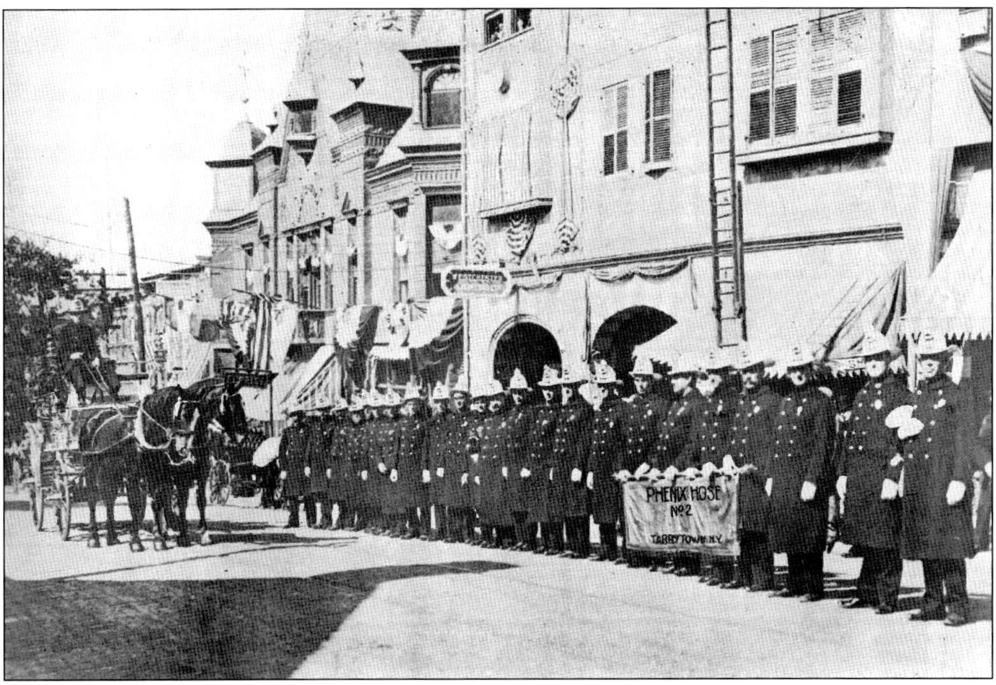


Local residents planned and participated in numerous grand celebrations during the 20th century. The Hudson Fulton Celebration in 1909 was arguably the most spectacular. Celebrating Henry Hudson's 1609 trip up the Hudson River and Robert Fulton's successful launching of the steamboat in 1807, the festivities lasted from September 25 to October 29 throughout the entire Hudson River Valley. Local volunteer firefighters, including these members of Phenix Hose No. 2, participated in several dress parades.

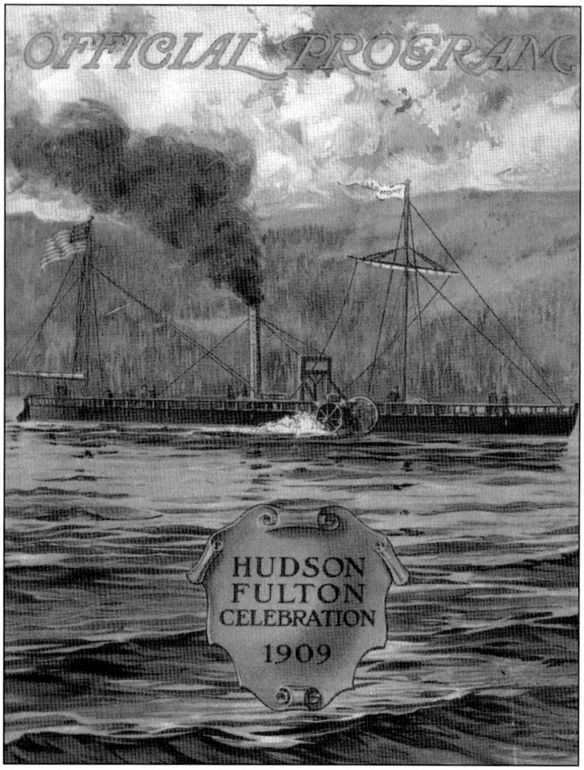


Each community published one or more programs detailing local events. Under the leadership of John Gross, the local committee from the Tarrytowns planned an enormous parade followed by an evening of fireworks on September 28, 1909, the lighting of beacon fires in Tarrytown Heights (simulating the communication fires of native peoples), formal dinners, afternoon picnics, dances, and local participation in the great naval parade on the river.

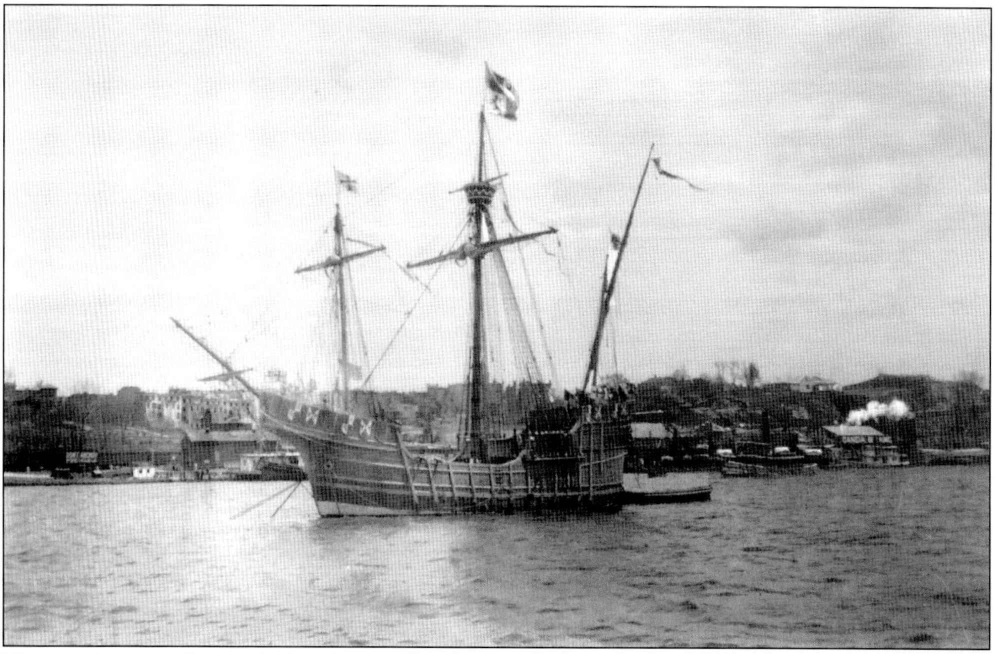

The naval parade boasted a flotilla of 1,542 ships including the U.S. Navy's entire Atlantic Fleet. A replica of the *Half Moon*, built at the Royal Ship Yards in Amsterdam by master craftsmen in the Netherlands, was one of the most popular ships in the parade. At a cost of $40,000, the "new" *Half Moon* was launched on April 15, 1909, and arrived in Tarrytown on September 27.

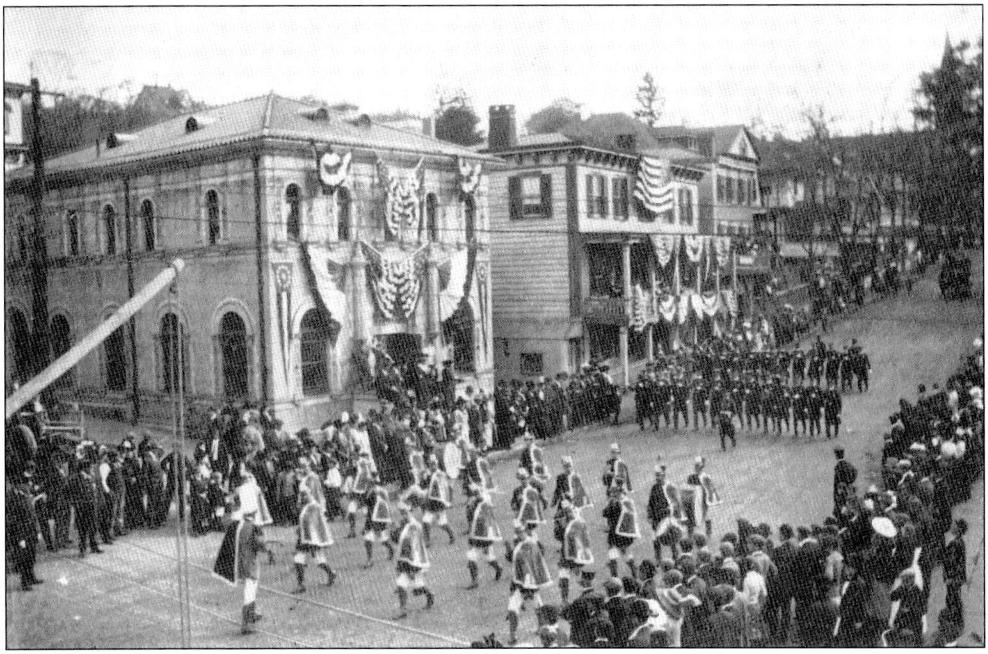

Thousands of residents and visitors turned out for what became the largest parade that has ever traveled down Broadway through the villages. Over 50 floats and nearly an equal number of bands passed by houses decorated with red, white, and blue bunting. The parade included regiments of British, French, and German marines.

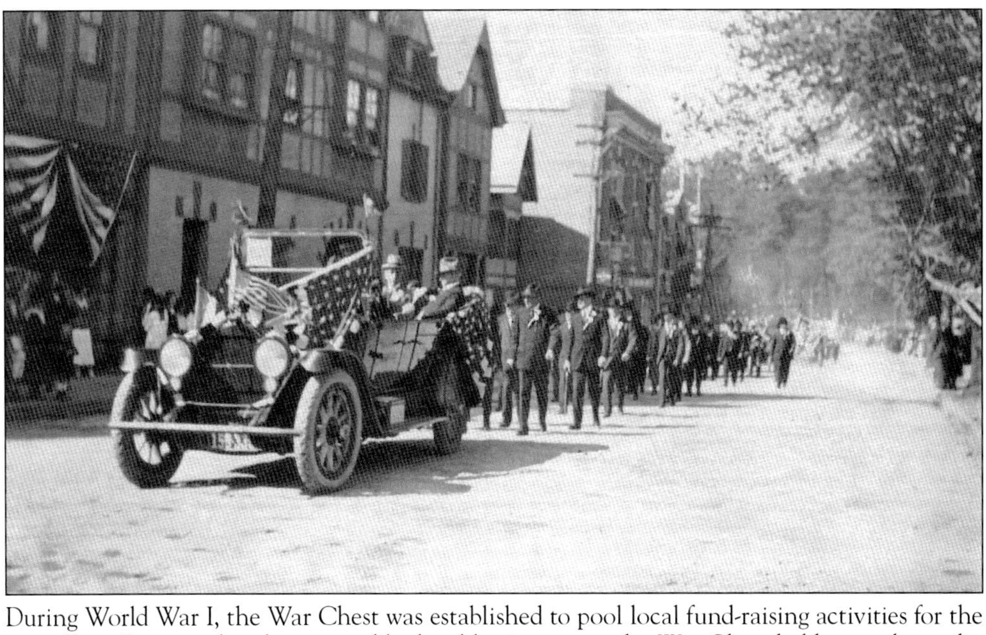

During World War I, the War Chest was established to pool local fund-raising activities for the war effort. Organized and supported by local businessmen, the War Chest held annual parades and other fund-raising celebrations. By 1919, local contributions to the Red Cross totaled $112,305, with the War Chest contributing over 90 percent of those dollars. The 1918 War Chest parade is pictured here.

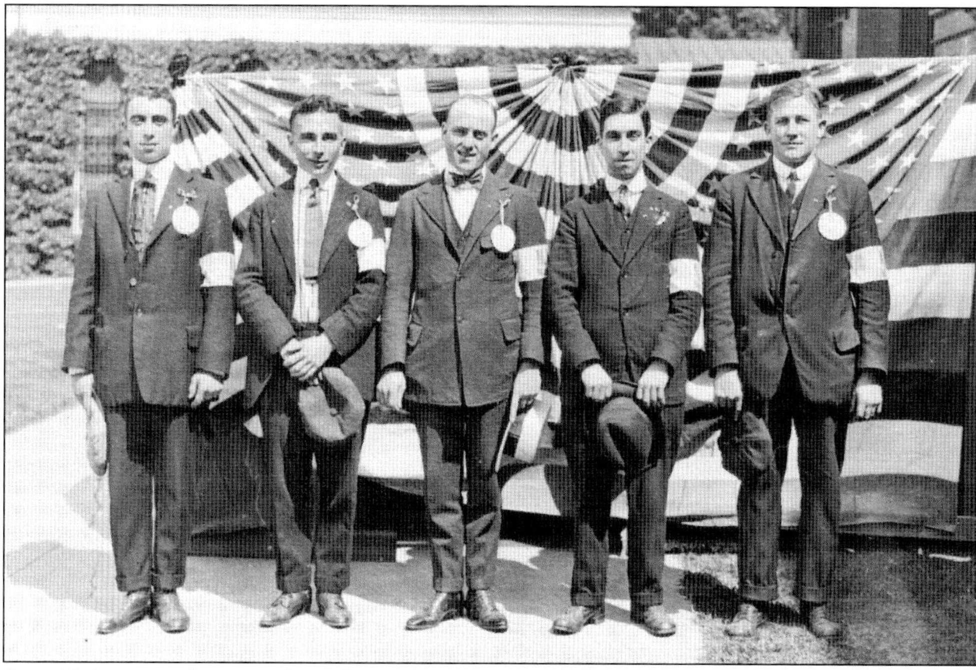

Over 700 men and women from the Tarrytowns served during World War I. After the armistice was signed, numerous commemorative events were held, including the Welcome Home Celebration on October 9, 1919. On that day, a memorial was unveiled along Broadway in front of Washington Irving High School (now the Landmark Condominiums). During the dedication ceremony, several local veterans were recognized for their service during the "war to end all wars."

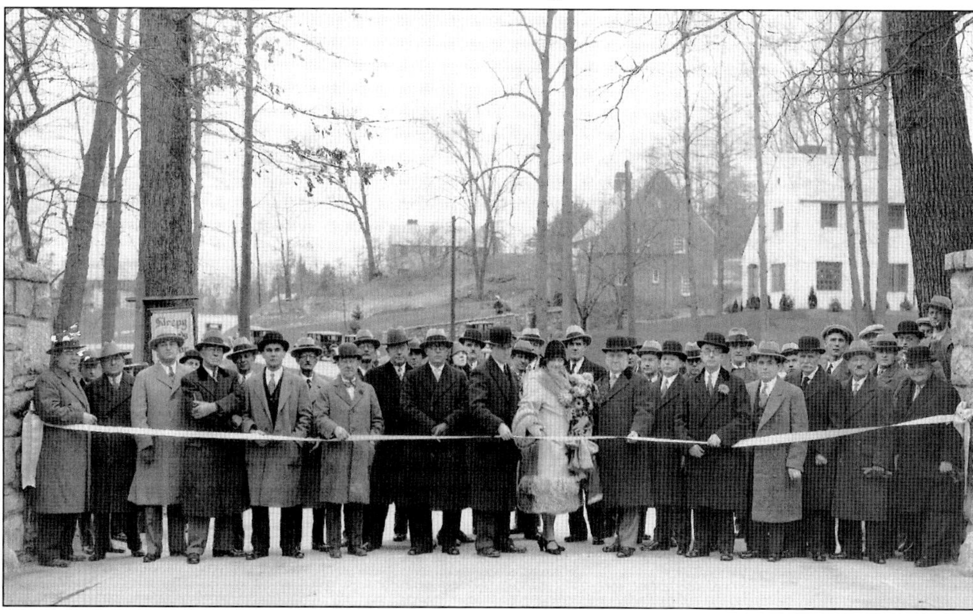

In 1927, Sleepy Hollow Manor, Inc., purchased 53 acres of the former John C. Fremont estate in order to create a housing development containing unique houses with private roads and a full-service maintenance plan. The ribbon-cutting celebration featured local politicians and businessmen from both villages and an unidentified Metropolitan Opera star.

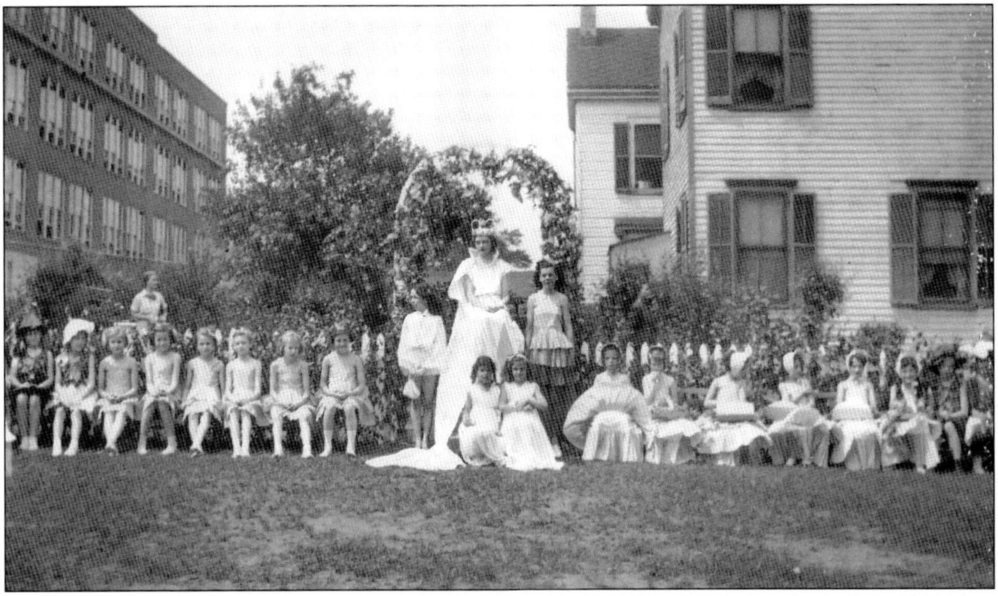

Each spring, May Day was celebrated in North Tarrytown. Shown here with students from her court is 1937 May queen Sylvia Page. The photograph of celebrants was taken in front of the old North Tarrytown High School.

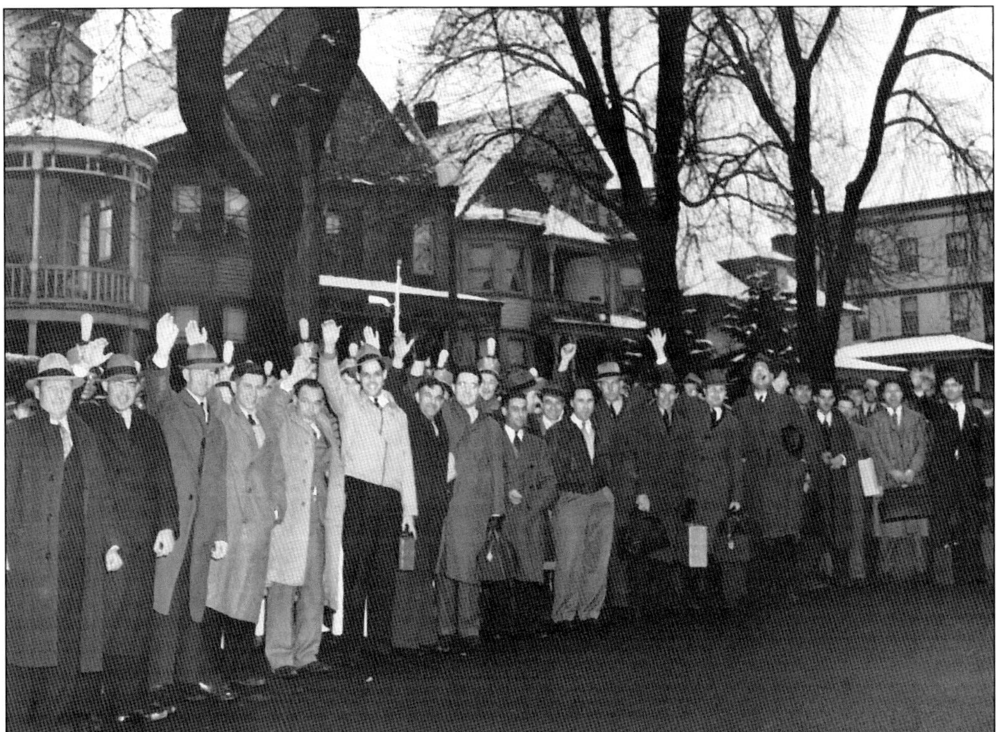

After the attack on Pearl Harbor catapulted the country into World War II, Tarrytowners responded to the call of duty. Here local draftees wave good-bye on their way to the Tarrytown train station in 1942. Family and friends said farewell while members of local bands played patriotic songs.

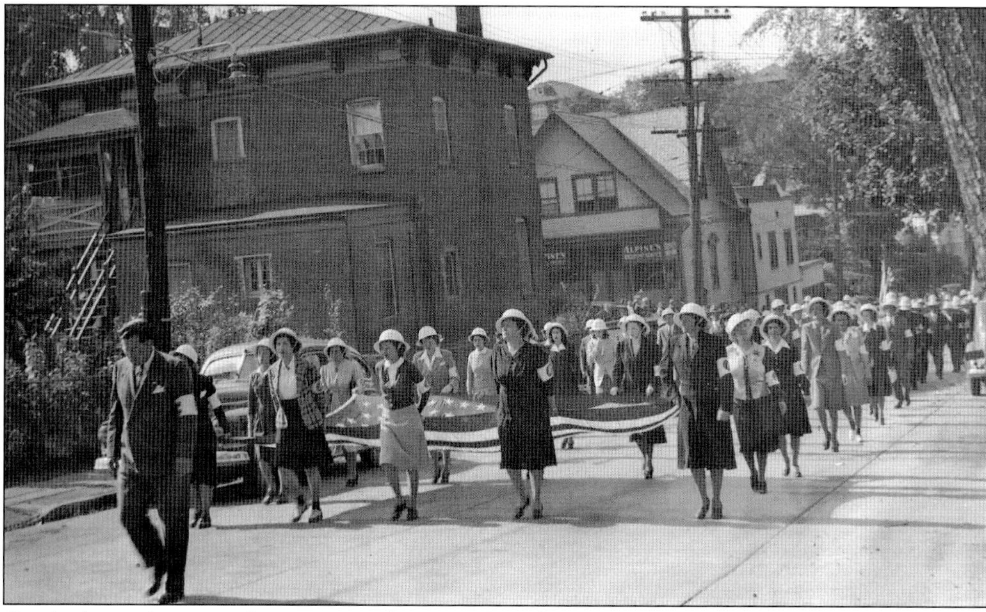

On the home front, residents scrimped, rationed, and saved to support the war effort. As they did in World War I, local residents contributed to the War Chest. Several fund-raising campaigns and War Chest parades were held to support the Red Cross and other organizations gathering supplies for the troops. In this image, the Women's Auxiliary is shown marching up Central Avenue during the 1944 War Chest parade.

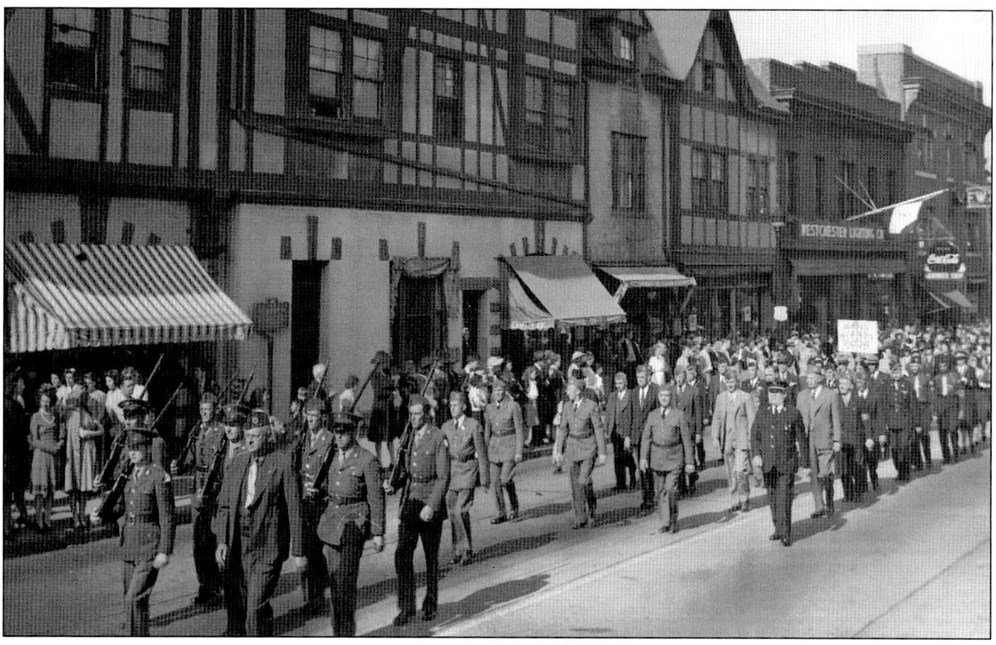


Near the end of World War II, the Honor Roll Dedication Parade was held in 1944 in tribute to the many local residents who were serving overseas. The parade passed by the temporary honor roll (at right, not shown), which was erected in front of the F. R. Pierson School that year. The names of 71 servicemen who paid the ultimate price were later immortalized on the World War II monument in the northeast corner of Patriots Park.

The United Nations officially came into existence on October 24, 1945, when the charter was ratified by China, France, the Soviet Union, the United Kingdom, the United States, and a majority of other signatories. In 1947, when the organization was just two years old, Tarrytown and North Tarrytown were chosen as America's "Model Community" to promote peace, American awareness, and support of the UN.

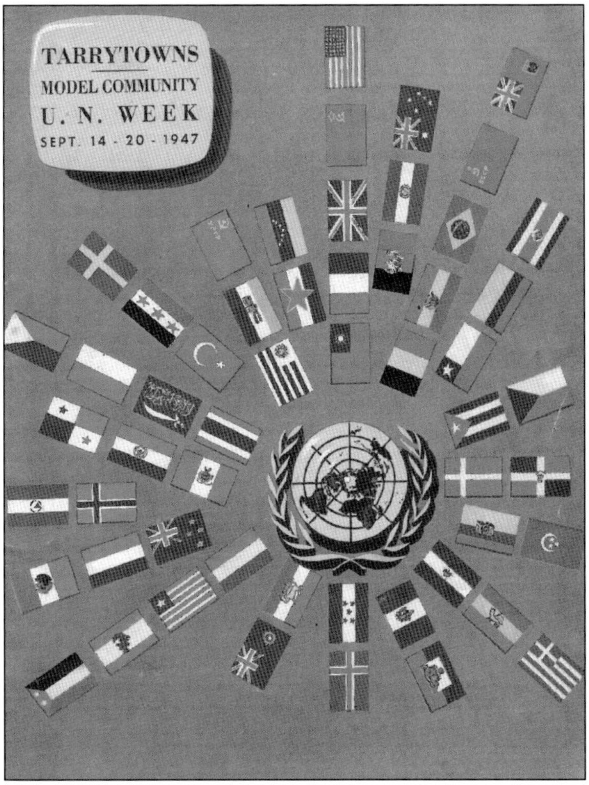


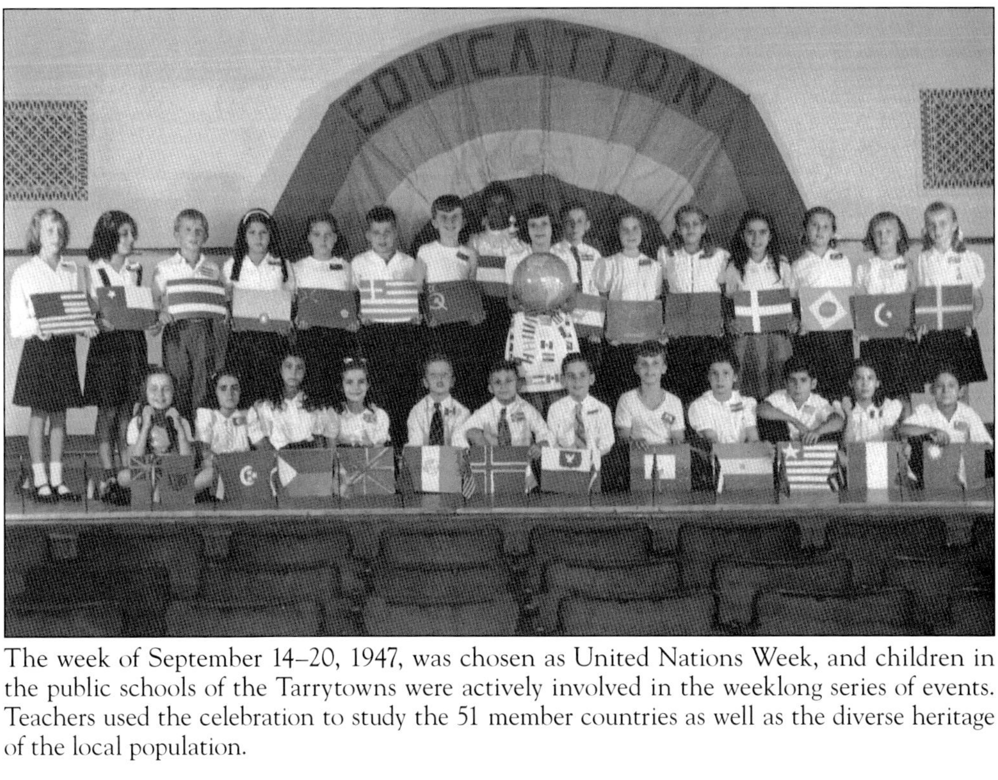


The week of September 14–20, 1947, was chosen as United Nations Week, and children in the public schools of the Tarrytowns were actively involved in the weeklong series of events. Teachers used the celebration to study the 51 member countries as well as the diverse heritage of the local population.

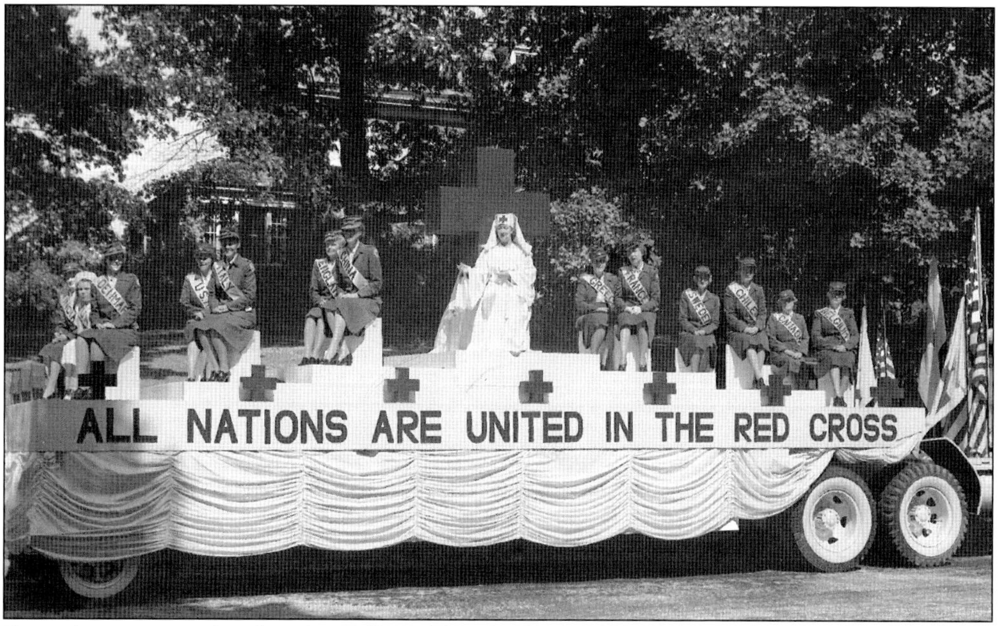


Special services in the churches followed by an afternoon service at Washington Irving High School opened the celebration. Nightly entertainment by groups representing UN member countries continued throughout the week. A gala parade on September 20, dedicated to the United States, brought the festivities to a close. The local chapter of the National American Red Cross entered one of the most popular and prize-winning floats.

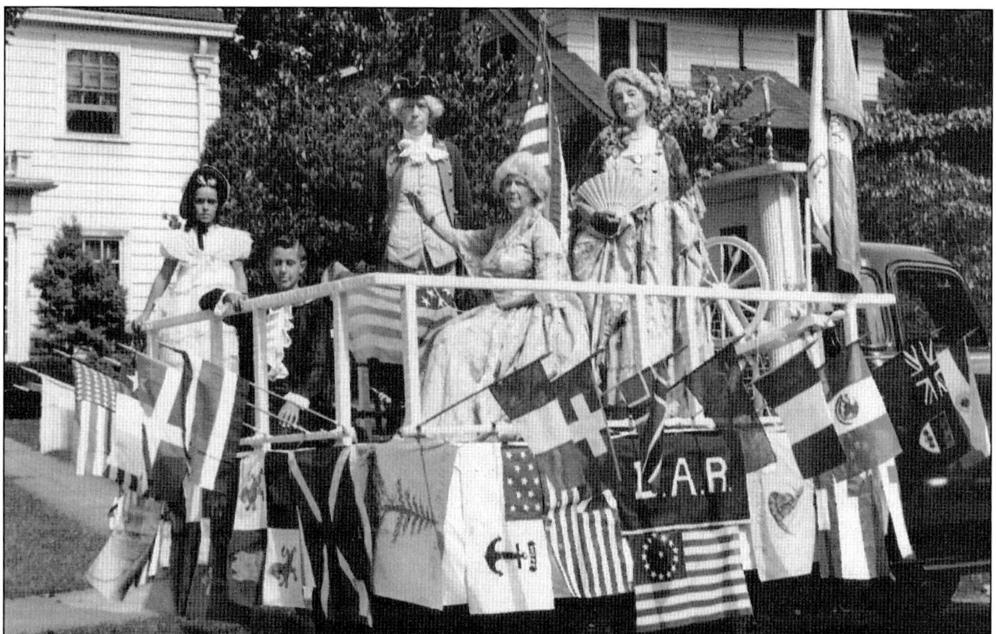

Ladies from the Tarrytown chapter of the Daughters of the American Revolution (DAR), founded in 1925 with Sarah Grey Case as organizing regent, wore their colorful colonial costumes for the DAR float. Participants included members from Tarrytown, North Tarrytown, and the surrounding communities.

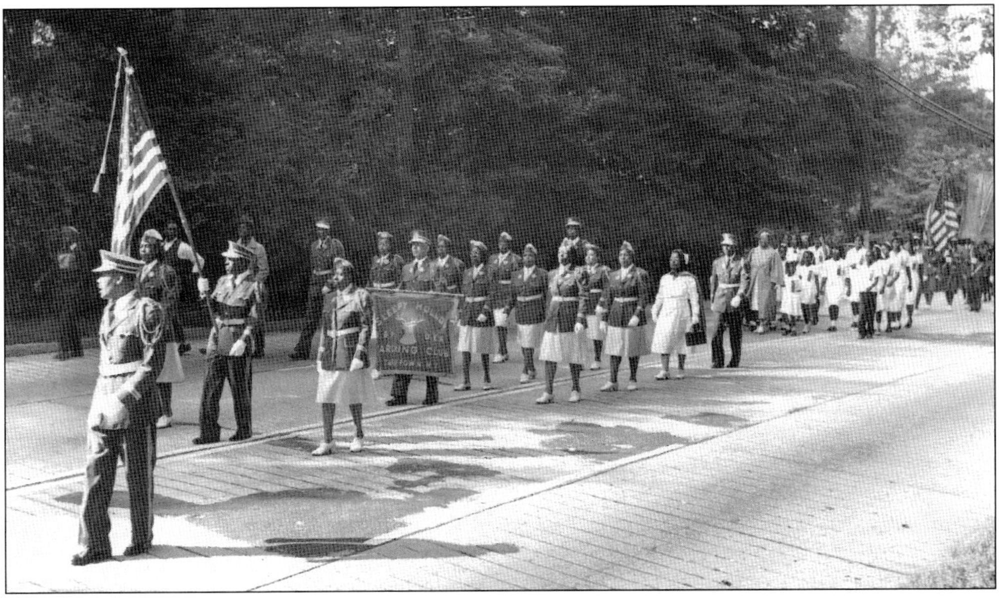

The parade involved 6,300 participants representing 75 organizations, 30 floats, and 50 bands. An estimated 50,000 spectators lined the streets. Marchers included contingents of the army, navy, air corps, fraternal organizations, volunteer firefighters from Tarrytown and North Tarrytown, Boy Scouts, Girl Scouts, veterans, the Red Cross, service clubs, labor unions, and the Sleepy Hollow Marching Club.

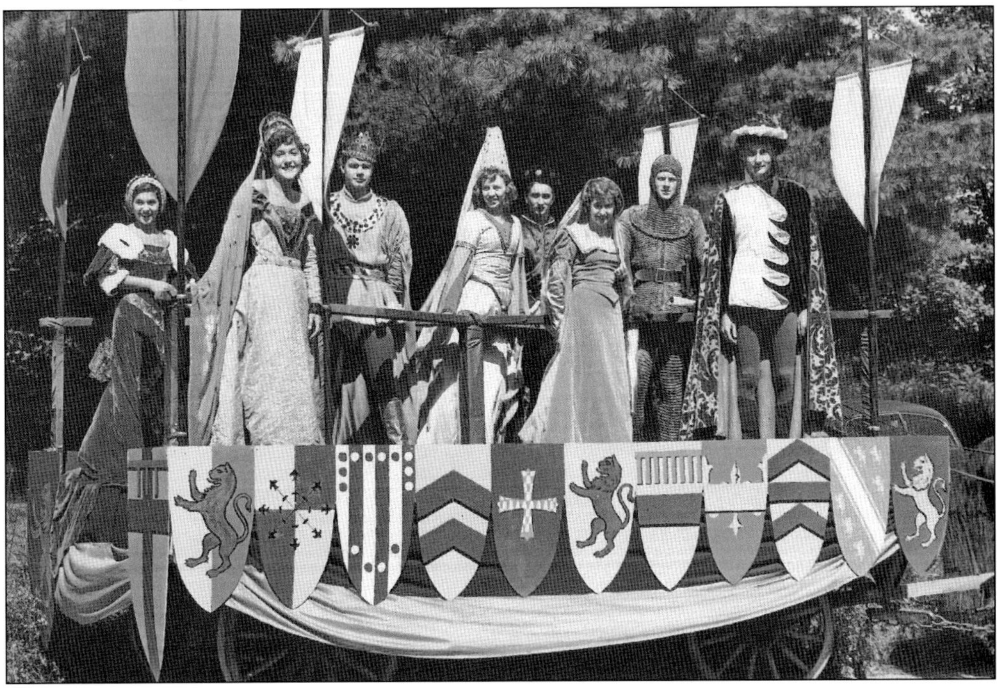

The parade, which lasted 2 hours and 15 minutes, started in Philipse Manor and ended at the Washington Irving High School stadium. One of the most popular and appealing floats depicted the Magna Carta, with men and women attired in medieval dress accompanied by knights on horseback.

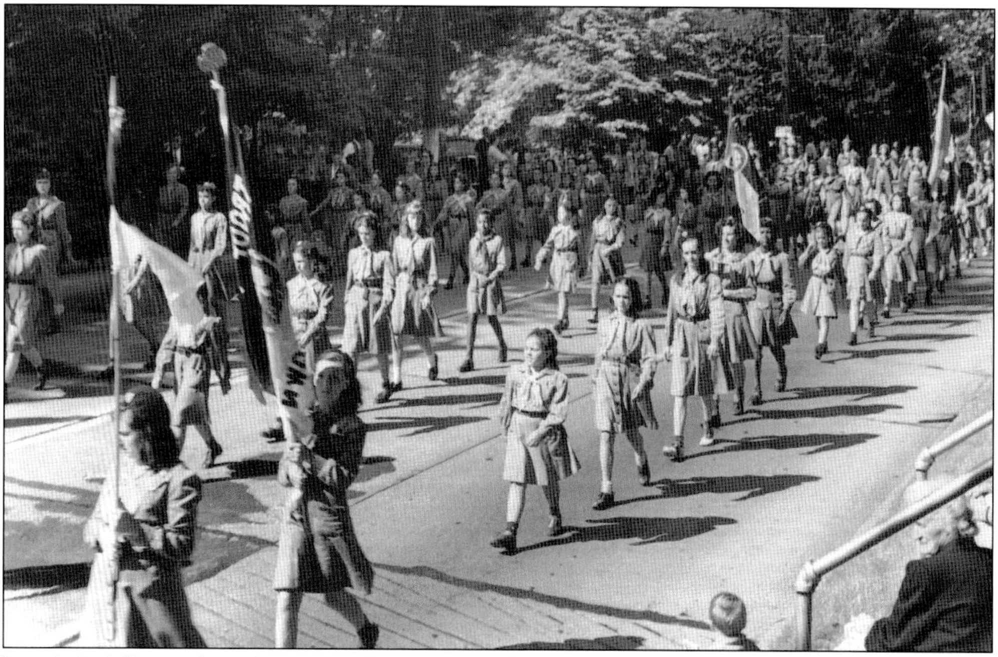

Local Girl Scouts have been marching in parades since they were formed in 1919 under the sponsorship of Mrs. John D. Rockefeller Jr. (Abby Aldrich), with headquarters at the First Reformed Church. The troops were open to all girls of North Tarrytown, Tarrytown, and Pocantico Hills and ranged in age from 7 to 17.

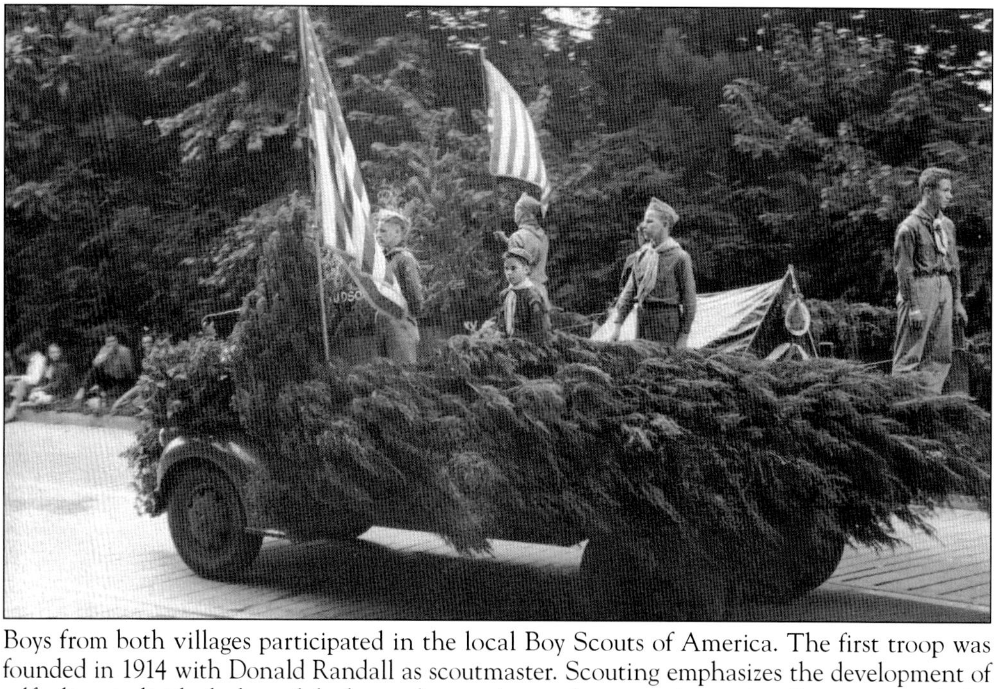

Boys from both villages participated in the local Boy Scouts of America. The first troop was founded in 1914 with Donald Randall as scoutmaster. Scouting emphasizes the development of self-reliant individuals through badge work, camping, and community service. Every year, both the Boy Scouts and Girl Scouts march in community-sponsored parades as well as special occasion celebrations such as the UN Parade.

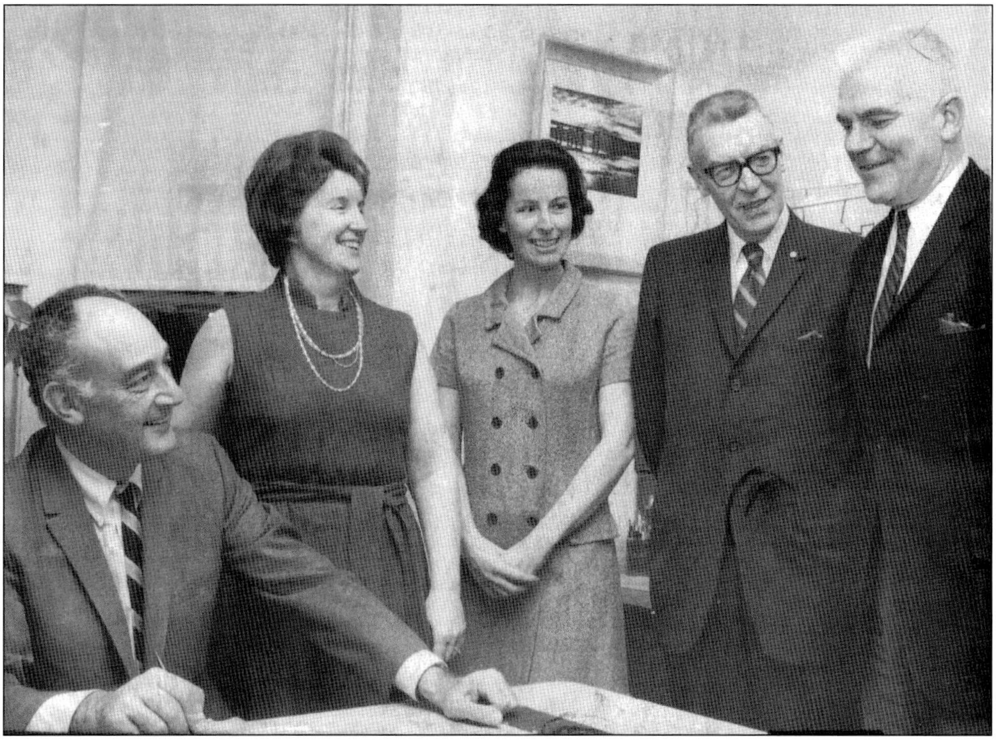

After the state passed the General Village Law that authorized local hamlets with the power to set up their own police and fire departments, the Village of Tarrytown incorporated in 1870. In 1970, the Centennial Committee began planning a lavish weeklong celebration. Mayor Anthony Veteran (far right) appointed David Loew (left) to head the 15-person committee that included (from left to right) Elizabeth Mascia, Ann Phillips, and George Condit.

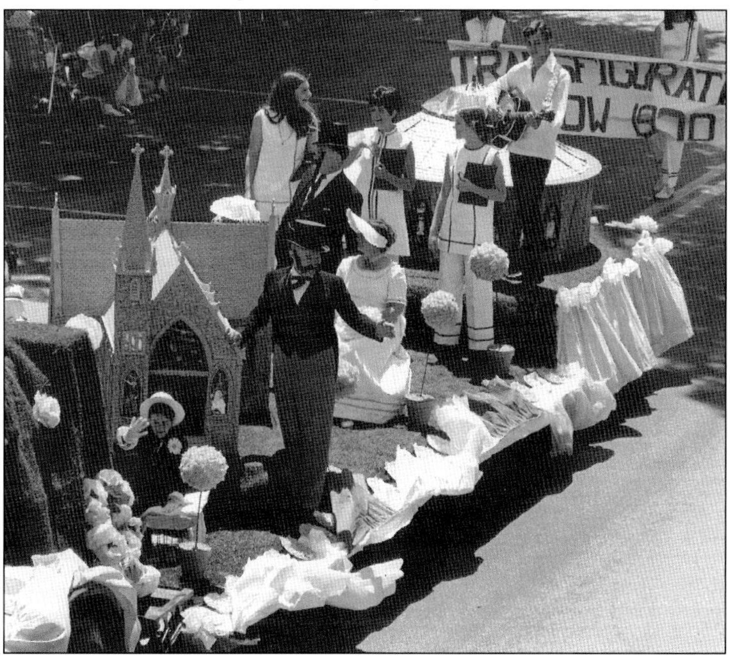

The Tarrytown centennial celebration took place during the week of June 6–13, 1970. Events included a fishing derby, a battle of the bands, picnics, the crowning of a centennial queen, an old-fashioned wedding, a commemorative play, and a large parade. The parade was held on the final day and included dozens of floats created by local service organizations commemorating the different events in Tarrytown's history.

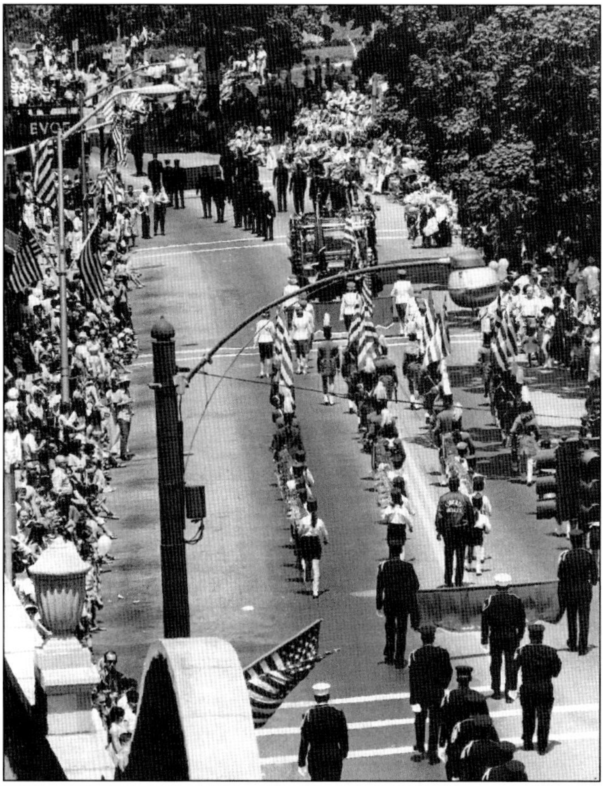

Thousands of residents and visitors lined the parade route along Broadway from south of the Tappan Zee Bridge to Sleepy Hollow High School. Many of the spectators were dressed in historic costumes as they watched 33 bands and 6,000 marchers.

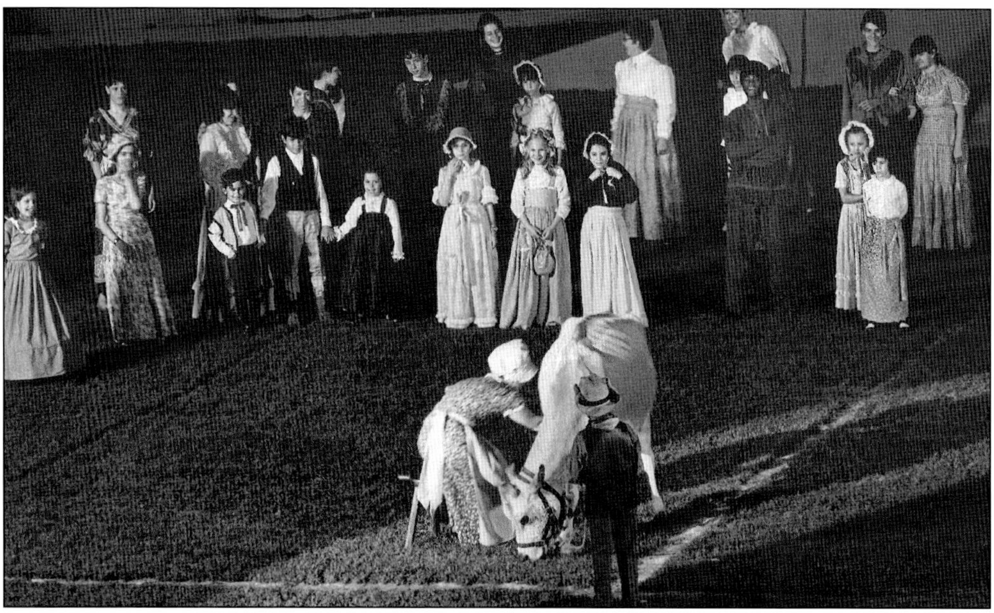

During Centennial Week, a play that focused on different events in the history of the village was presented each evening on the athletic field at Washington Irving Junior High School. *Tarrytown: A View from the Tappan Zee* was narrated by Centennial Committee members and had a cast of hundreds. The *Tarrytown Daily News* reported that there were more than 2,000 attendees at each performance.

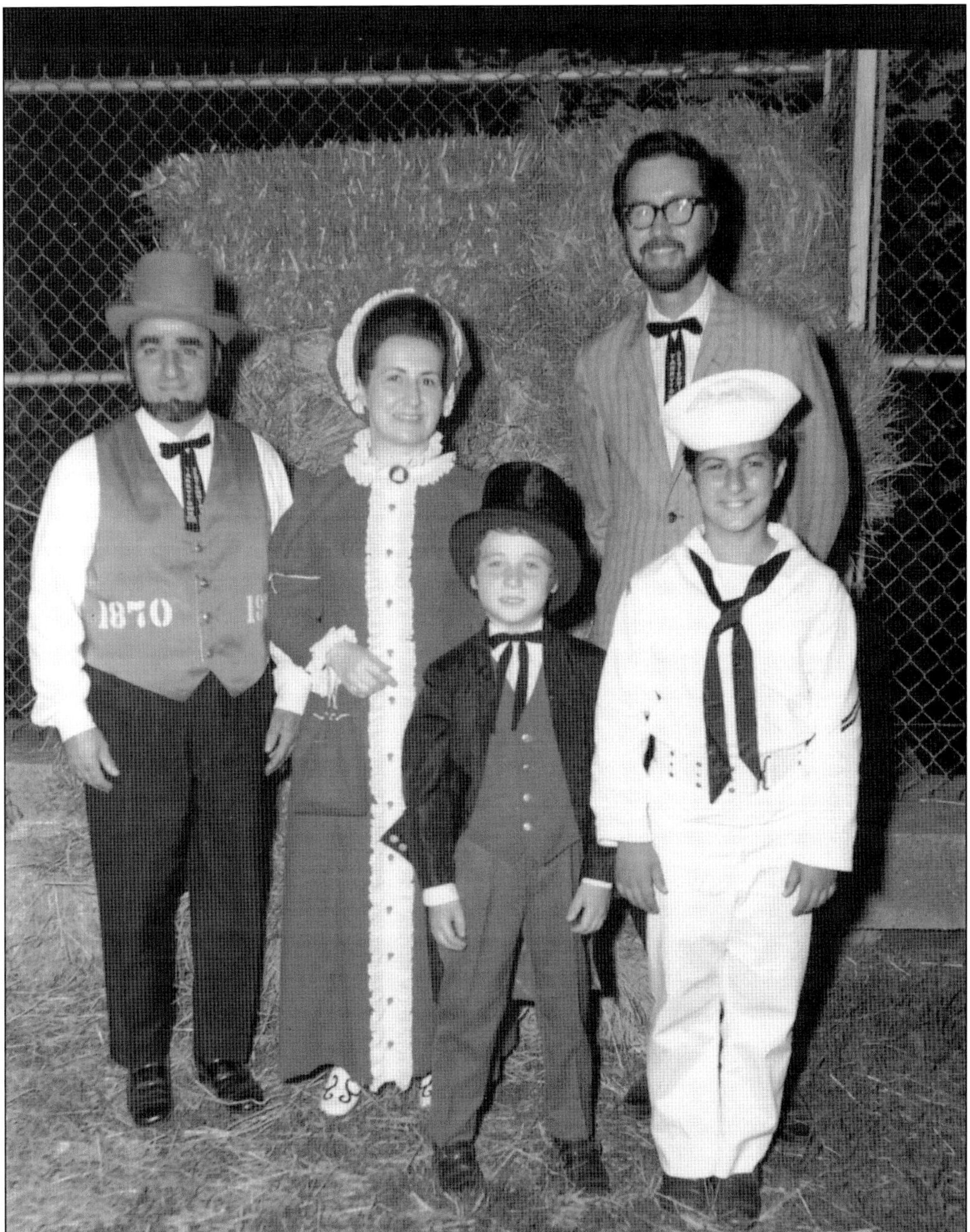


Together with their family, Charles and Lorraine Annicchiarico dress in historical costumes to celebrate the Tarrytown centennial. Lorraine provided numerous handmade costumes for all the historical celebrations during the last three decades of the 20th century. From colonial soldiers' uniforms to women's swimming costumes of the 1920s, her detailed creations were the hit of local celebrations.

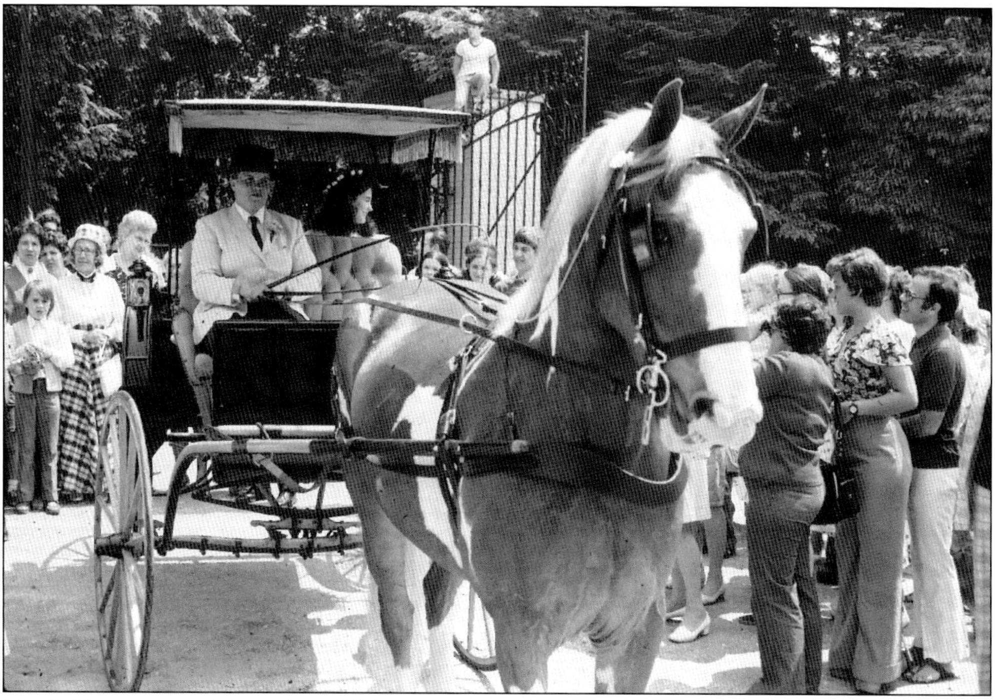

North Tarrytown celebrated its 100th anniversary for an entire year in 1974. Festivities included a flea market, a wedding, shows, and sporting events. Centennial bride Teresita Mastrapa was married on June 15 to James Dumas in the Old Dutch Church. Wearing a colonial-style wedding gown and accompanied by her father, she arrived in a horse-drawn carriage to cheers and applause. A public reception followed at Philipsburg Manor.

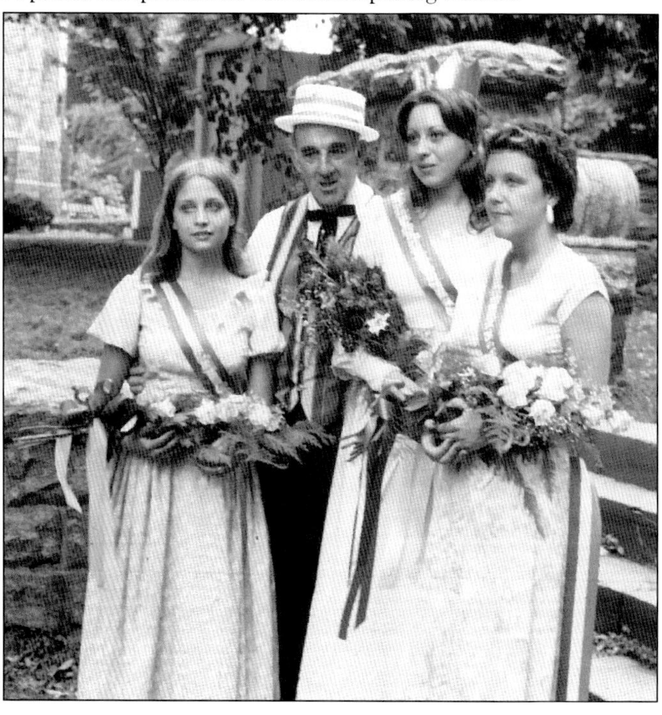

Georgianna Crouch was crowned the North Tarrytown centennial queen in Patriots Park on July 2, 1974. Pictured from left to right are Nancy La Caruba, Centennial Committee chairman Gabriel P. Hayes, Georgianna Crouch, and Noelle Righter. During the rest of the summer, the Italian, Portuguese, French, and Slovak clubs held colorful festivals. The entire community came together for a parade on October 12. A dinner dance at Marymount College on November 30 closed the centennial year.

Beth Albanese displays a cake depicting the Headless Horseman and Ichabod Crane at Philipsburg Manor. A monument celebrating Irving's *Legend of Sleepy Hollow* was dedicated in 1974 as part of the North Tarrytown centennial.

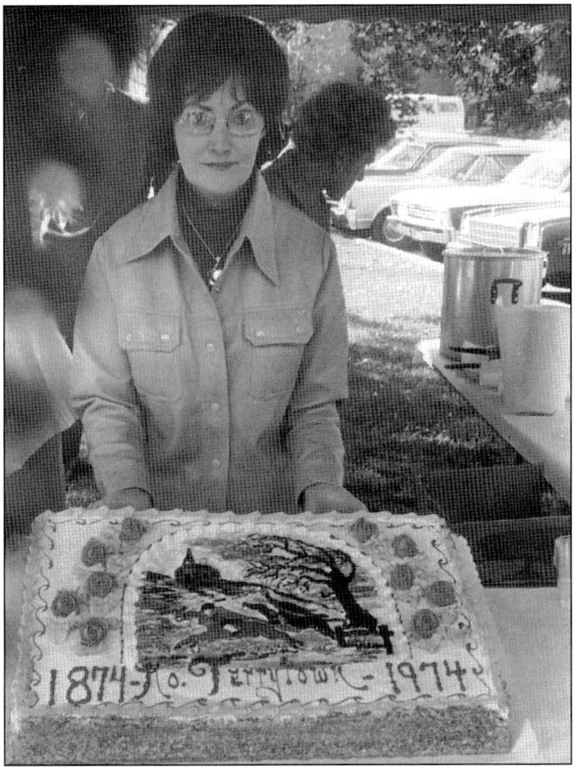


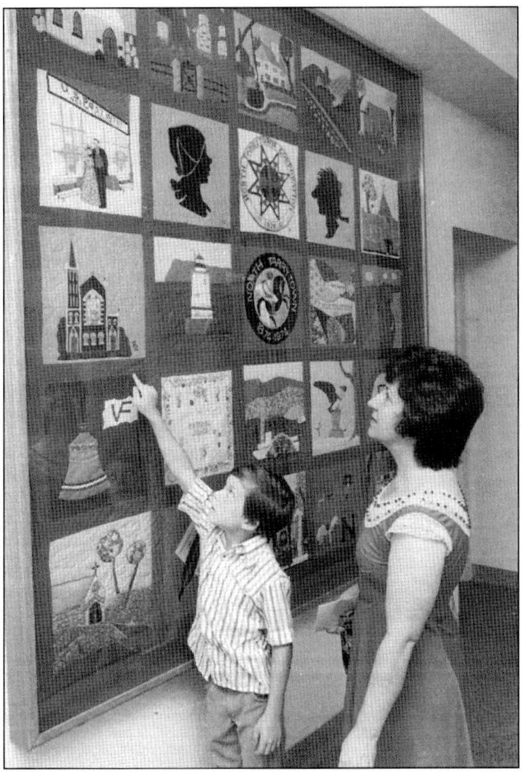

The bicentennial quilt, designed and made by women of the village between April and December 1975, depicts scenes of Sleepy Hollow country, including Village Hall, the post office, the Old Dutch Church, and Fremont Fountain. In addition to her work on the quilt, Lorraine Annicchiarico, a talented seamstress, is known for her handmade historical costumes and banners. The quilt is on display at Sleepy Hollow Village Hall.

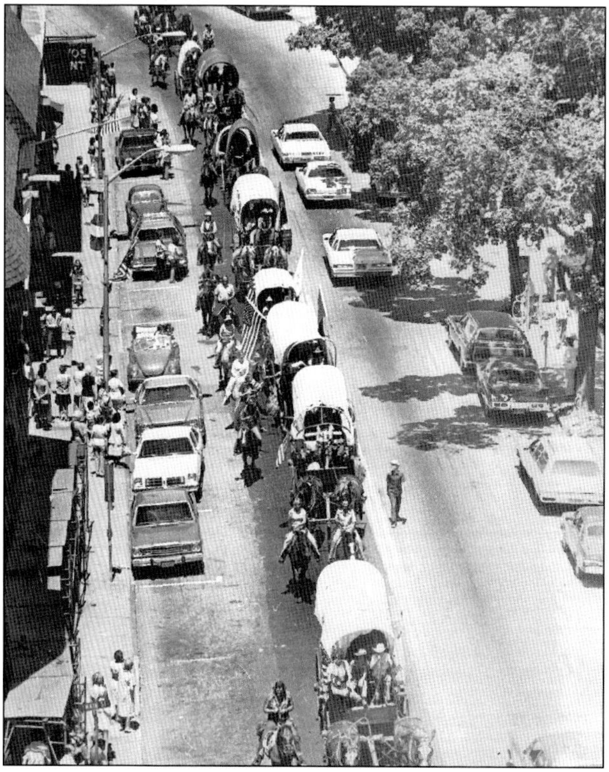

The U.S. bicentennial was celebrated in the villages with a weekend of nightly fireworks, parades, and a visit of 10 vessels from Operation Sail in the harbor. The Bicentennial Wagon Train came through Tarrytown to help commemorate the country's pioneer history.

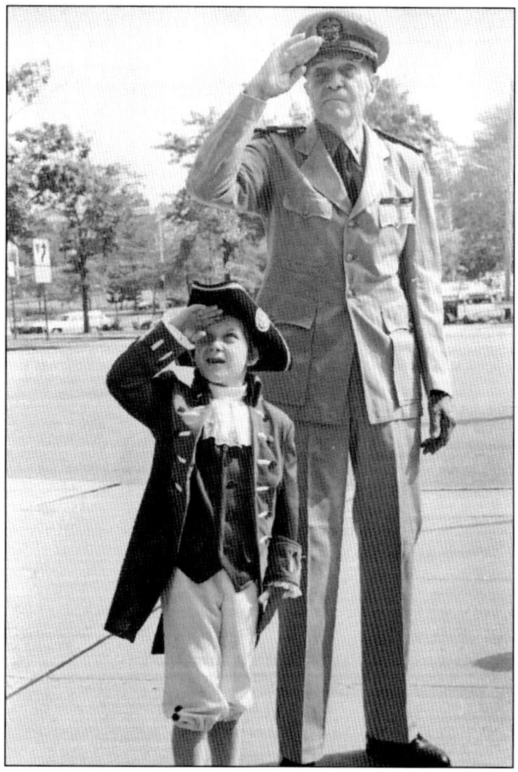

To celebrate the bicentennial, a parade was held on Sunday, July 4, 1976. Harry Storm, in his naval uniform, and an unidentified young patriot salute as the flag passes by. Church bells rang at 2:00 p.m. across the country to mark the signing of the Declaration of Independence.

# *Two*

# Associations

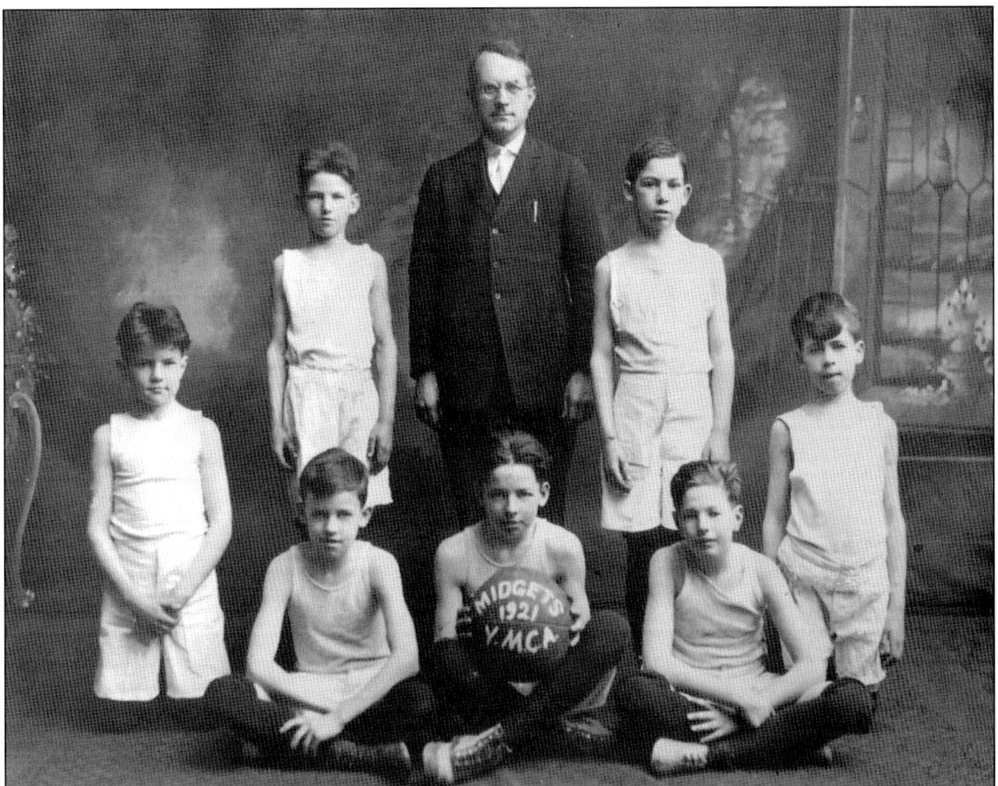


The 20th century saw the organization of numerous local associations. Each was established with the belief that individual members had responsibilities to society and their community. One of the earliest organizations was a branch of the Young Men's Christian Association (YMCA). Local banker and coach Robert Patteson was the driving force behind the new YMCA in 1903, and his Midgets basketball team was one of its most popular programs.

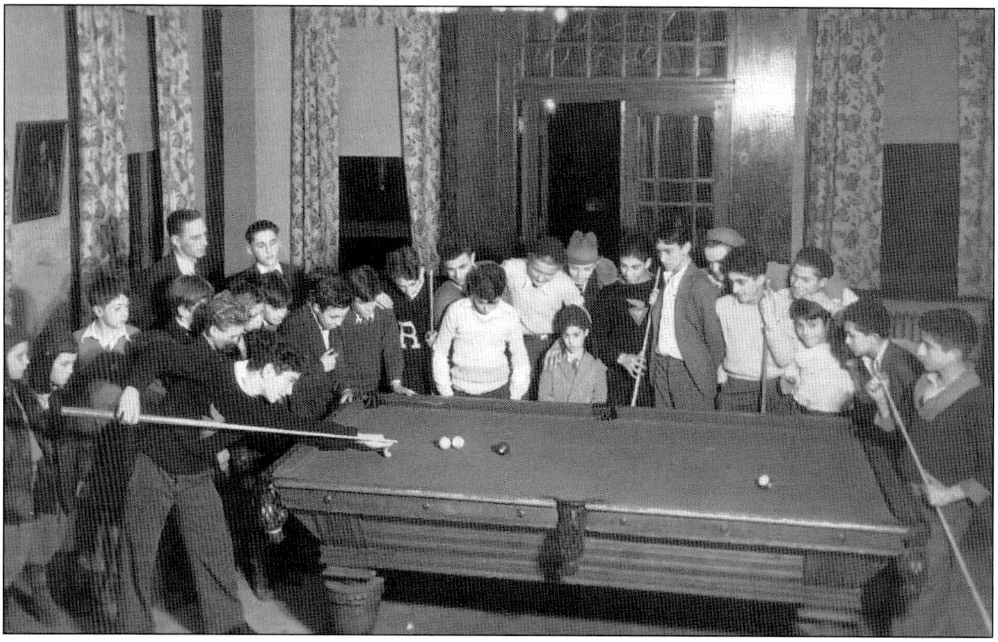

Throughout the 20th century, the YMCA had a strong influence over the youth of both villages. When the current Y was constructed in 1912, it provided a location for numerous sports and social programs. During the 1930s, the YMCA Camera Club documented the variety of programs offered. Pictured here are several unidentified boys playing pool in the billiards room.

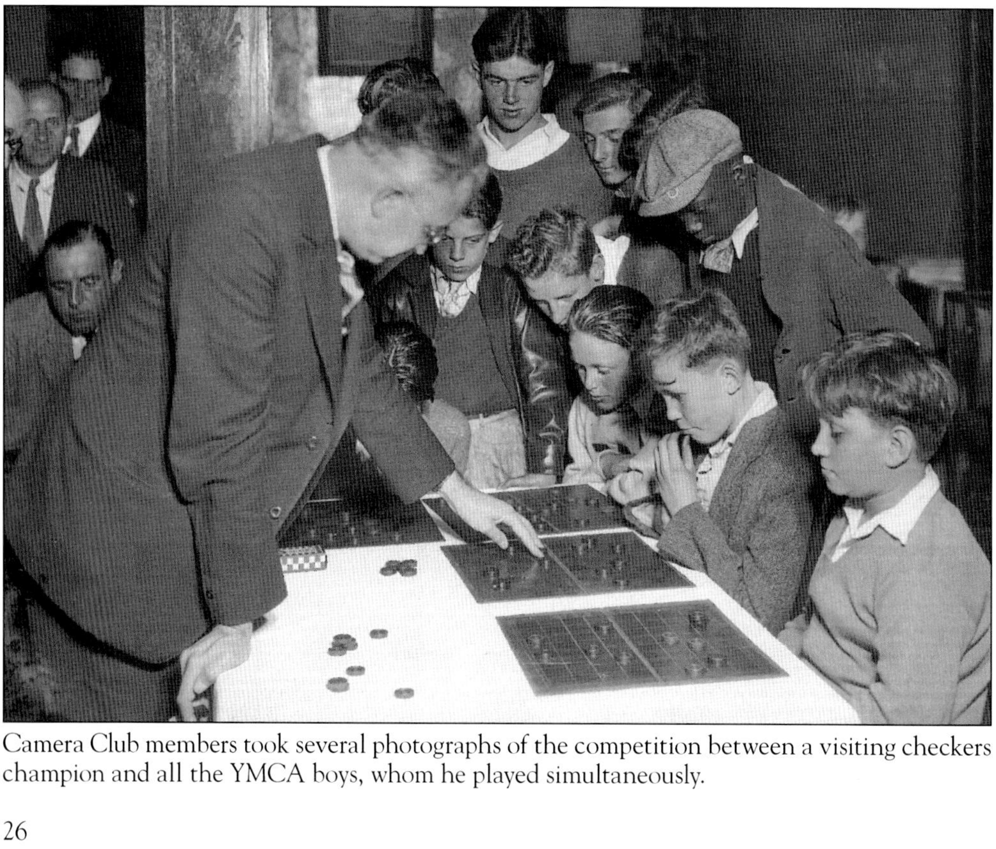

Camera Club members took several photographs of the competition between a visiting checkers champion and all the YMCA boys, whom he played simultaneously.

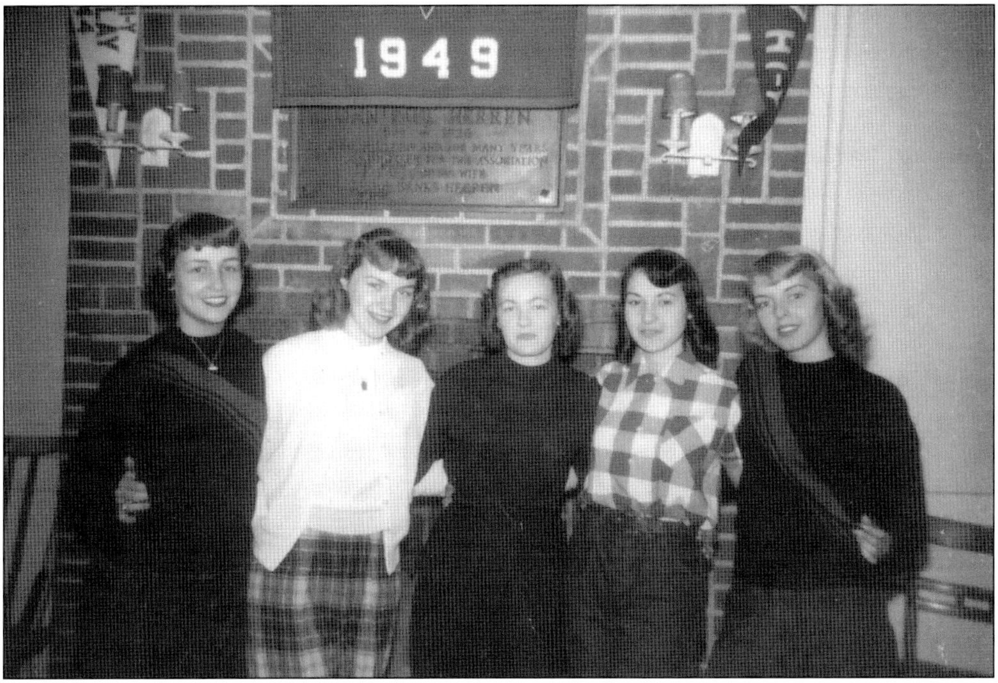


From the 1920s until the 1950s, high school students from both villages joined the HI-Y, a service and social club associated with the local YMCA. The goal of the club was to encourage personal development among the members. The young ladies above belonged to the 1949 North Tarrytown High School Girls HI-Y. Members pictured here are, from left to right, Grace Fariel, Greta Nilsson, Susan Jakl, Harriet Goldberg, and Joan Graham.

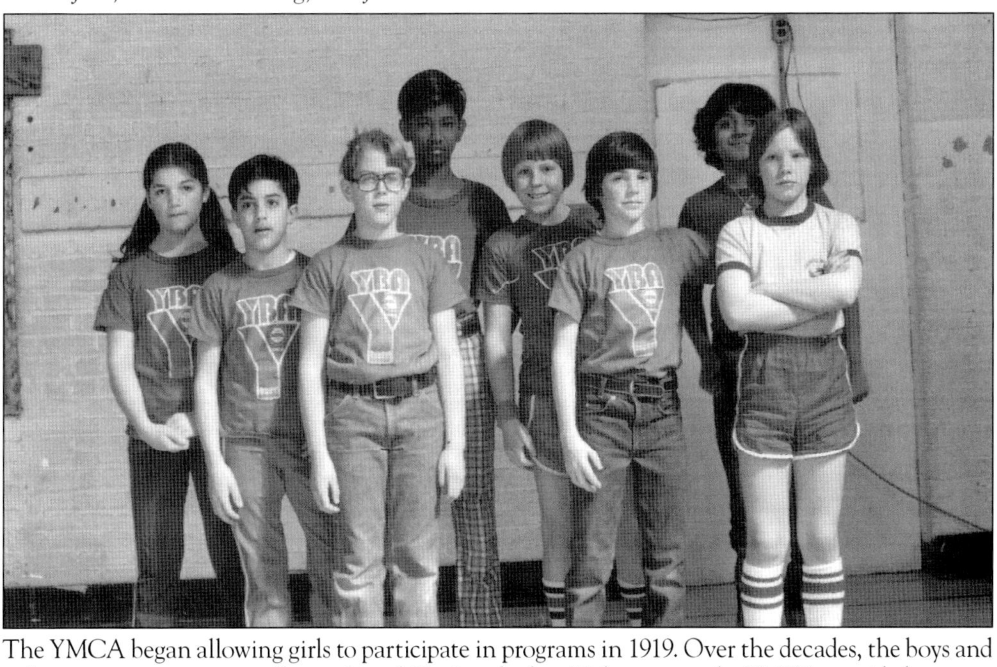

The YMCA began allowing girls to participate in programs in 1919. Over the decades, the boys and girls programs were eventually combined. During the late 20th century, the YMCA provided summer camp programs for local children as well as numerous family and adult participation programs.

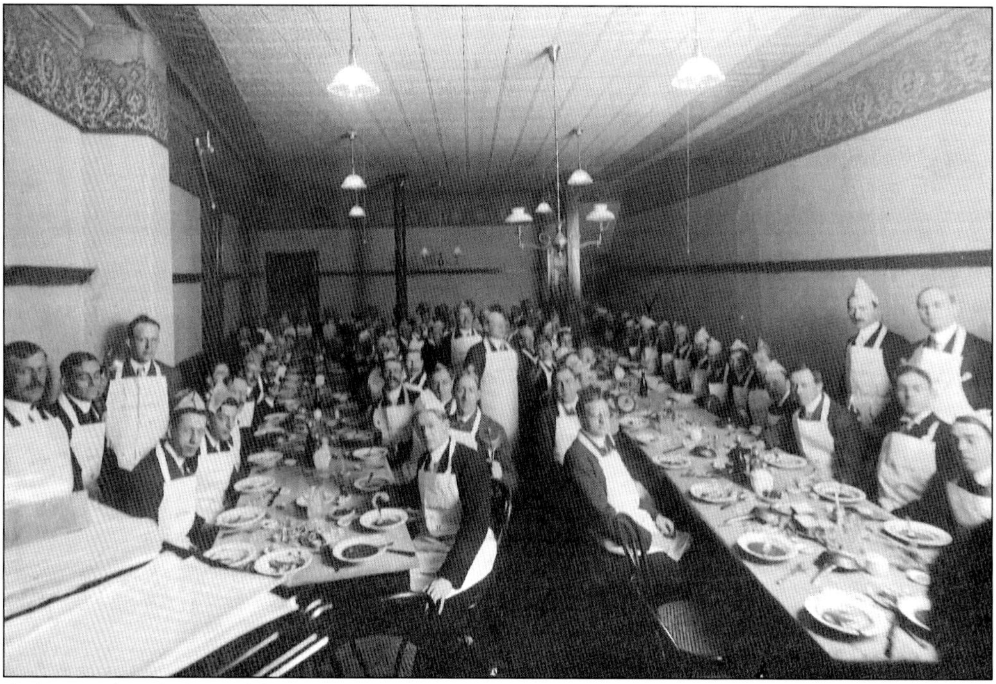

A fraternal and charitable organization, Solomon's Lodge No. 196 Free and Accepted Masons has been located at the Main Street Masonic Hall Temple in Tarrytown since the beginning of the 20th century. Members are shown above enjoying a lodge dinner.

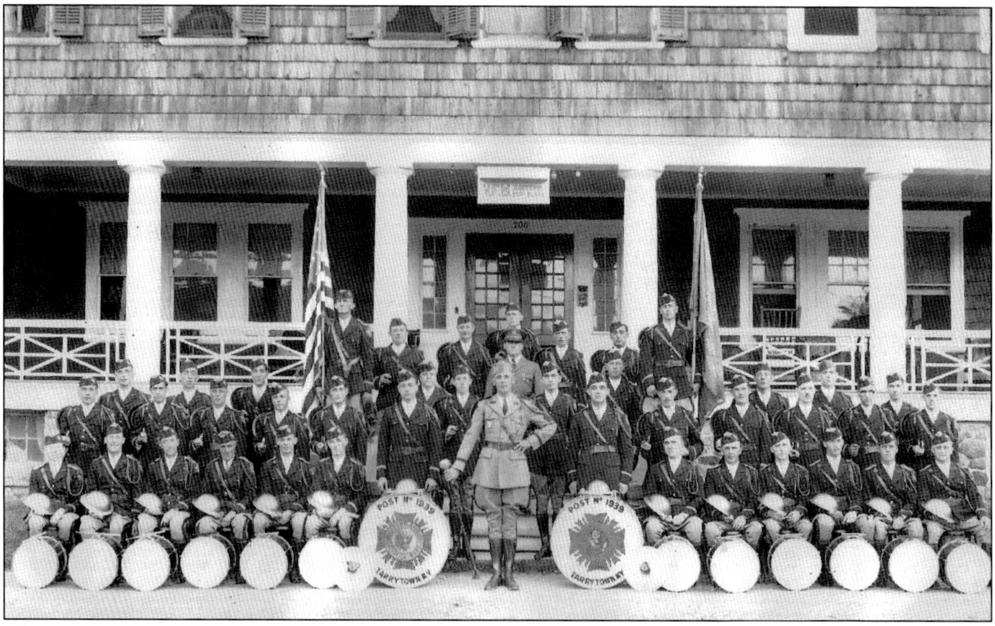

The Veterans of Foreign Wars Post 1939 was organized in 1930 during the Depression to help struggling, out-of-work veterans obtain government benefits. The post continues to be active in community service and marches yearly in the Memorial Day parade. The prize-winning drum and bugle corps, organized in 1932, has won more than 25 awards and trophies over the many years it has been in existence.

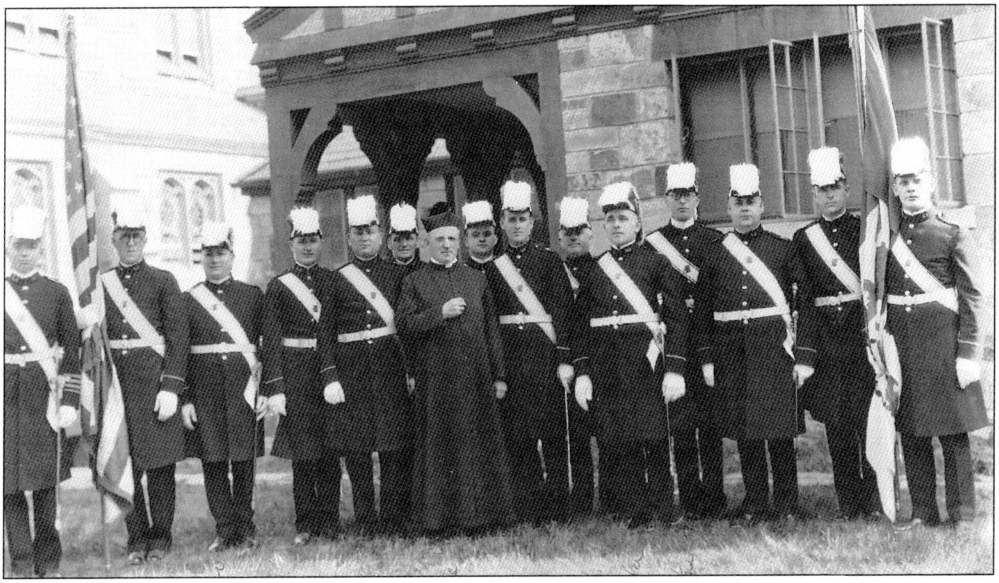

The Knights of Columbus, St. Elmo's Council 318, is a fraternal, charitable, and patriotic organization of Catholic men located on North Washington Street in Tarrytown. The *c.* 1930s color guard includes, from left to right, Fred Peters, John McElroy, Joseph Pellagrino, Thomas McGirl, John Crowley, George Kirby, Rev. W. J. Donohue (chaplain), Mike Nicolasi, John Pollard, William Ward, Vincent Stronski, Charles Hofgartner, Joseph O'Neil, unidentified, and Octo Specht.

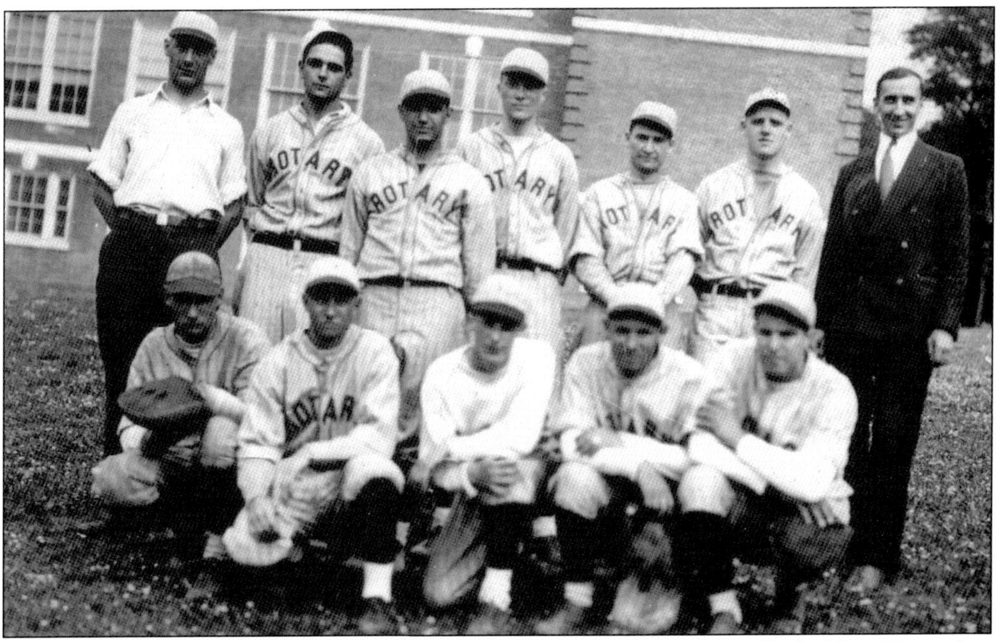

During the 20th century, numerous national service organizations established local branches across the country, one of which was the Tarrytowns branch of the Rotary Club, organized in November 1921. With the motto "service above self," local Rotarians have a distinguished history of raising funds for the Tarrytown Hospital (later Phelps Memorial Hospital), local scout troops, Westchester County Community College, and numerous small nonprofit groups. The 1925 Rotary baseball team is pictured above.

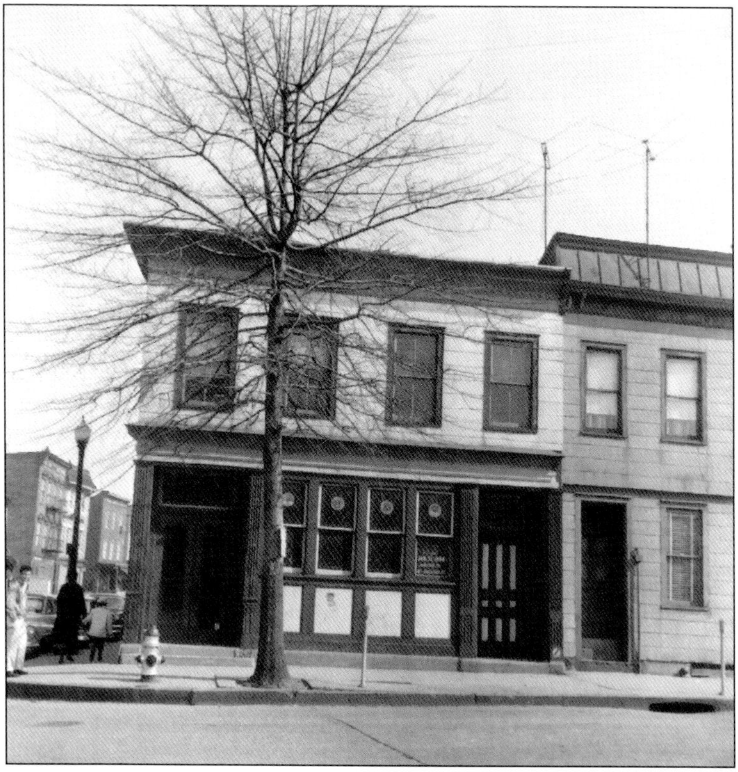

The Salvation Army was founded based on the following principle: "They serve God best who serve their fellow men." The group's first missionaries came to Tarrytown by boat and established themselves downtown early in the 20th century. They eventually replaced their original building, shown here, with their current headquarters at 115 Wildey Street in 1959.

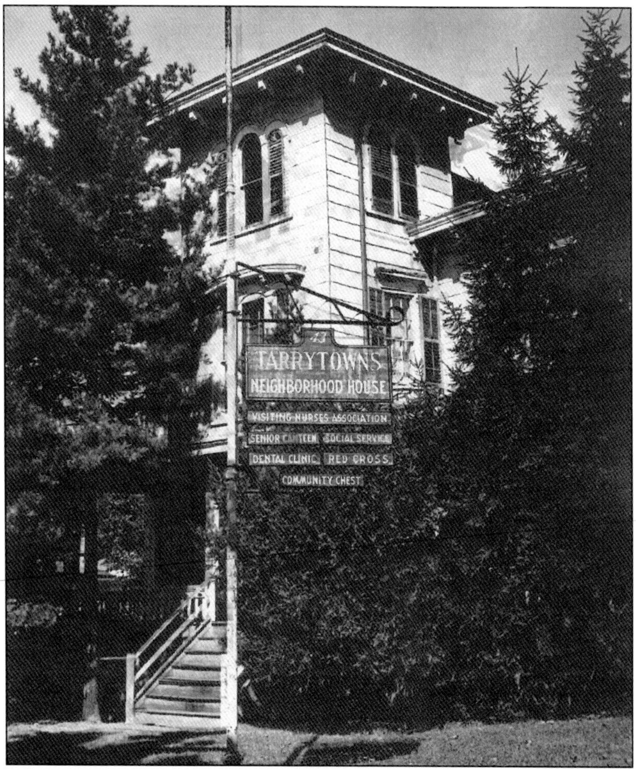


The Neighborhood House was founded in 1912 when the Women's Civic League donated a building for a community service center. In 1920, Cornelia Blakemore Warner purchased a large house on Wildey Street for the group's permanent home. The multitude of programs the organization supported is evident on the sign in front of this building, which was replaced in the early 1960s with a modern brick structure.

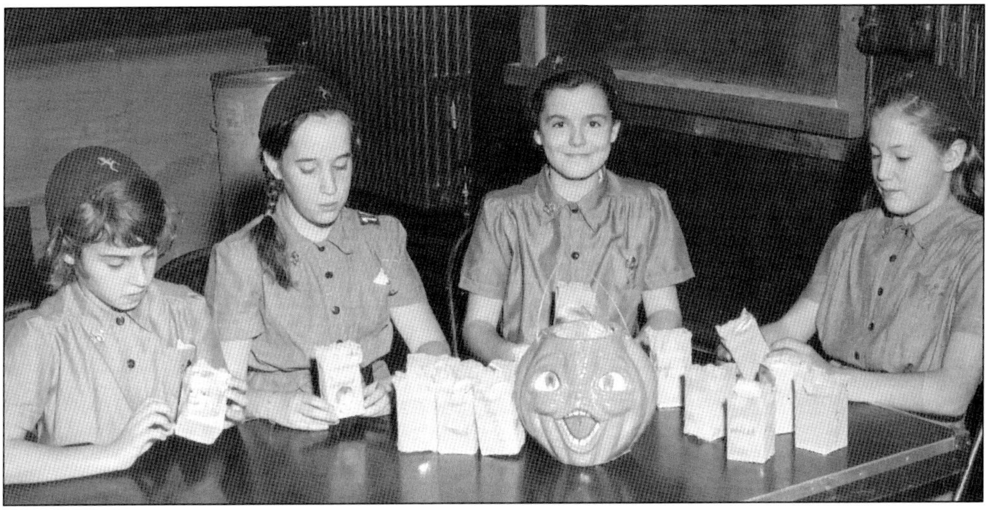

The Brownies are a younger girl version of the Girl Scouts dedicated to building confidence, character, and self-esteem. Brownies ranged in age from six to eight years old, and all interested girls were welcome. Shown here working on a Halloween project in 1956 are, from left to right, unidentified, Mary Scott, Susan Ridgeway, and Gail Brooks.

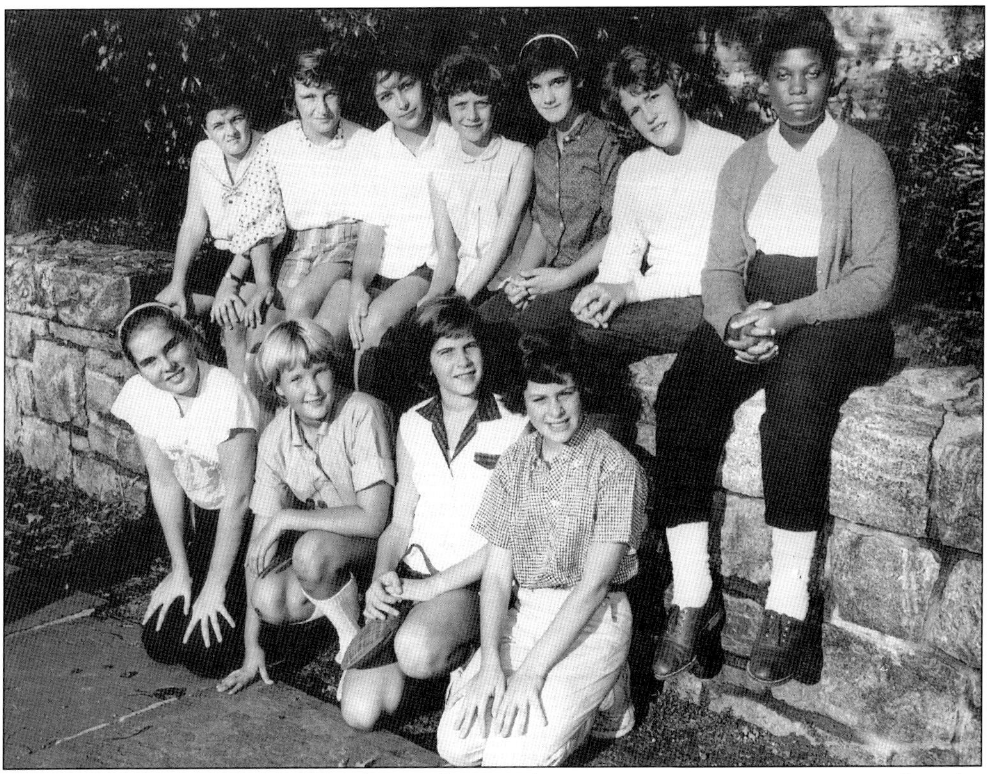

The Girl Scouts of the Tarrytowns have volunteered at numerous community events such as the Historical Society, Inc.'s annual Strawberry Festival. Here local scouts are pictured on a 1959 outing. They are, from left to right, (first row) Nancy McGlashan, Karen Swanson, Lynn Myman, and Betsy Brodt; (second row) Susan Hongach, Pat Zaicek, Mary Lynn Shaw, Linda Celtruda, Michele Rufle, Gail Brooks, and Cynthia Smith.

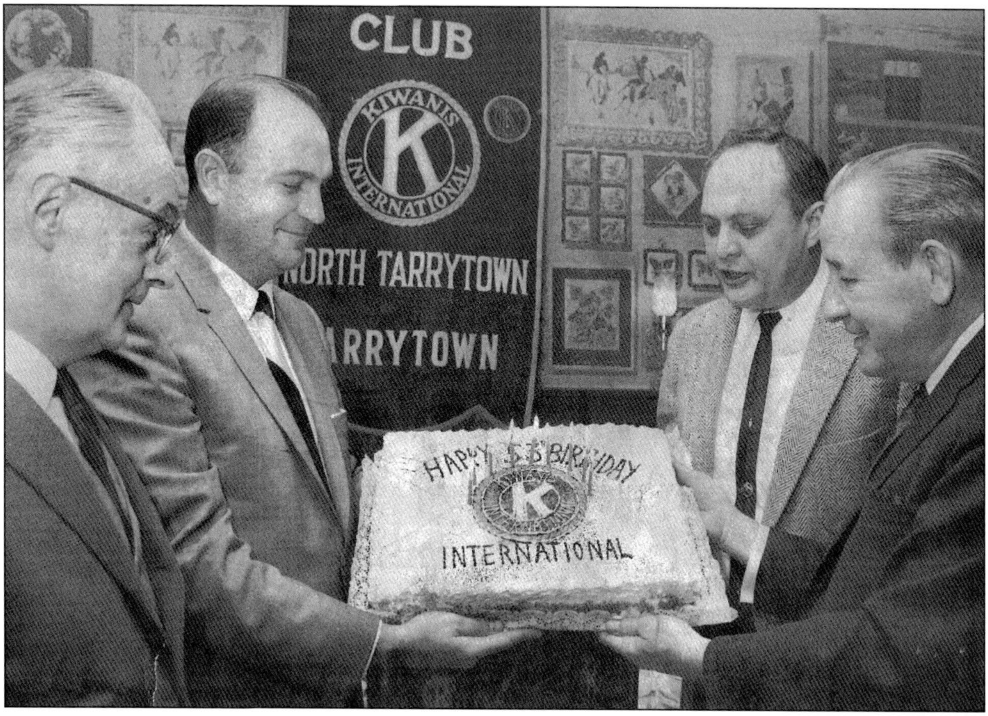


Organized in 1938, the local Kiwanis Club was part of the international association dedicated to "changing the world one child and one community at a time." Locally, the club supported numerous scholarships and senior programs. From left to right, Ed Beck, John Garibaldi, John Biros, and Ralph Mattison celebrate the 53rd anniversary of Kiwanis International in 1968.

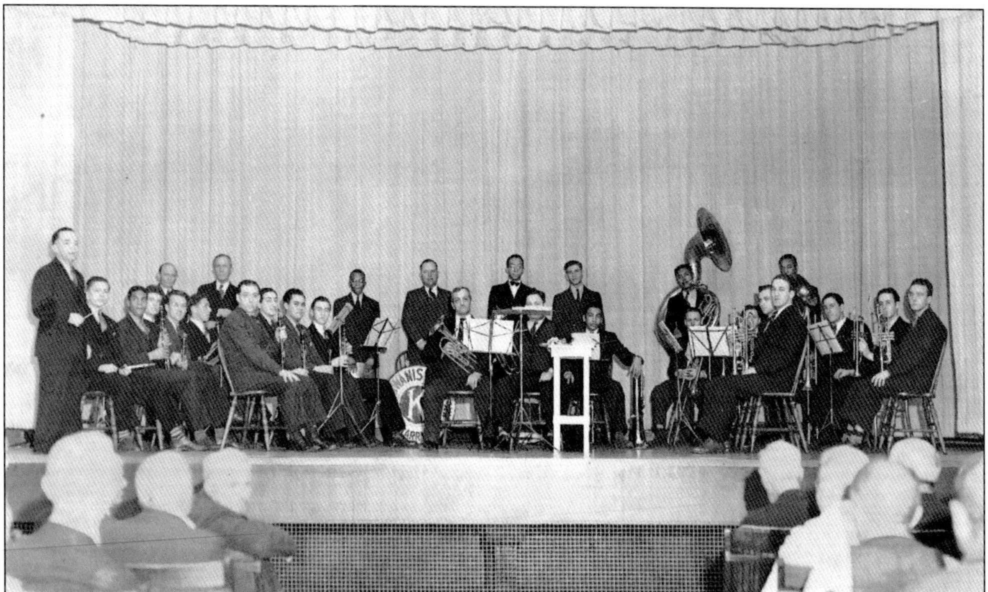

The Kiwanis Club had a large band that performed at numerous events to raise funds for local charities. During much of the 20th century, the Kiwanis sponsored the Key Club at Sleepy Hollow High School in order to encourage students to participate in local philanthropy.

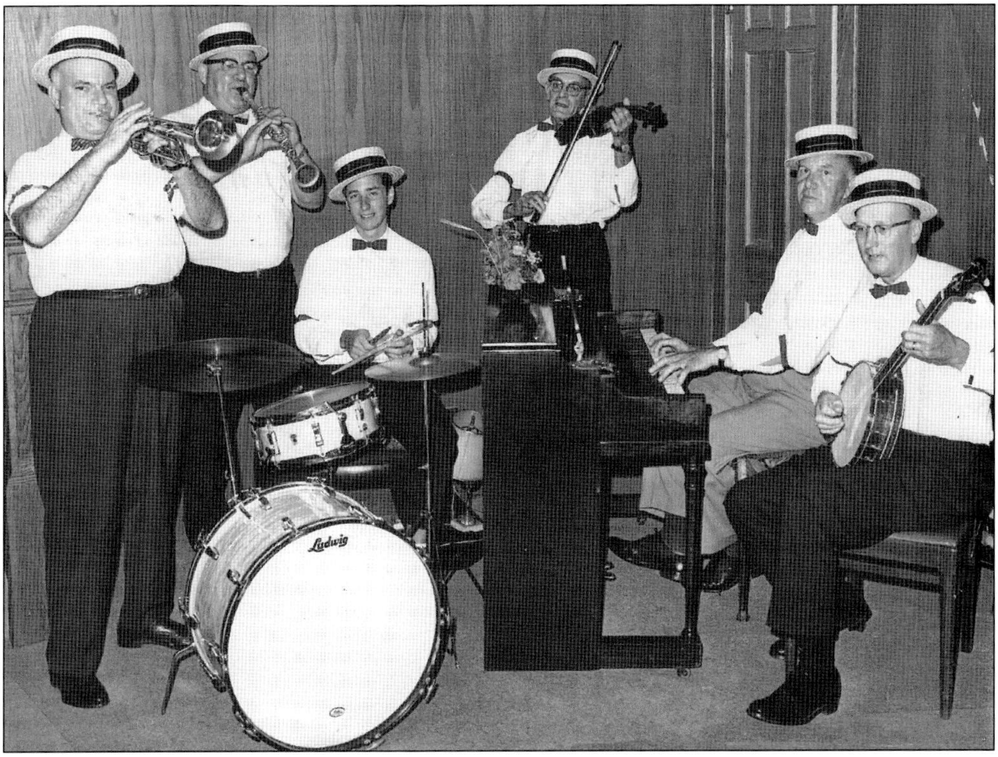


A chapter of the Lions Club—which stands for Liberty, Intelligence, and Our Nations Safety—was organized in Tarrytown in 1924. During the 1960s, the club held a series of musical entertainment shows called the *Lions Roar* to raise funds for financing the construction of the current Neighborhood House. The organization's Dixieland band included, from left to right, Howard Bush, Carl Hackett, Robert Hubbel, Seymour Levy, Herbert Hall, and Graham Hubbel.

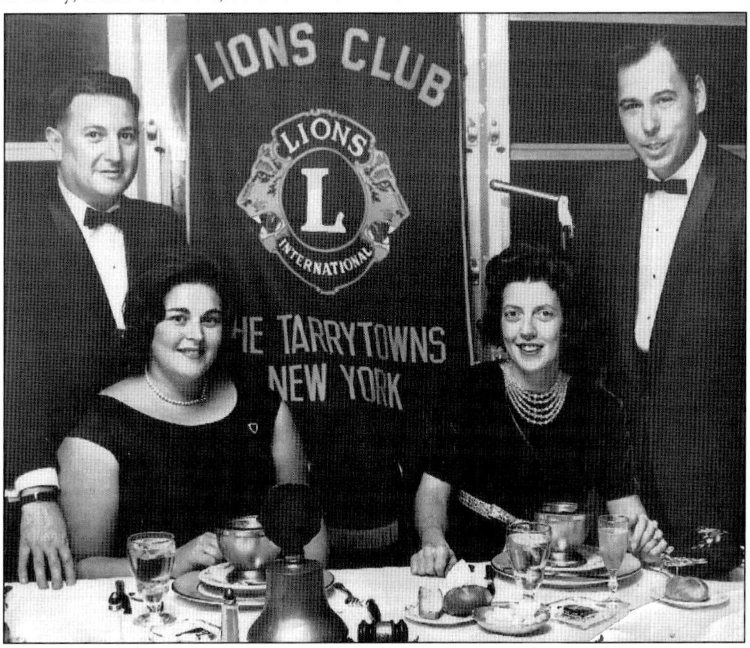


The Lions were local businessmen who volunteered to raise funds for cancer and eye disease as well as other local charities. The Lions Club provided members with outings, entertainment, and annual dinners. Pictured here are Dr. and Mrs. Melvin Kaplan (left) and Paul and Audrey Wheatley (right) at one of the annual dinners in the 1960s.

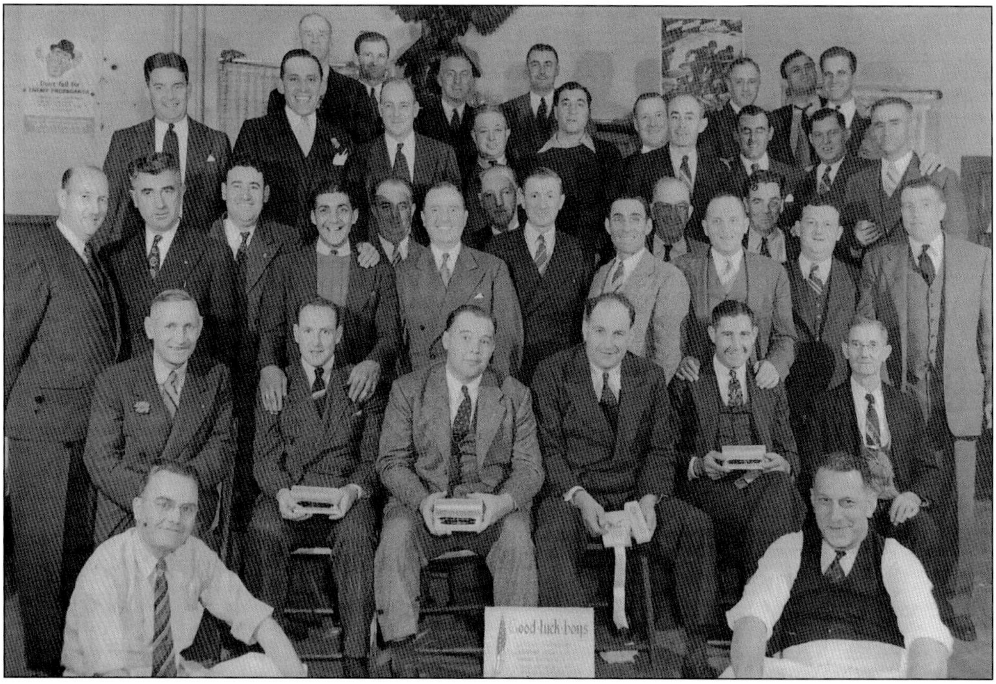

A group of businessmen who wanted to create a charitable organization united in the "spirit of liberty, truth, justice and equality" founded the Fraternal Order of the Eagles in 1898. The local branch of the Eagles began meeting in North Tarrytown in 1901, and women were invited to join in 1945. Charities supported by the Eagles during the 20th century included the Salvation Army, the Neighborhood House, and Warner Library.

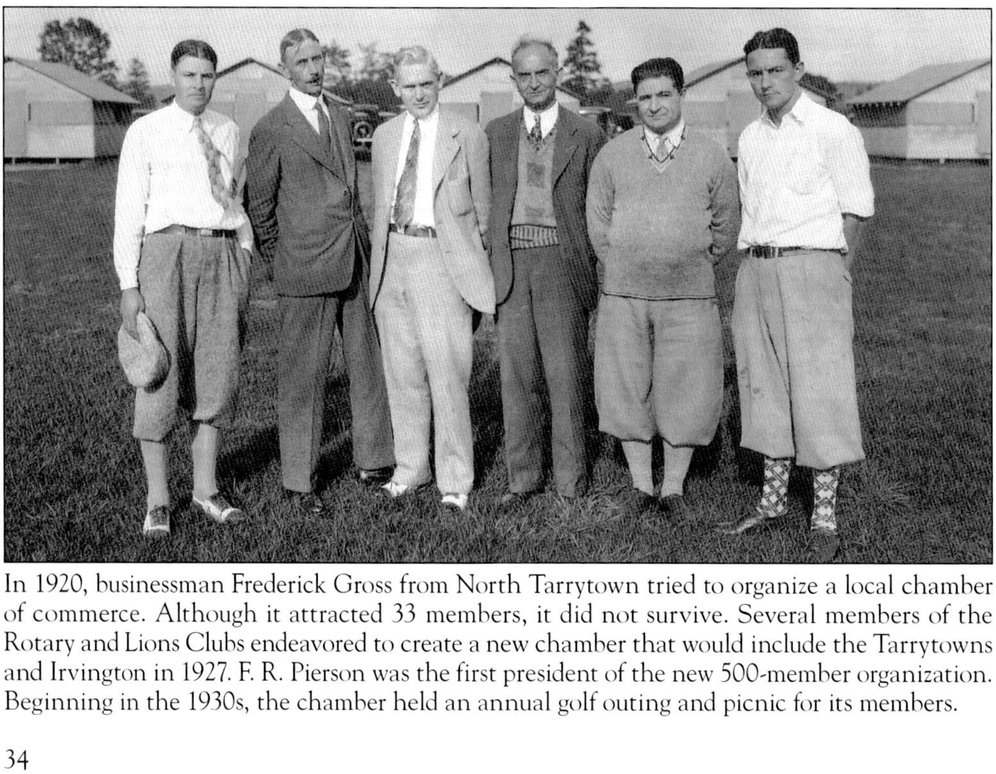

In 1920, businessman Frederick Gross from North Tarrytown tried to organize a local chamber of commerce. Although it attracted 33 members, it did not survive. Several members of the Rotary and Lions Clubs endeavored to create a new chamber that would include the Tarrytowns and Irvington in 1927. F. R. Pierson was the first president of the new 500-member organization. Beginning in the 1930s, the chamber held an annual golf outing and picnic for its members.

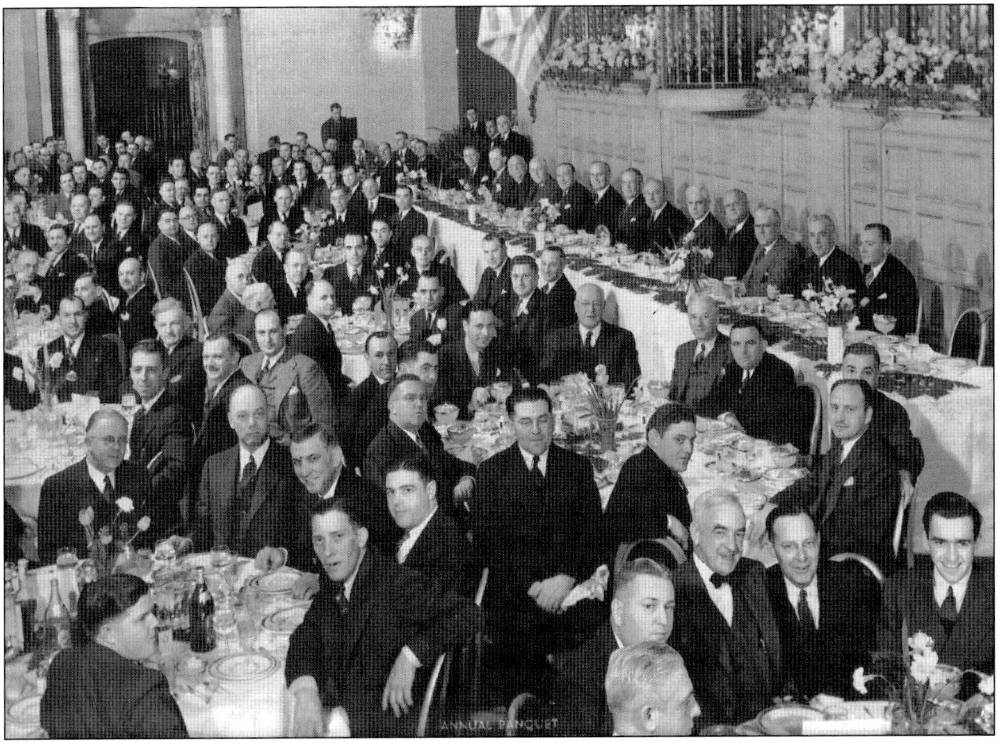


During the 20th century, the number of chamber members continued to grow as the group worked to "promote the civic, economic and social welfare" of the community. Pictured here is the annual banquet held at the Westchester Country Club in 1940. In 1966, the organization officially changed its name to the Sleepy Hollow Chamber of Commerce.

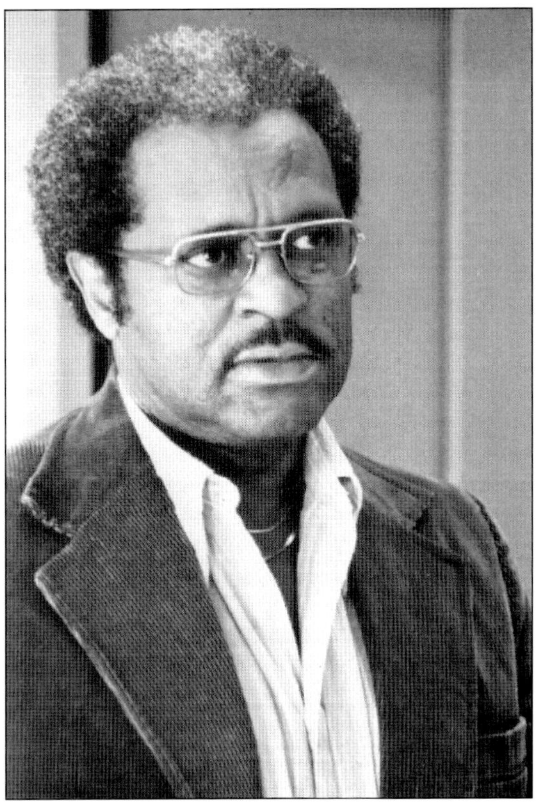

Beginning in 1942, the chamber annually honored local citizens and/or organizations that had performed extraordinary service to the community, naming them as the Person or Organization of the Year. The 1997 Person of the Year was William Burnette, chosen for his many years of service to the community as a guidance counselor at Sleepy Hollow High School. In this position, Burnette prepared thousands of local students for a lifetime of achievement.

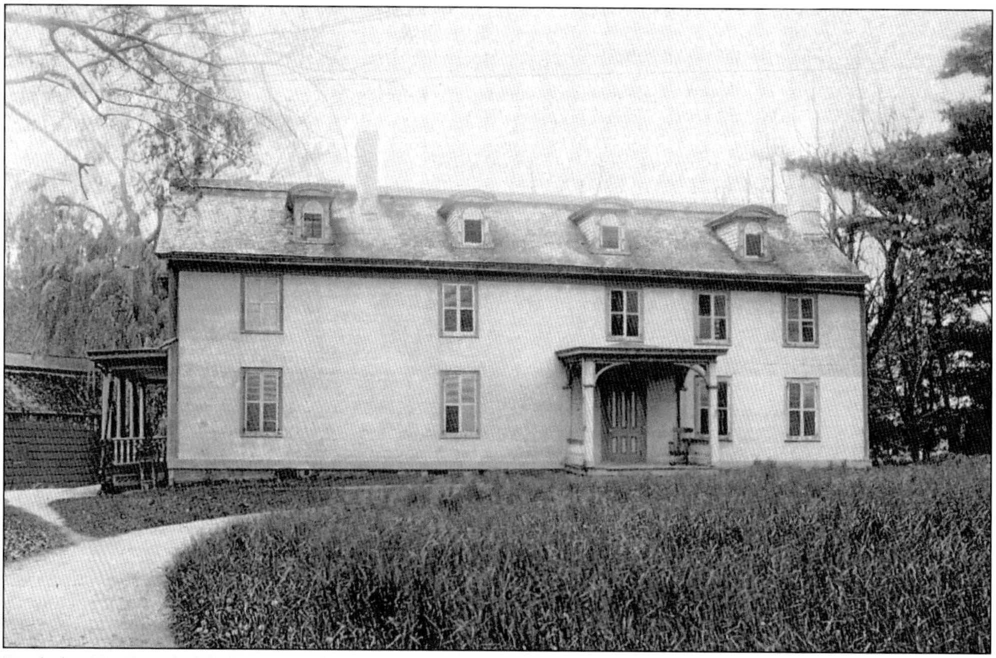

Built by Frederick Philipse in the 1680s, the Upper Mills Manor House, or Philipse Castle, was made of stone. Gerald Beekman purchased the property after the American Revolution and added a wooden extension in 1785. After the death of Cornelia Beekman in 1847, the property had a series of owners. By the beginning of the 20th century, the house was in need of renovation.

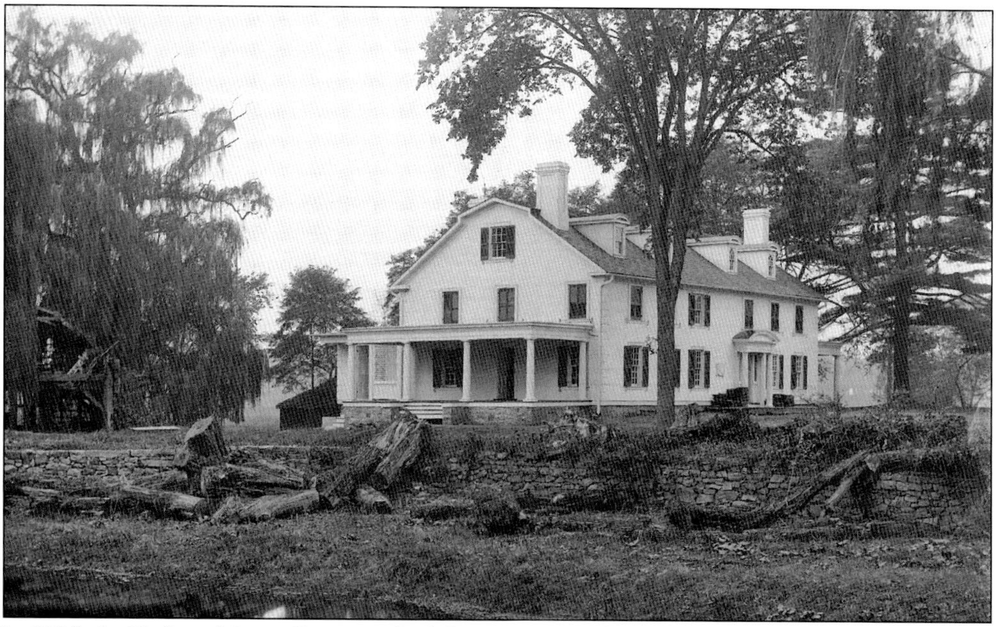

In 1906, the Philipse Manor Company had the entire outside of the building covered with stucco, which served to preserve the original structure for future restoration. Between 1911 and 1915, Philipse Castle was operated as an inn; in 1916, it was sold to actress Elsie Janis, who held the property until 1937. The Historical Society, Inc., acquired it at auction with funds from John D. Rockefeller Sr.

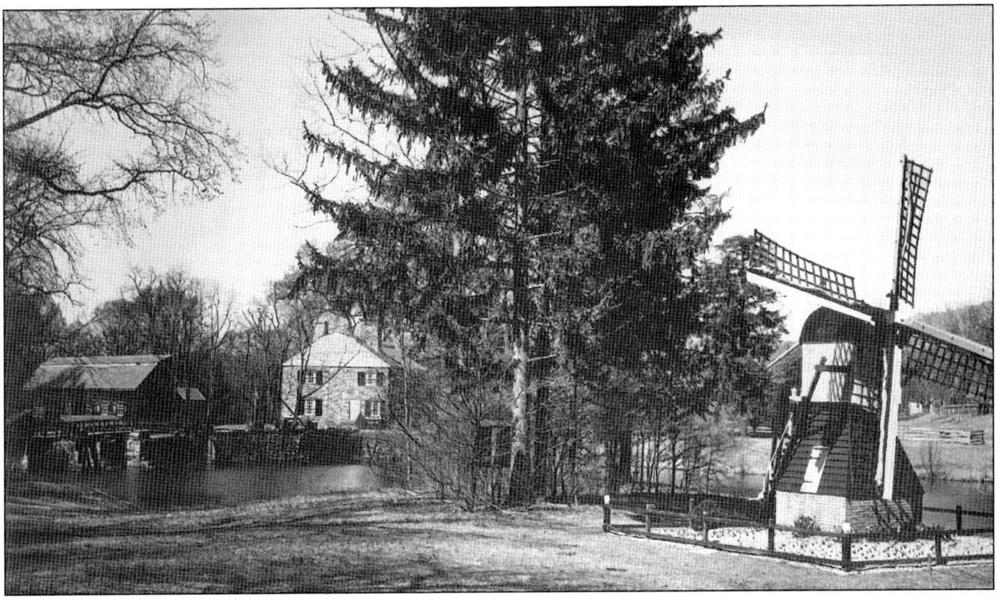

The Historical Society, Inc., began restoring the house, retaining the Beekman wing and uncovering the original stone exterior. Renovations were completed in 1943, and the society operated the site until about 1950. Promotional pamphlets declared that "Philipse Castle is Full of Fine Exhibits" and is the "most complete re-creation of early Dutch manorial life in America." A 26-foot windmill, or *wipwater-molen*, fabricated by Dutch craftsmen became part of the restoration and a major attraction.

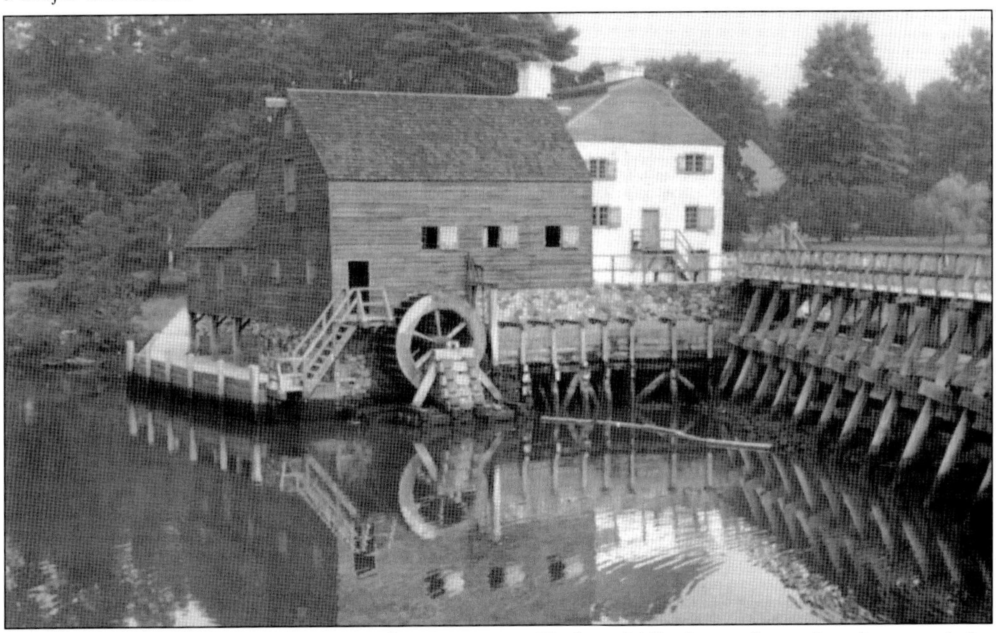

In 1951, Sleepy Hollow Restorations (later Historic Hudson Valley) was formed and restored the property back to the 1720–1750 period. After extensive archaeological, architectural, and documentary research, the dam, gristmill, and wharf were rebuilt, and all of the additions were removed from the original stone house. In 1969, visitors entered the reopened restoration via a wooden footbridge over the restored dam. It was dedicated as a national historic landmark in 1971.

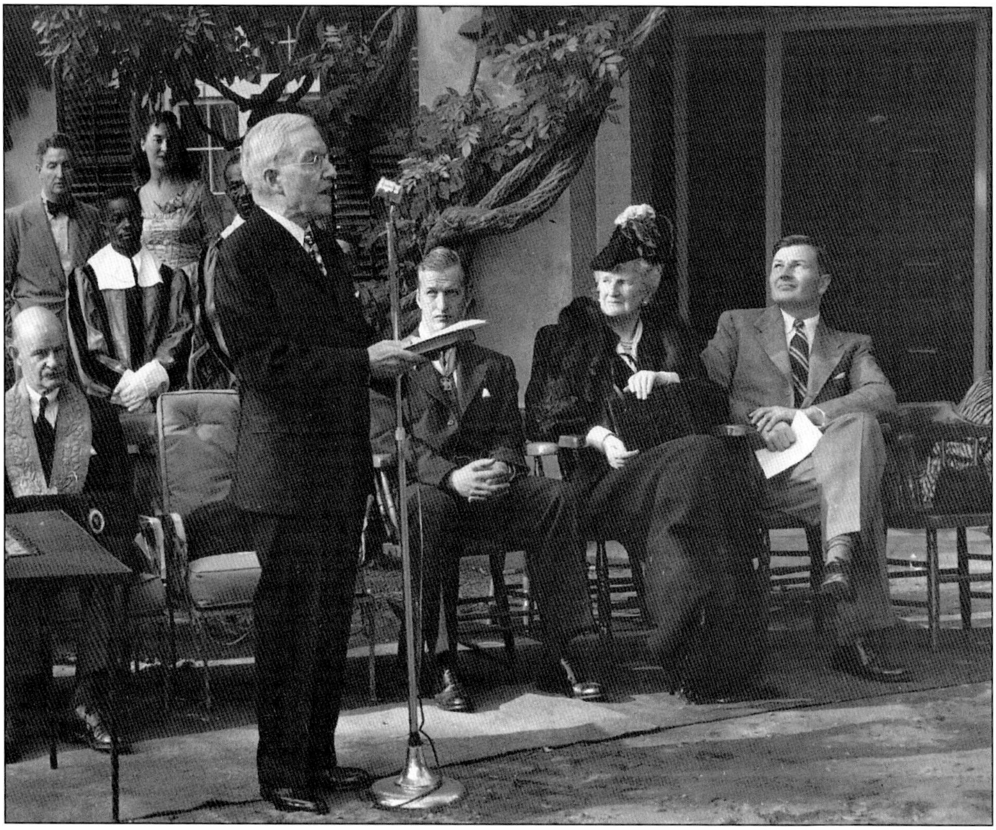

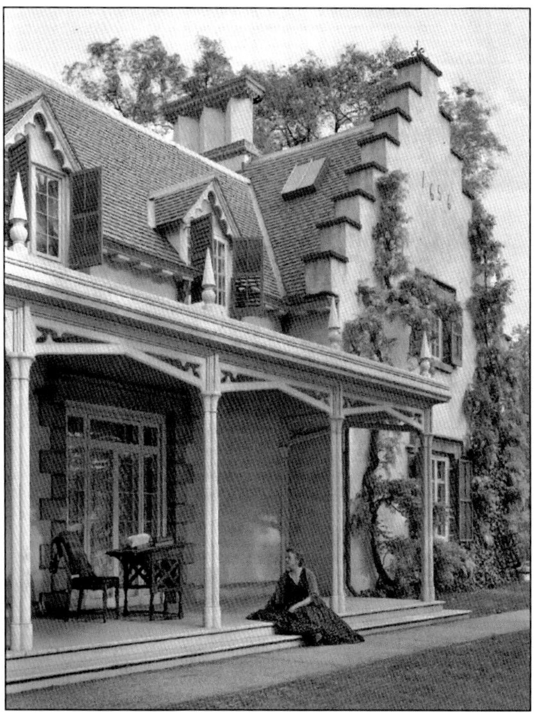

In 1945, John D. Rockefeller Jr.'s Sealantic Fund purchased Sunnyside, Washington Irving's home. The restored site opened in 1947 and has been a popular destination for all ages ever since. John D. Rockefeller Jr. is shown speaking at the opening ceremony. Seated from left to right are unidentified, Washington Irving III (a descendant of Irving's brother), Abby Aldrich Rockefeller, and David Rockefeller. In the background are members of the St. Nicholas Society.

Sunnyside tour guides, dressed in hoop skirts, greet visitors on the front porch. The landscape and gardens have been carefully tended to resemble the gardens that Irving enjoyed from 1835 to 1859, including an original wisteria vine that continues to bloom. Sunnyside and Philipsburg Manor are both operated by Historic Hudson Valley.

# *Three*

# Children at School

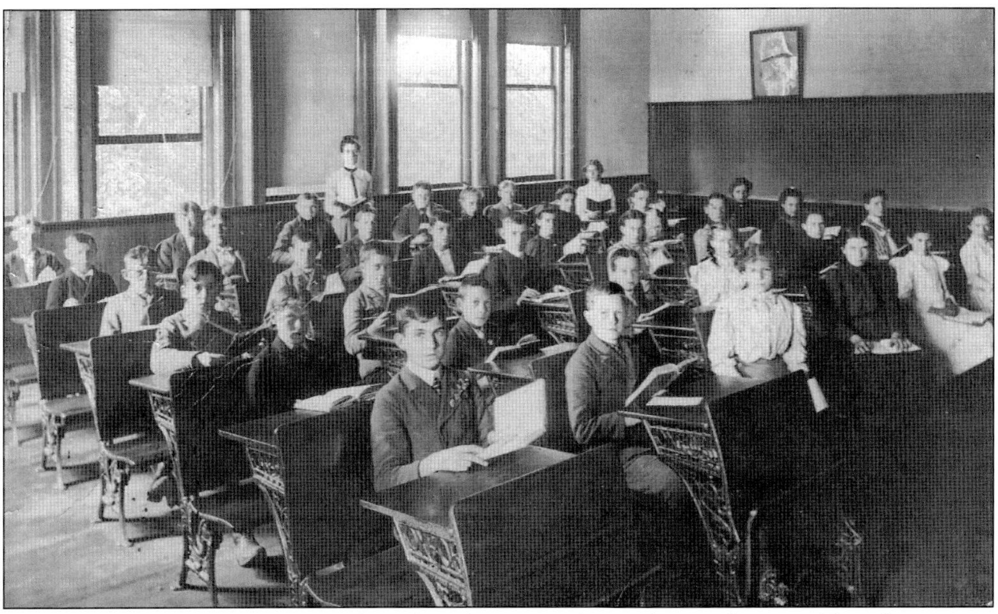

Tarrytown and North Tarrytown have long histories of providing inclusive public education to their residents. During the 20th century, the two public school systems grew rapidly until they were combined in the 1950s. This photograph depicts a typical classroom in the former North Tarrytown High School building in 1902. The building, which stood on Beekman Avenue, was constructed in 1899 and demolished in 1957.

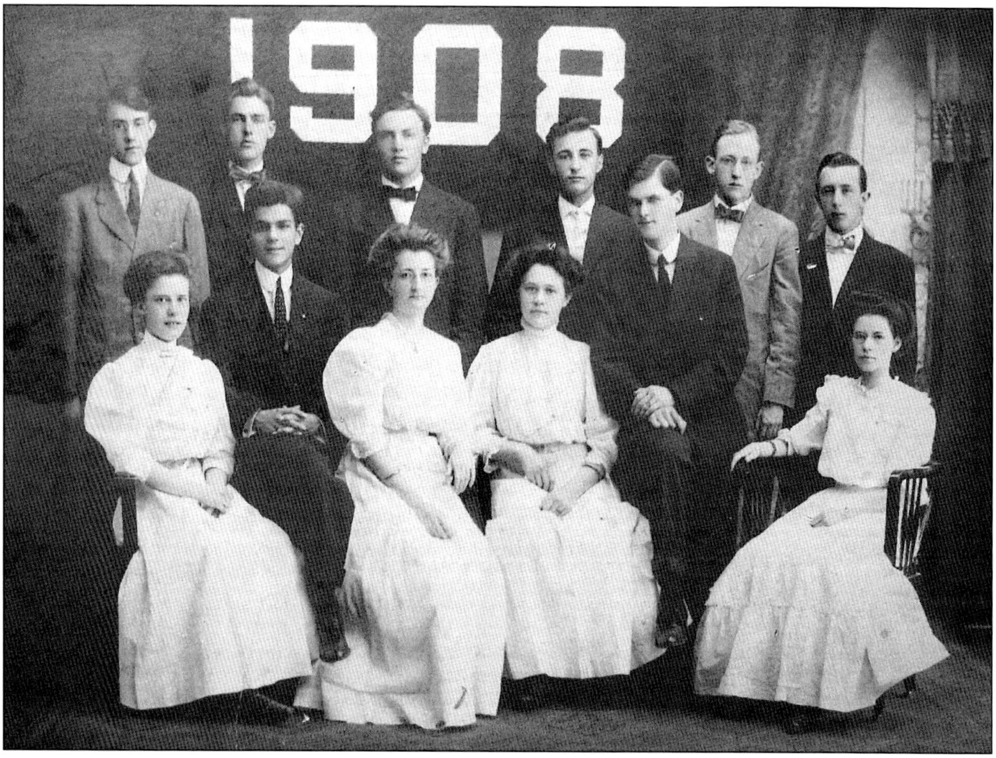


At the beginning of the 20th century, the first Washington Irving High School (later renamed F. R. Pierson School) was utilized for all grade levels. During the first decade, graduating classes were small in number. The class of 1908, pictured above, included George Andrews, Helen Wicks, Gladys Campbell, Robert Patteson, Dorothy Richards, Maud White, Bayard Allen, Frederic Croke, George Curtiss, Harold Frost, James Losee, and Richard Wright.

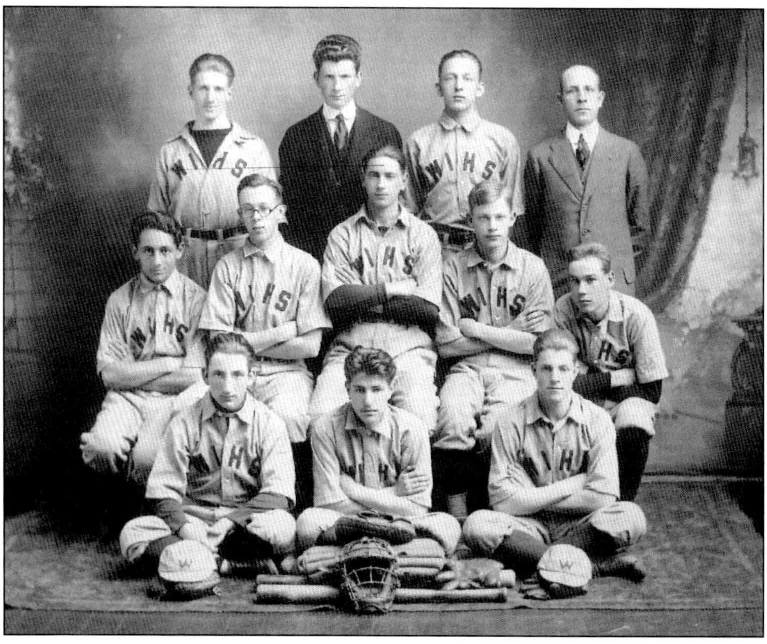

The 1916 Washington Irving High School baseball team is pictured here. George Martin was the student manager. Shortly after graduation, several of the boys in this photograph joined the U.S. Military and served in World War I.

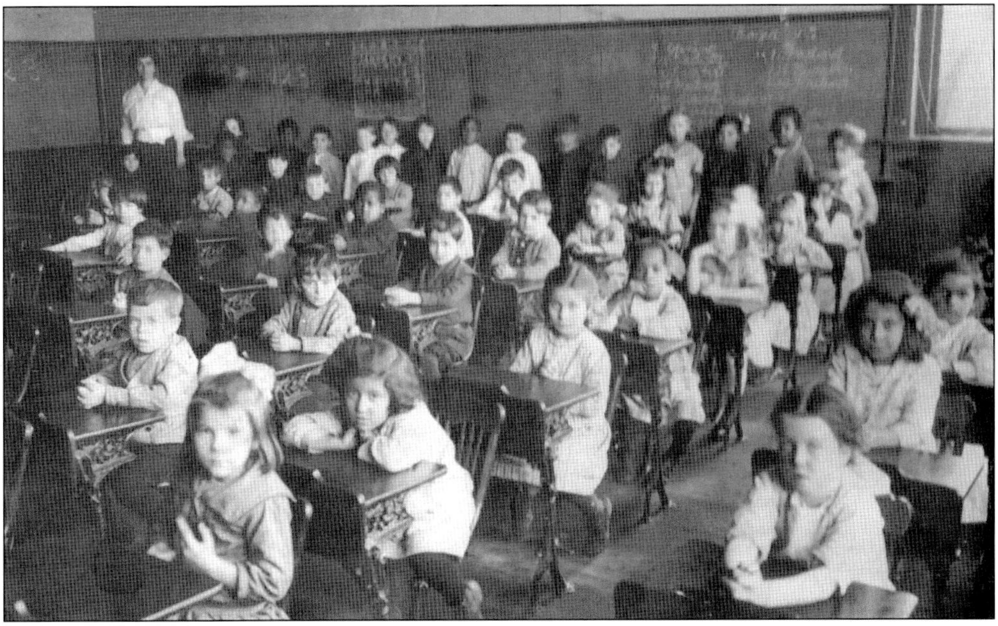

In 1896, a one-room elementary school building was constructed next to the 1865 schoolhouse on Sleepy Hollow Road in North Tarrytown. This school building was actually the third and final built in that location, with each being called the Sleepy Hollow School. Pictured above is the open classroom around 1915. The Sleepy Hollow School remained in service until 1932, when the Pocantico Hills Central School opened.

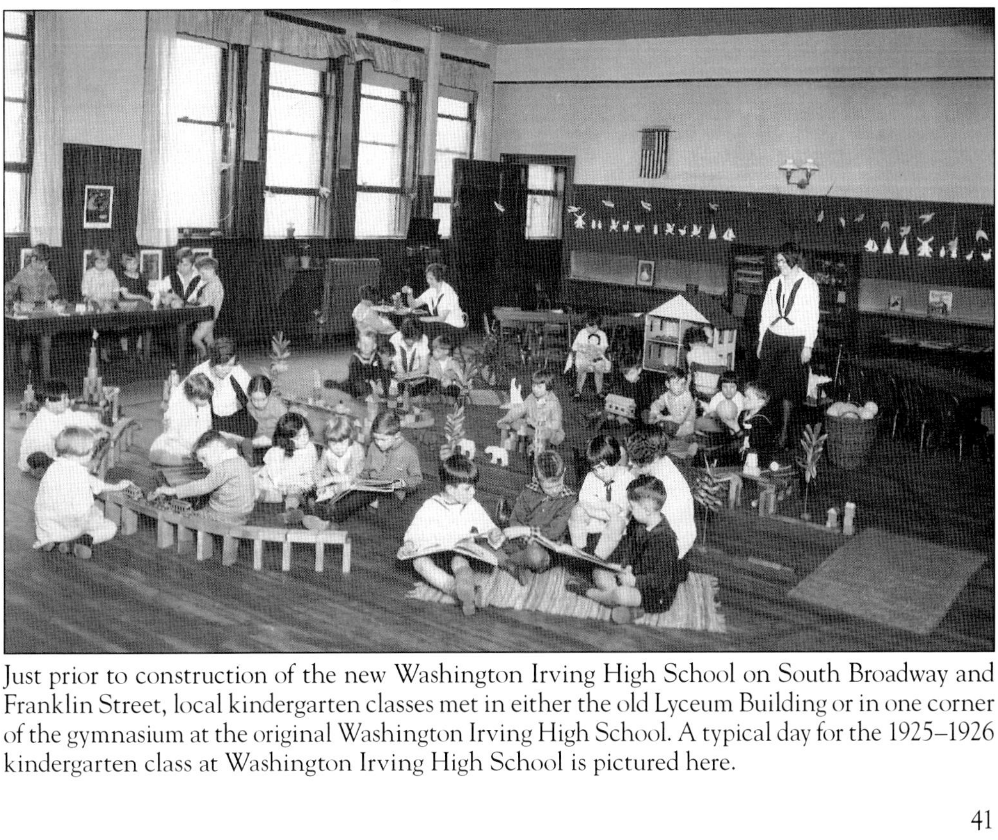

Just prior to construction of the new Washington Irving High School on South Broadway and Franklin Street, local kindergarten classes met in either the old Lyceum Building or in one corner of the gymnasium at the original Washington Irving High School. A typical day for the 1925–1926 kindergarten class at Washington Irving High School is pictured here.

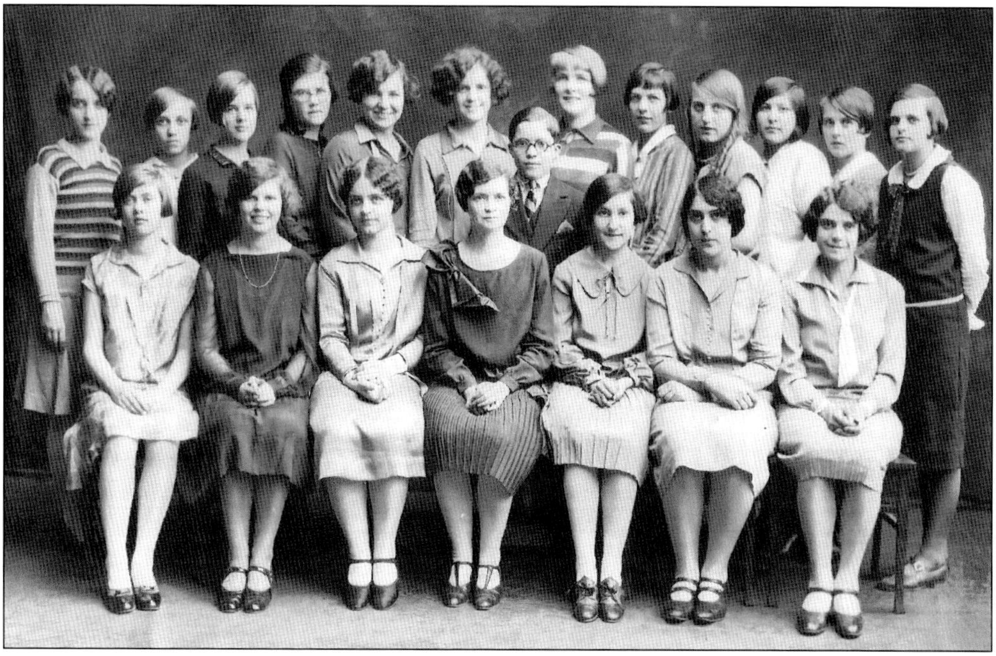

This photograph shows the North Tarrytown High School French Club in 1927. According to local yearbooks, the purpose of the club was to "bring about a better understanding of French life and customs while acquiring fluency in French speech." Club activities included playing French games, singing French songs, and serving delicious refreshments.

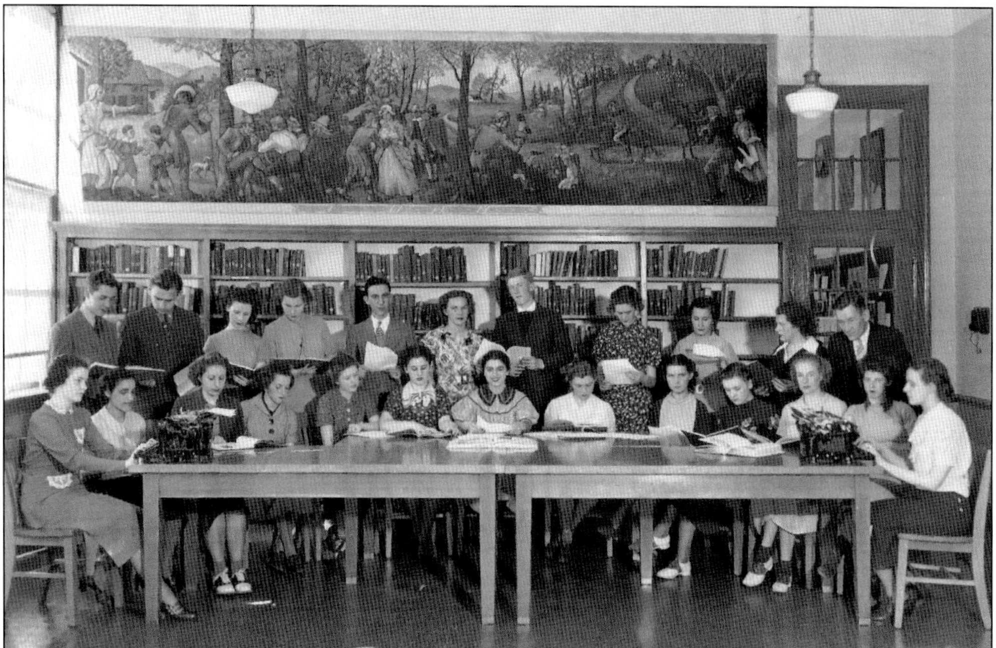

The North Tarrytown High School yearbook staff of 1937 is pictured above. The staff of the *Headless Horseman* included five editors: Yetta Alter, Lucille Johnson, Sylvia Page, Margaret Schneider, and Ann Walsh.

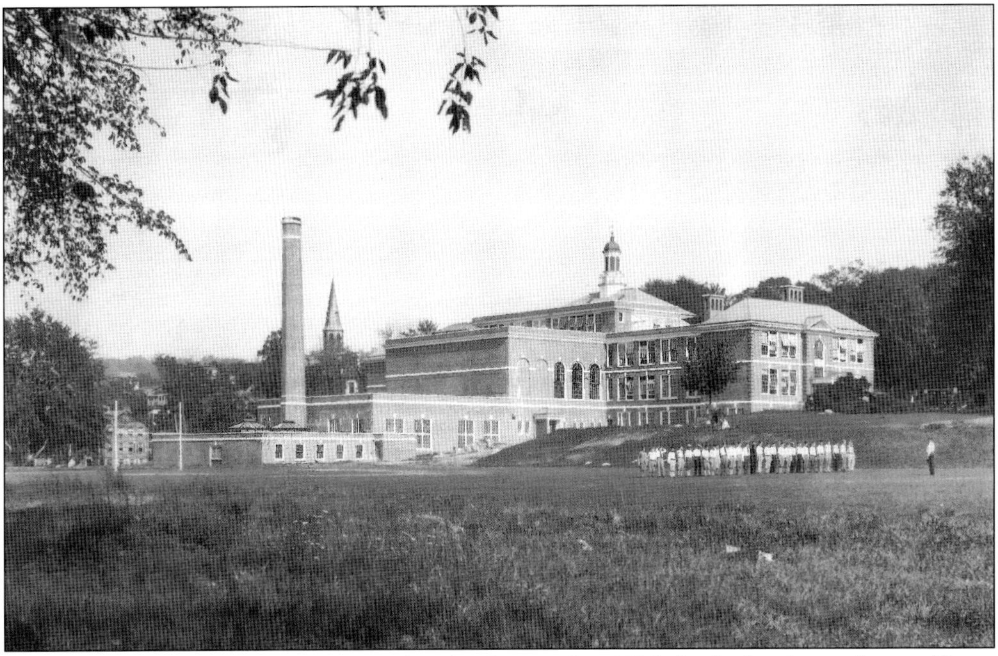

When the new Washington Irving High School opened in 1925, the facility boasted several large athletic fields. A *c.* 1930 view shows the fields, bleachers, and rear of the new school building. The field soon became a gathering spot for local celebrations and events.

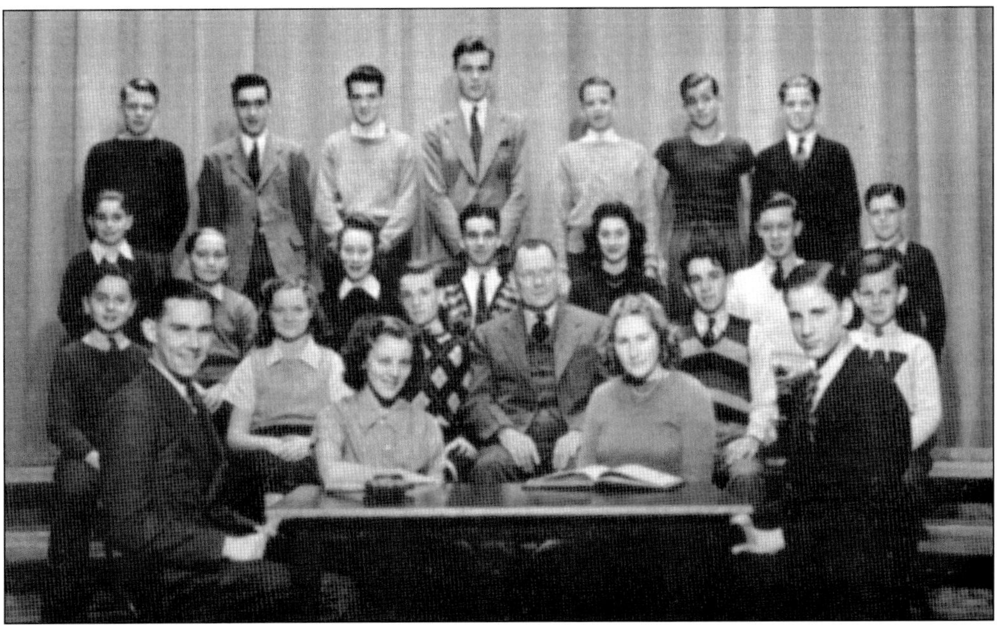

The class officers of the 1940 student council at Washington Irving High School included, from left to right, (first row) Ernst Steurer, president; Elizabeth Verrone, treasurer; Margaret Prideaux, secretary; and Richard Hartline, vice president. Oscar F. Koch, principal and faculty advisor, is seated in the center of the second row.

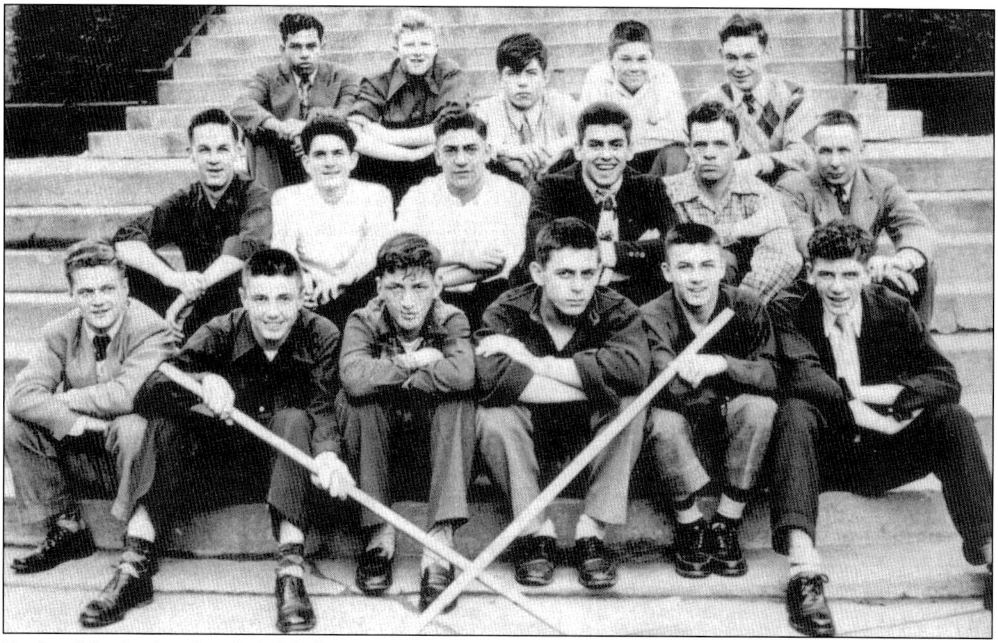

Each of the high schools fielded teams in a variety of sports. The Washington Irving High School 1949 hockey team included, from left to right, (first row) Daniel Rizzi, Walter Ceconi, John Kucich, John Gileno, Robert Collin, and Roman Windas; (second row) John Fiala, Angelo Paolantonio, Francis Galgano, Joseph Occhipinti, Robert Nichol, and coach Harold Rasbeck; (third row) Andrew Garrant, Arthur Weeks, Edward Garman, Robert Maher, and Joseph Partlow.

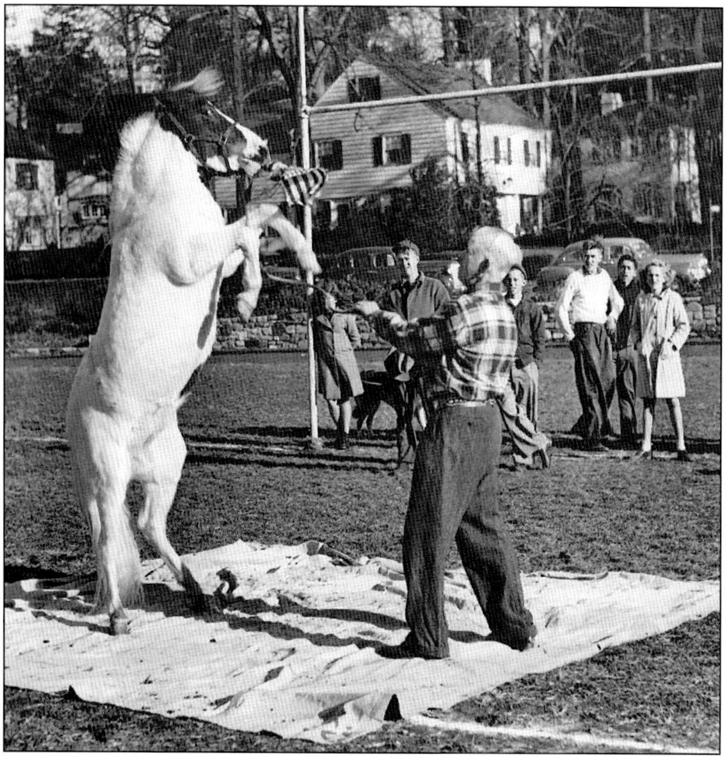

Seen in this 1950s image, Snowball was the beloved mascot for North Tarrytown High School from 1941 until 1957. Each day on their way to and from school, students passed by the spirited Mexican pony as he grazed in front of his home on the corner of Howard and Pocantico Streets. Snowball was originally owned by Willette Fitzpatrick and came to numerous sporting events each year.

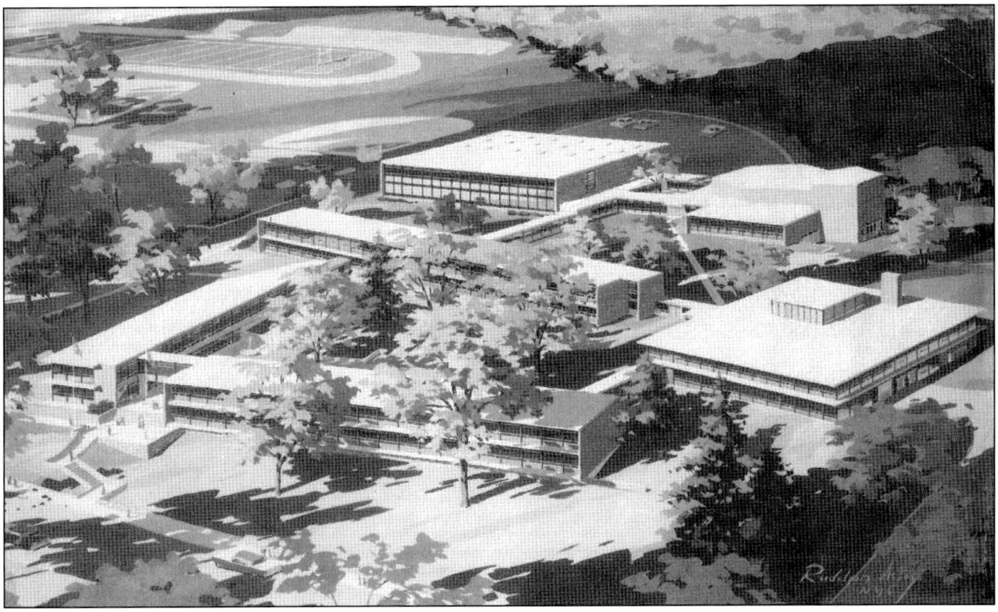

Beginning in 1920, public debates took place regarding the consolidation of the public schools in the two villages. Although consolidation was finally approved by a vote in 1949, it was not until 1957 that the combined Sleepy Hollow High School opened. For a total cost of $3,955,000, the site was purchased, architects Perkins and Will from White Plains designed the building, and general contractor Stewart Muller from Croton completed the land improvement and construction.

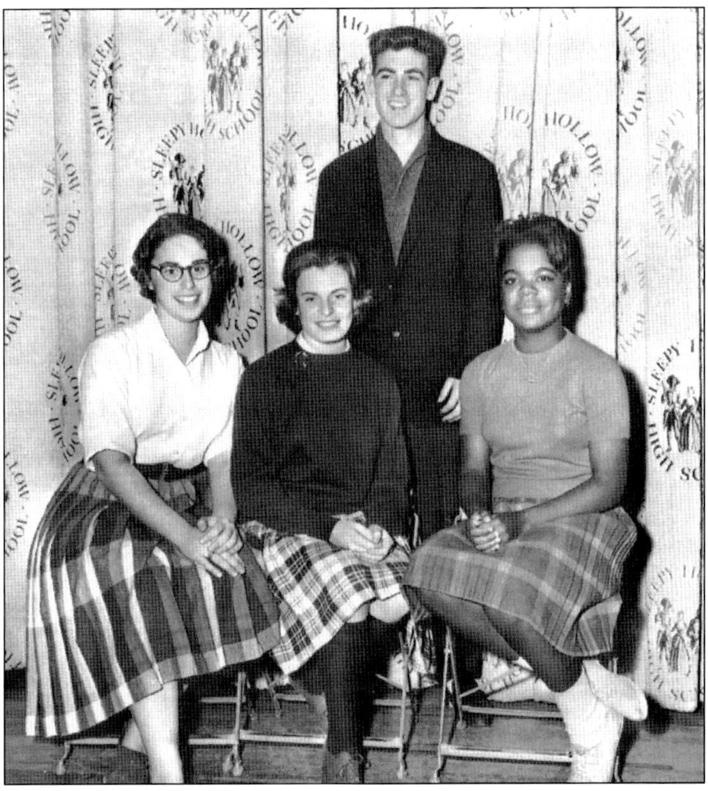

In 1961, the sophomore class officers at Sleepy Hollow High School included, from left to right, Carole Kuster, Toby Sladkus, Charles Brockner, and Naomi Cardwell.

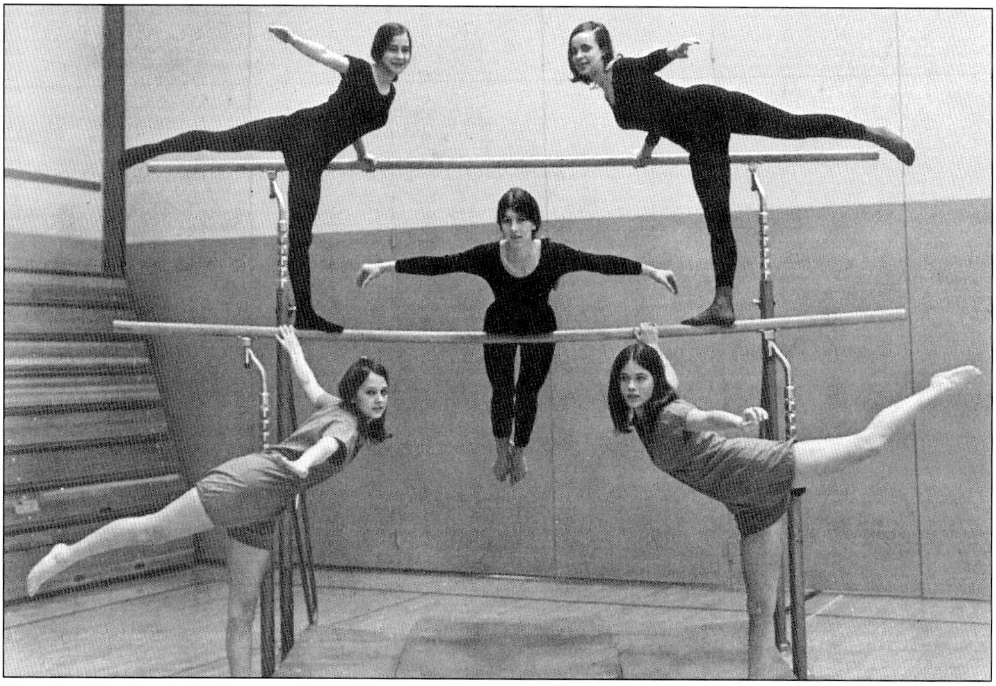

Coached by Linda Pellinger, the 1969 girls gymnastics team met twice a week. The team included, from left to right, (first row) G. Ettlemyer and Susan Crosbie; (second row) C. Fairlie, N. Bibbo, and Barbara Chebetar.

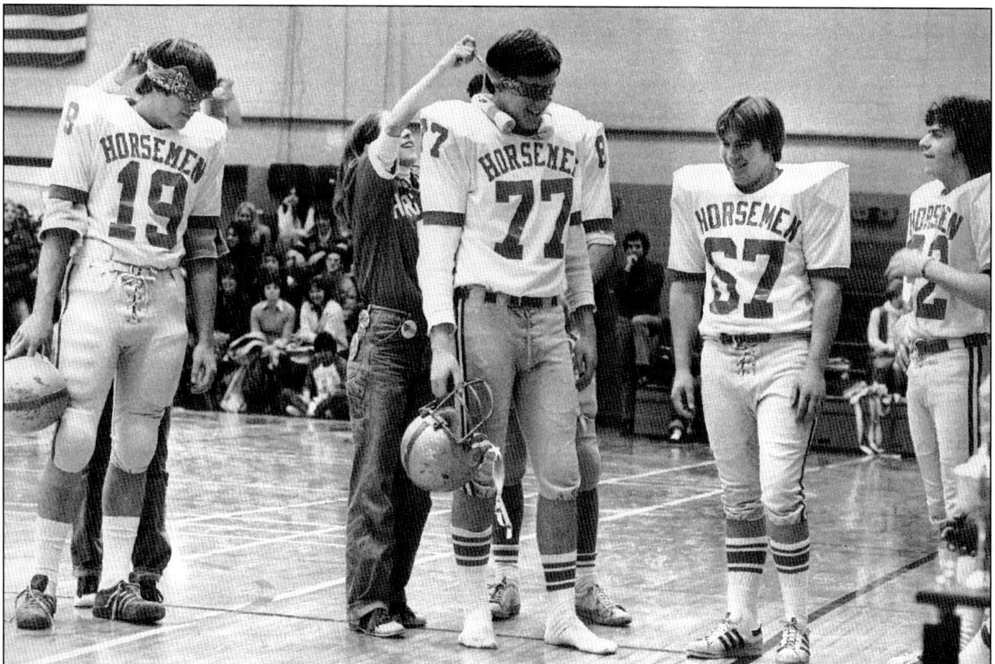


Once the schools were consolidated during the second half of the 20th century, Ossining High School became the major sports rival of the new Sleepy Hollow High School. Here a cheerleader is blindfolding football players at a pep rally on November 16, 1979.

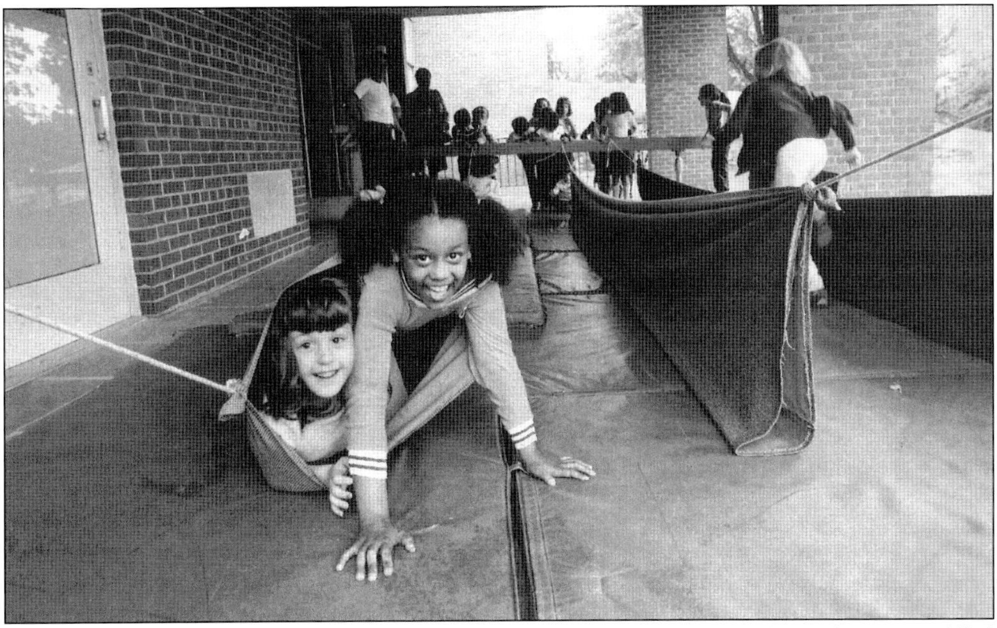

During the 1970s, the students and staff at Sleepy Hollow High School planned an event-filled day called Joy Day, where students were able to partake in a variety of crafts, music, and athletic activities. This program spread to adjacent John Paulding School, where the staff held Fun Day for the students for several years. Here Rena Pasalides and Fanny Rojas are shown participating in the 1981 Fun Day.

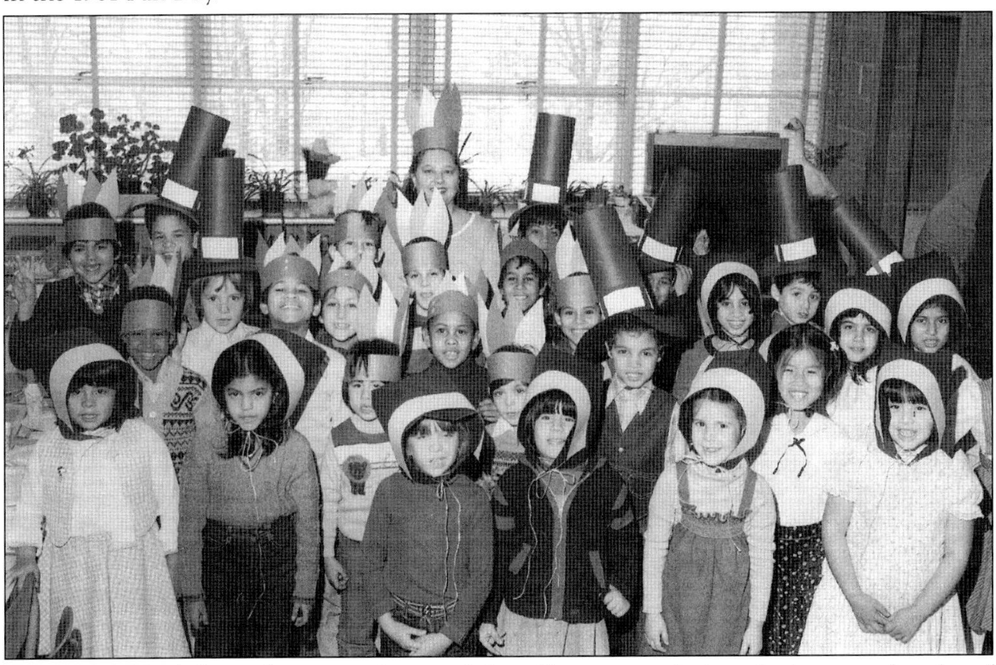

As the non-English speaking population of the villages grew during the last two decades of the 20th century, the number of English as a Second Language (ESL) teachers and classes also increased. Ana Lissabet and her multicultural ESL class at John Paulding School are shown above celebrating Thanksgiving in November 1980.

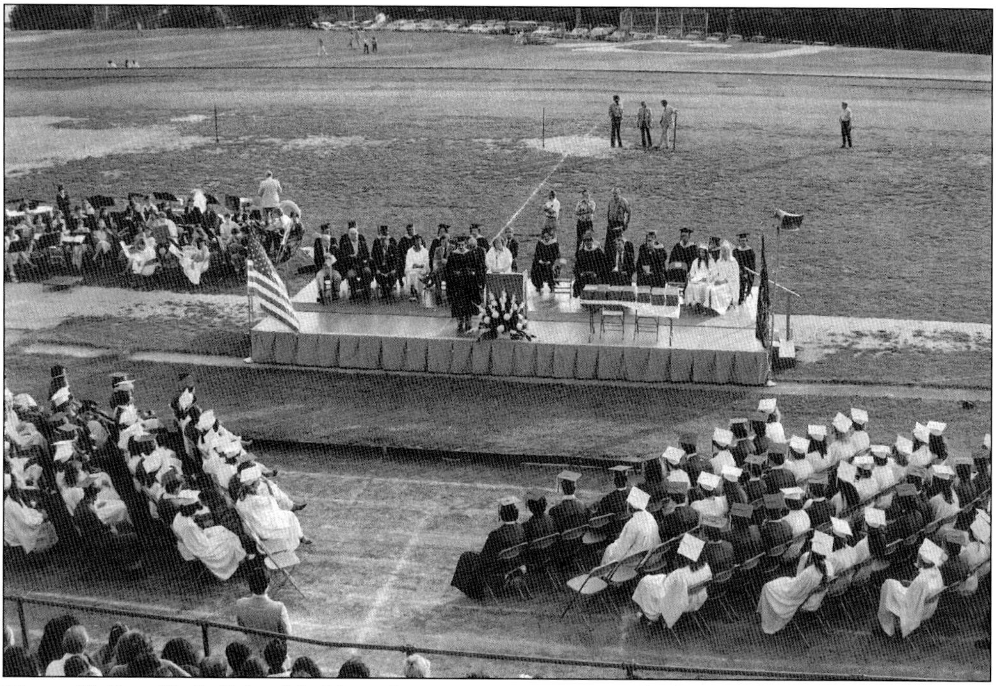

Sleepy Hollow High School held graduation ceremonies on the large athletic field behind the school. In this photograph, school board president Julie Wolf and principal Joseph Di Palermo are shown preparing to hand out diplomas to the class of 1980.

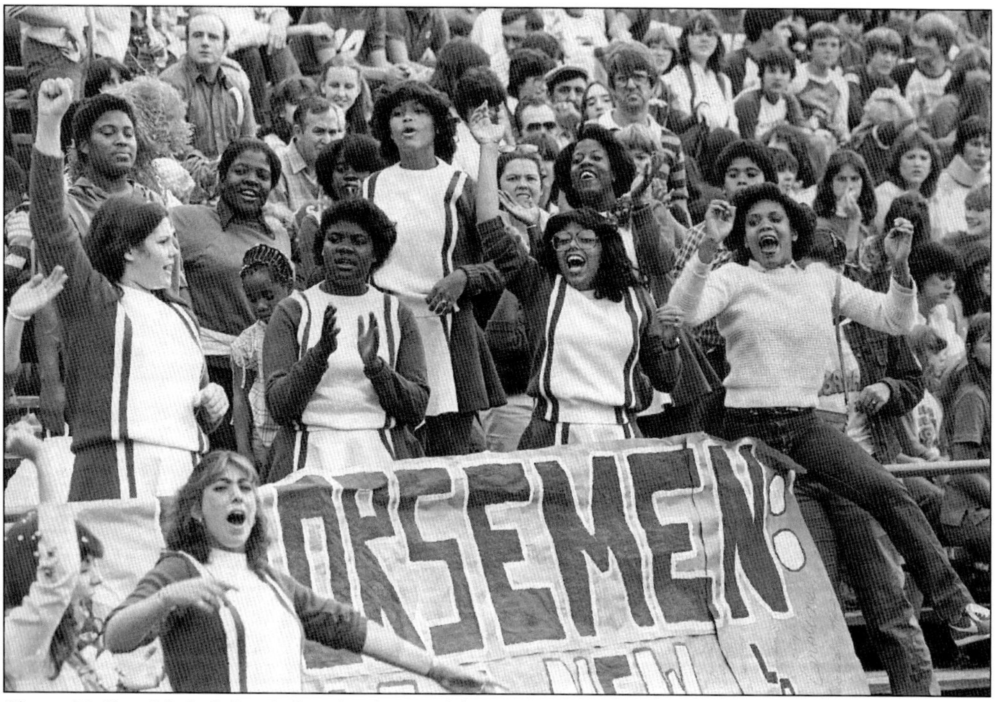


Sleepy Hollow High School cheerleaders and fans celebrate after the Horsemen score a touchdown during a game in September 1981.

# *Four*

# POLITICS AND POLITICIANS

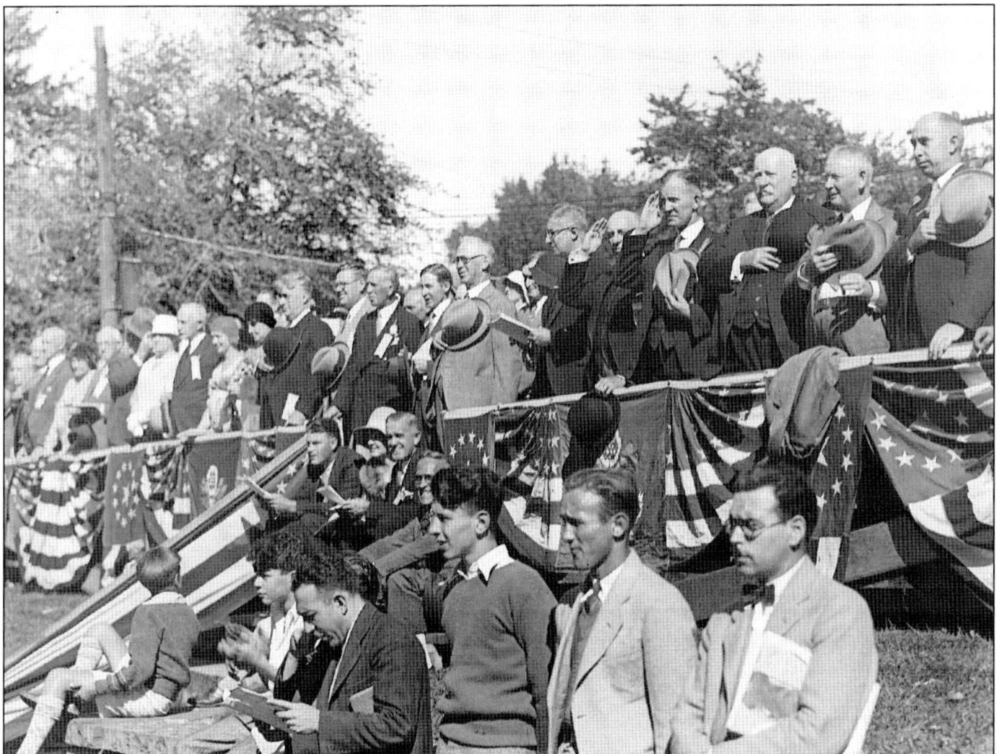

One of the earliest issues that united local politicians was the elimination of the street-level grade crossing near the Tarrytown train station. The issue came to a head following the death of Judge Frank V. Millard at the crossing. A decision was finally reached to build a bridge over the tracks to save lives. After the completion of the H-Bridge, a ceremony was held at Washington Irving High School on October 3, 1925.

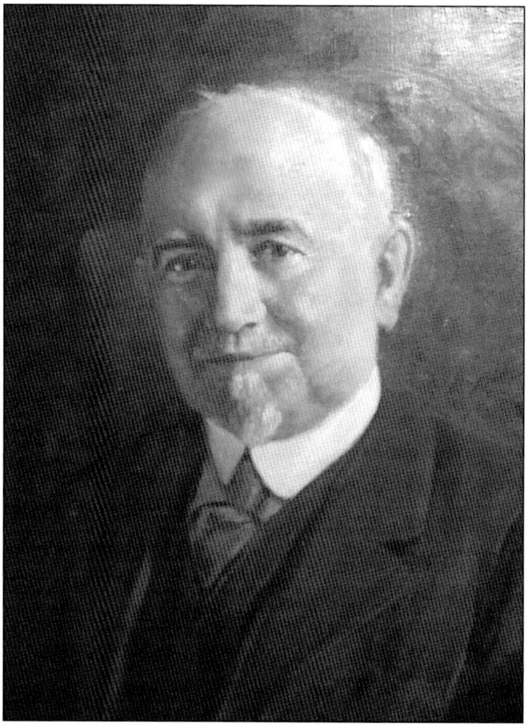

Frank Romer Pierson was a beloved local florist and importer of flower bulbs from Holland, France, and Japan. From 1910 until 1921, Pierson served as Tarrytown's village president. During that time, Broadway was unpaved, and the village trustees were split over whether to use blacktop or Hastings block to improve the road. Pierson broke the tie by voting in favor of blacktop, prompting locals to call the paved road Pierson's Pie Crust.

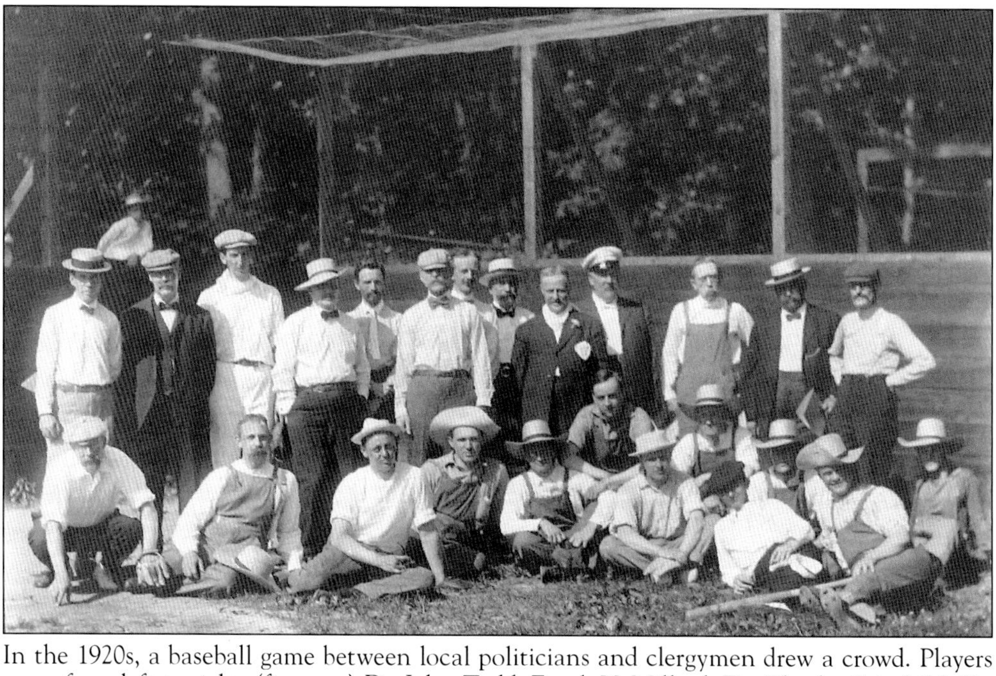

In the 1920s, a baseball game between local politicians and clergymen drew a crowd. Players were, from left to right, (first row) Dr. John Todd, Frank V. Millard, Dr. Charles Fairchild, Dr. McBean, John Ewing, Winfield H. Morse, two unidentified, Hugh Thornton, Gerald Fitzgerald, Charles Millard, and Fred Russell; (second row) Rev. Arthur Mabon, Ike Requa, Ray Strong, Dr. Erdman Brandt, Dr. John Robertson, Dr. Luke Fleming, Dr. Howard Coles, Dr. Nicholas Freeland, Dr. William Moorehouse, W. H. Ely, Clarence Davison, Jim Requa, and Dr. Owen Igoe.

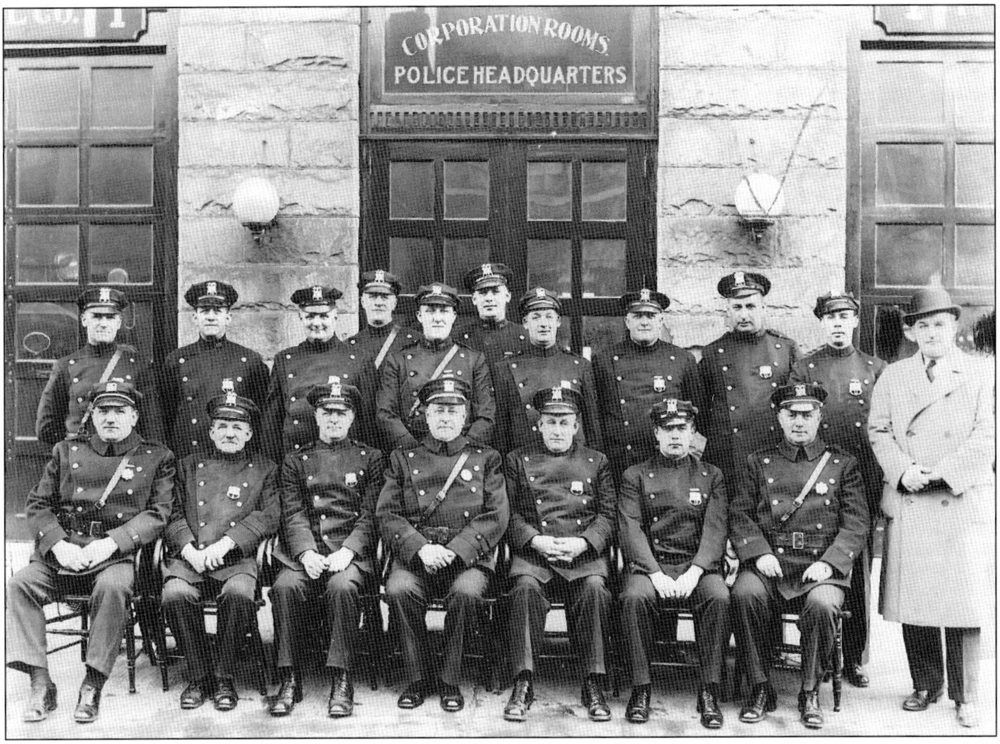


During the early 20th century, the village government for Tarrytown was located in the Vanderbilt Building, often called the Corporation Building, on Main Street. The building housed the police department, two volunteer fire companies, the office of the village engineer, and the trustees meeting room. The village shared the building with Solomon's Lodge No. 196 Free and Accepted Masons. Behind the structure was the village jailhouse.

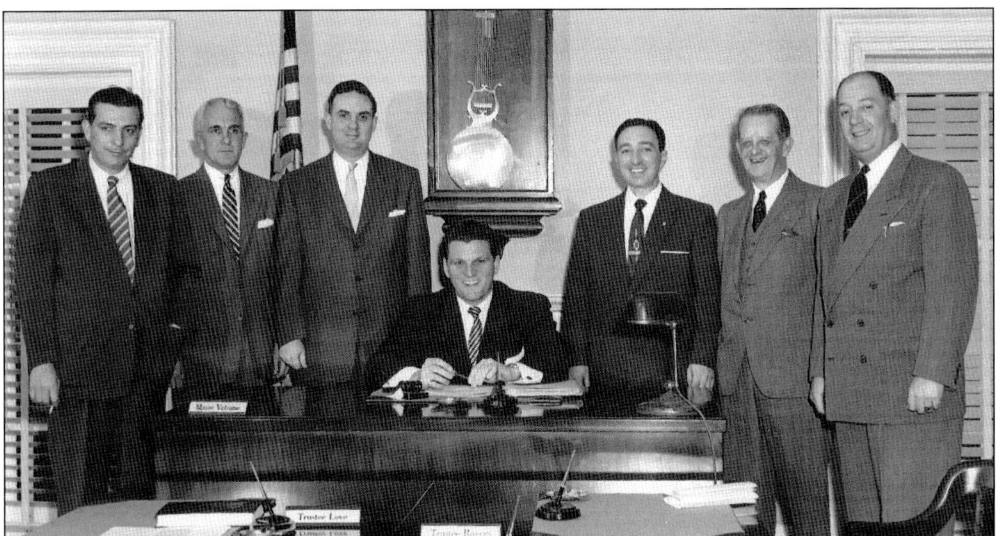

Edward N. Vetrano was elected mayor of Tarrytown in 1951 and served until 1957. He is pictured above with his board of trustees in Village Hall. From left to right are Roy Moffett, Kenneth Lyden, William Love, Mayor Vetrano, Charles Brietenbach, Embree Rogers, and Roger Martin.

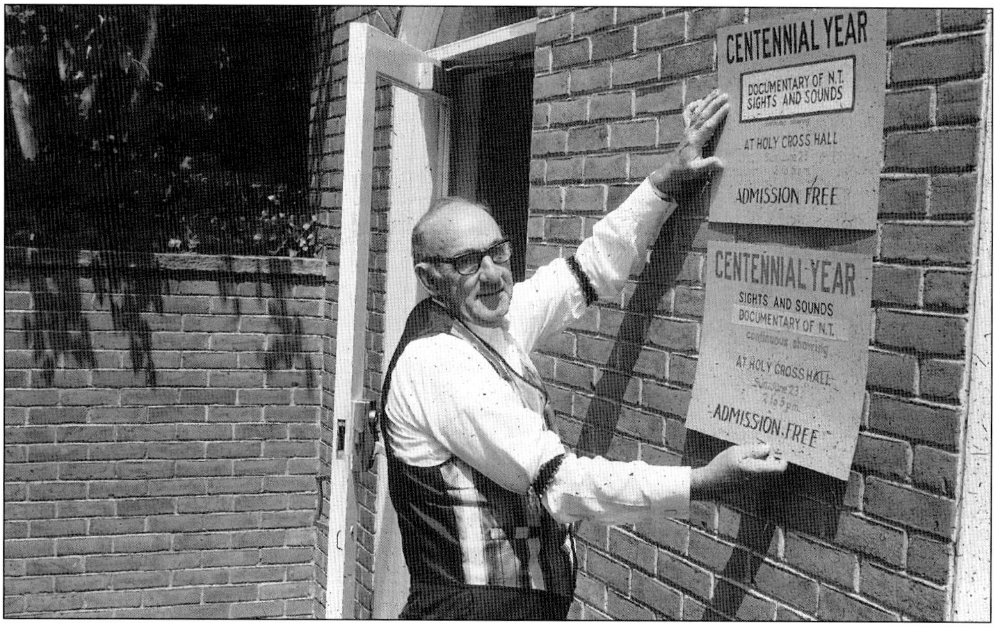


North Tarrytown centennial chairman Gabriel Hayes was village mayor from 1950 until 1961. Born in North Tarrytown, he lived almost his entire life in the village. When he returned from the Second World War, Hayes became guidance director at North Tarrytown High School (later Sleepy Hollow) and served until 1973. A grand knight of St. Elmo's Council of the Knights of Columbus, he was known for his dedication to education, church, government, and community service.

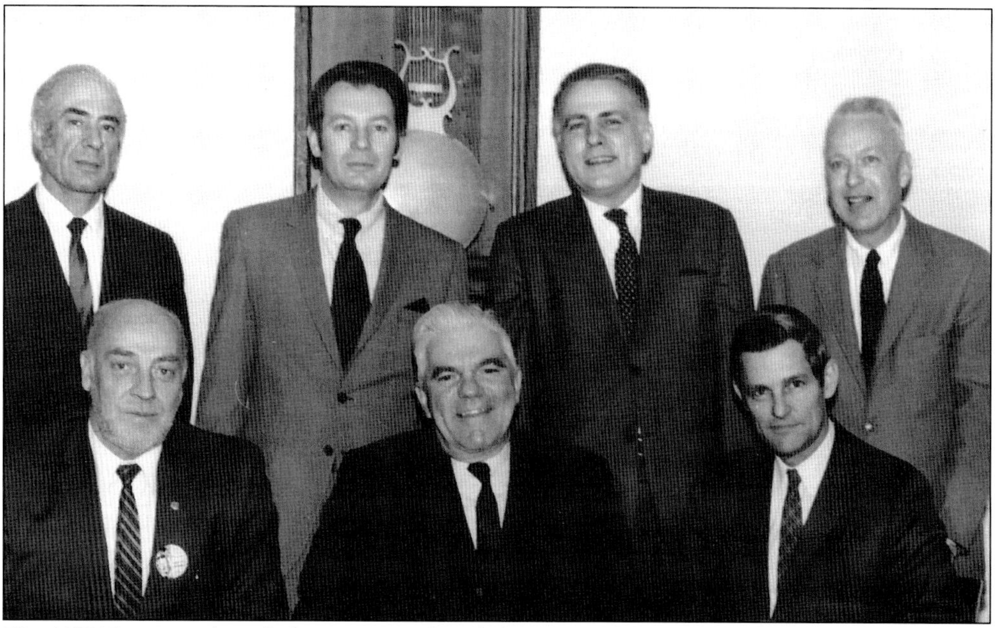

The 1970 Tarrytown board of trustees are, from left to right, (first row) Bill Basher, Mayor Anthony Veteran, and George Case; (second row) Ray Calore, Ray McGovern, John Bonomi, and Patrick Byrnes. Veteran served as Tarrytown mayor from 1959 until 1973. He was also a nine-term Greenburgh town supervisor. Like most local politicians, he held a regular full-time job. For over 25 years, Veteran was employed by the neighboring Elmsford School District.

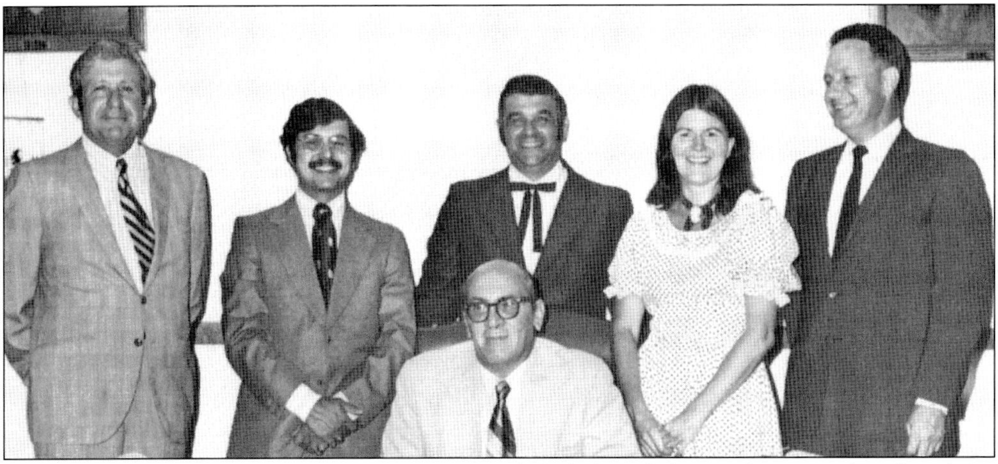

The 1974 North Tarrytown board of trustees included, from left to right, Ugo Checchi, Philip Zegarelli, John Malandrino, Emilie Spaulding, and James Timmings. Mayor James F. Galgano is seated in front. A sixth trustee, Patrick Munroe, is missing from the picture. Malandrino, with his ribbon tie, and Spaulding, in colonial dress, are costumed for the North Tarrytown centennial.

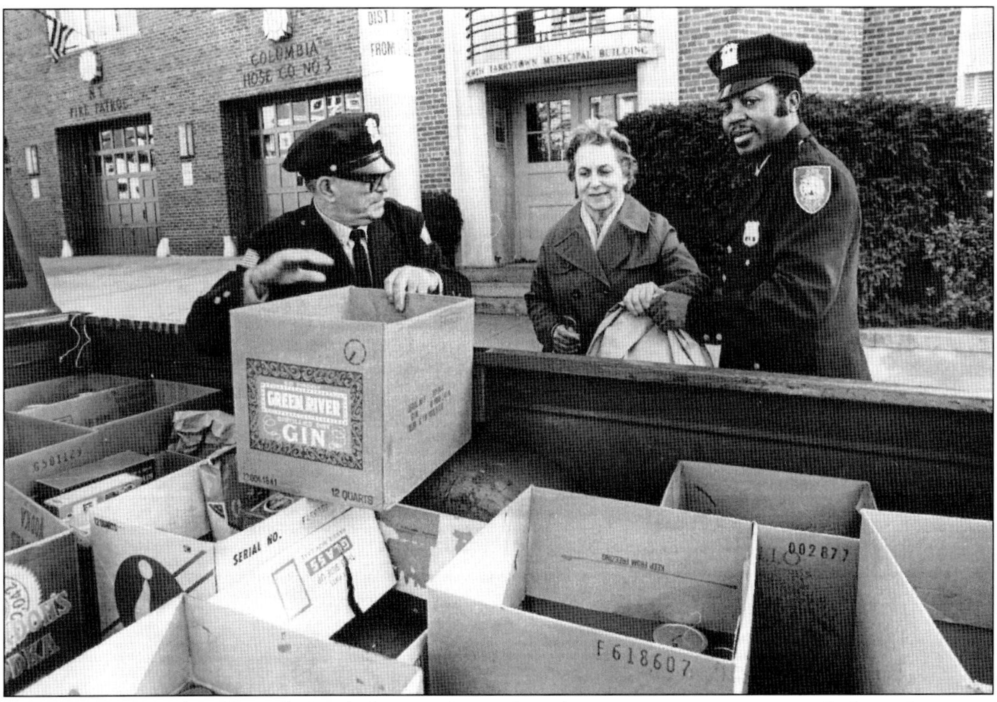


The auxiliary police have helped the regular police force in various ways, including directing traffic and helping with crowd control during community events. Shown here in front of the North Tarrytown Police Station assisting Elizabeth Maenza during a 1976 food drive are auxiliary policemen Tony DeOrio (left) and Teddy Wilcher.

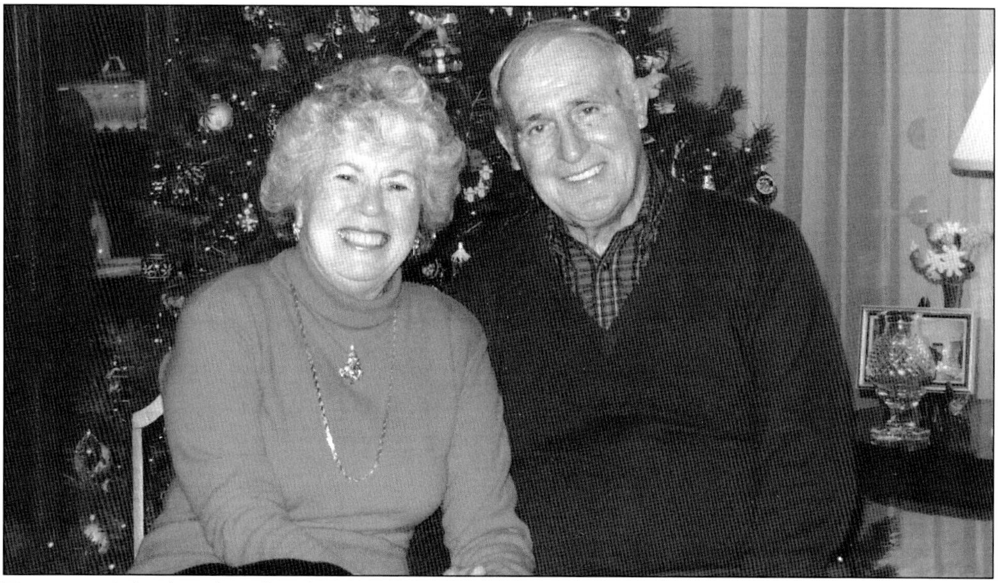

Tarrytown's husband and wife mayors, Eileen and Patrick Pilla, have a combined 27 years in public service. Pat became a trustee in 1972, was elected mayor in 1975, and served until 1983. Not to miss a beat, Eileen became a trustee that same year. She was elected mayor in 1987 and served until 1999. When the Pillas were not at village meetings, they could be seen visiting local shops and restaurants.

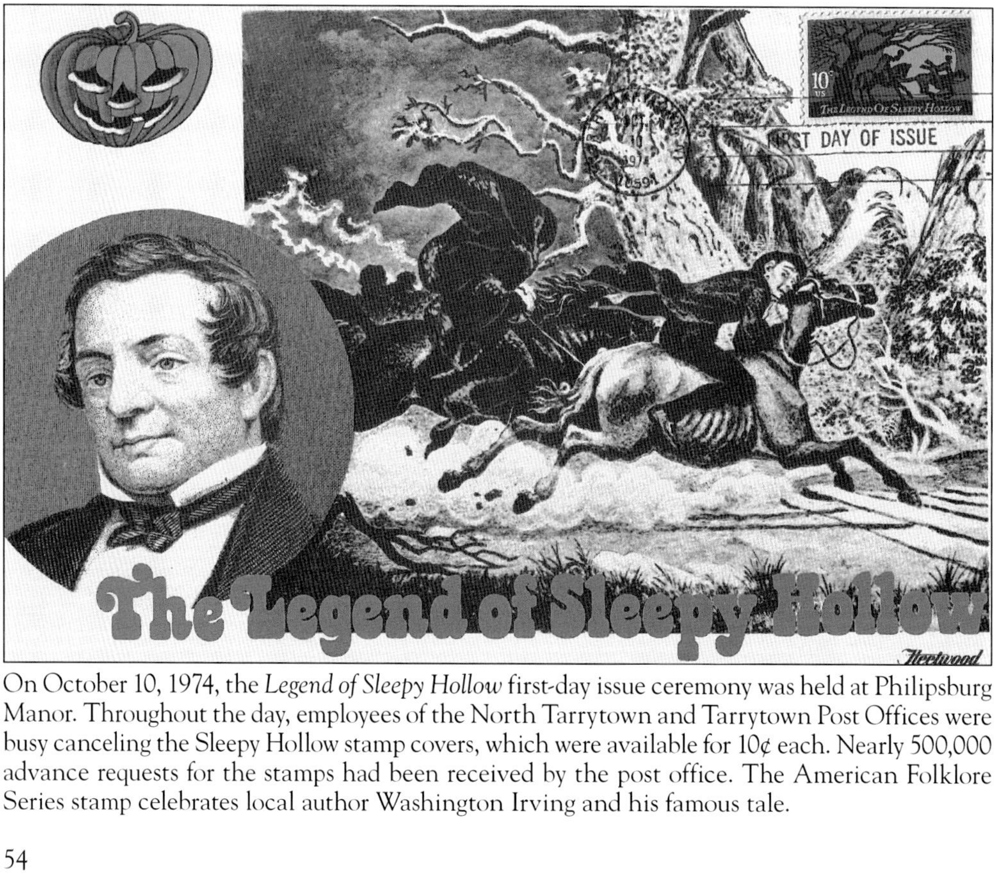


On October 10, 1974, the *Legend of Sleepy Hollow* first-day issue ceremony was held at Philipsburg Manor. Throughout the day, employees of the North Tarrytown and Tarrytown Post Offices were busy canceling the Sleepy Hollow stamp covers, which were available for 10¢ each. Nearly 500,000 advance requests for the stamps had been received by the post office. The American Folklore Series stamp celebrates local author Washington Irving and his famous tale.

# *Five*

# The Tappan Zee Bridge

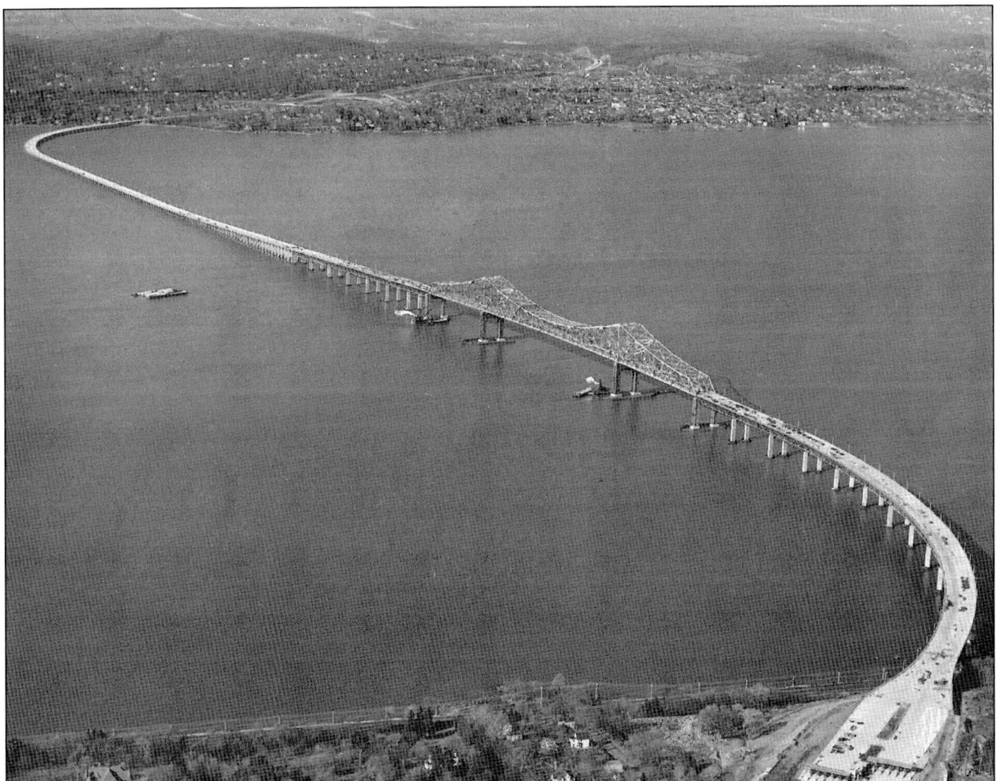

One of the most significant construction projects of the 20th century was the creation of the Tappan Zee Bridge. The pros and cons for the construction of a bridge between Tarrytown and Nyack had been the subject of heated debates since the 1930s. Eventually the economic need for a vital transportation link across the Hudson River outweighed the negatives, and the New York State Senate passed a bill in 1951 to eliminate any potential legal obstacles.

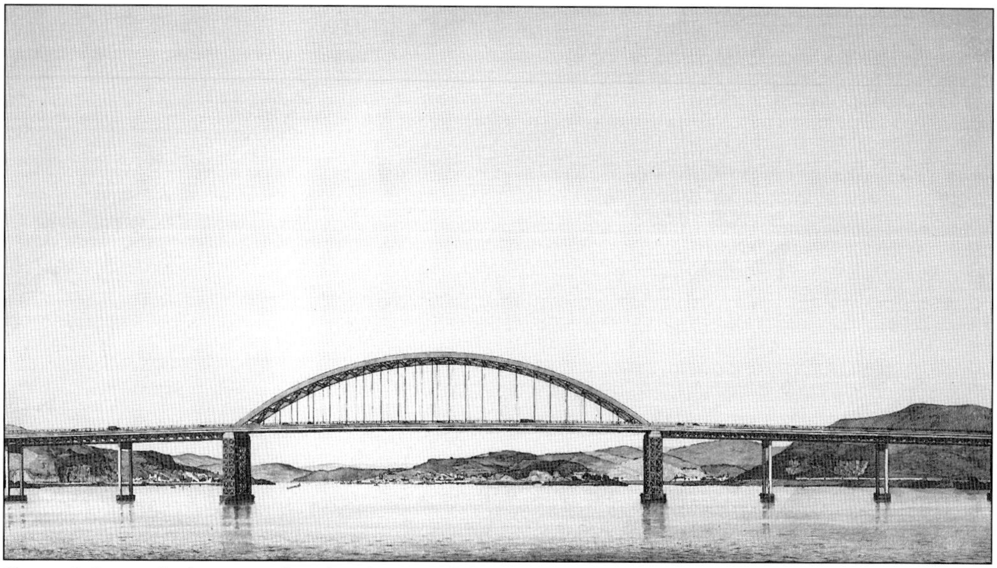

One of the early favorites for the design of the new bridge was this 1,000-foot tied-arch span created by the engineers at the New York Thruway Authority. This design was created with the idea that a single contractor would be able to complete the construction. No contractors submitted bids for the project, and this design was scrapped.

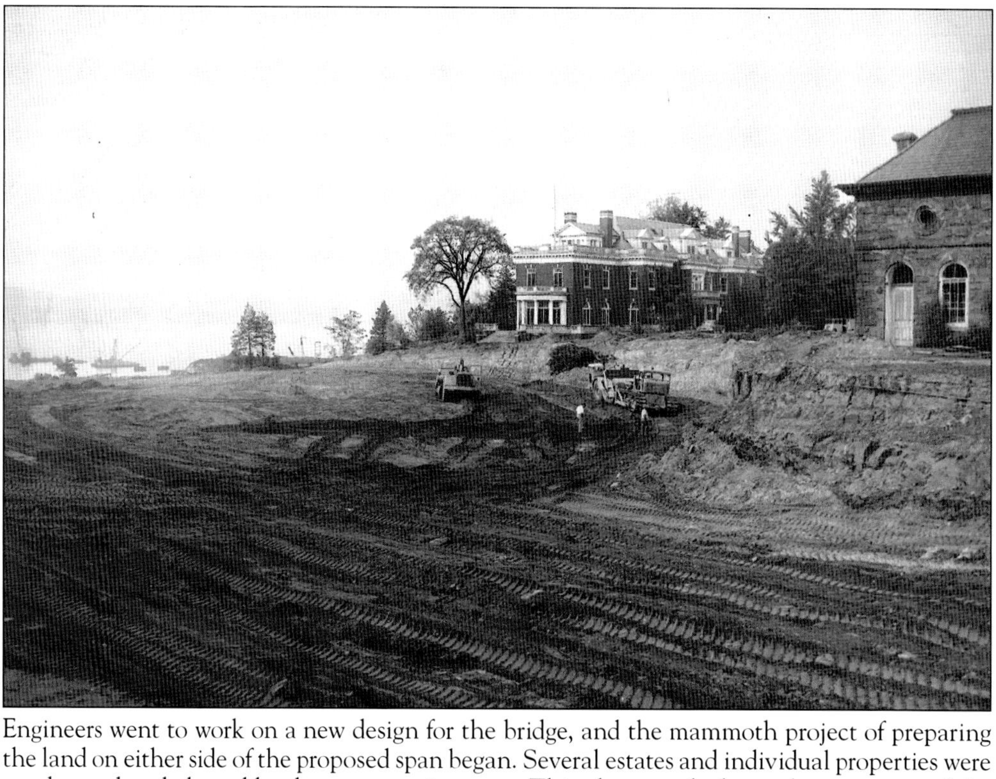

Engineers went to work on a new design for the bridge, and the mammoth project of preparing the land on either side of the proposed span began. Several estates and individual properties were condemned and cleared by the construction crew. This photograph shows the remnants of the Thomas Luke estate being razed in 1954.

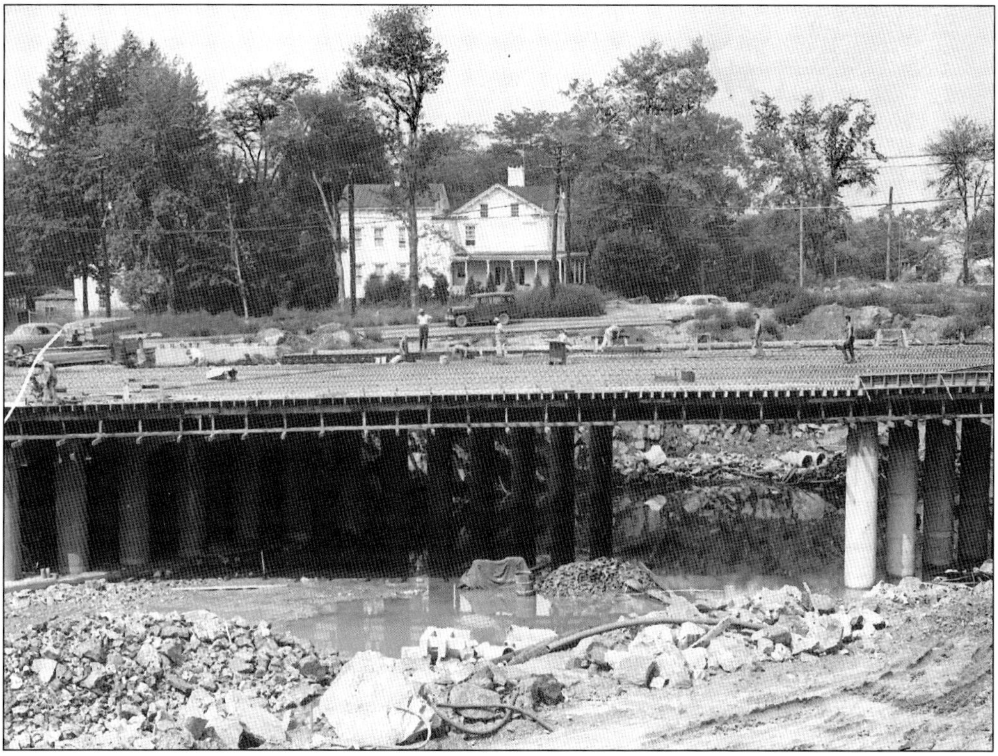

As part of ground preparation work during the early phases of construction, a large section of Broadway (Route 9) was altered to provide access for the New York State Thruway. The construction crew shown here is pouring concrete to build a new bridge to carry the traffic on Broadway over the planned thruway.

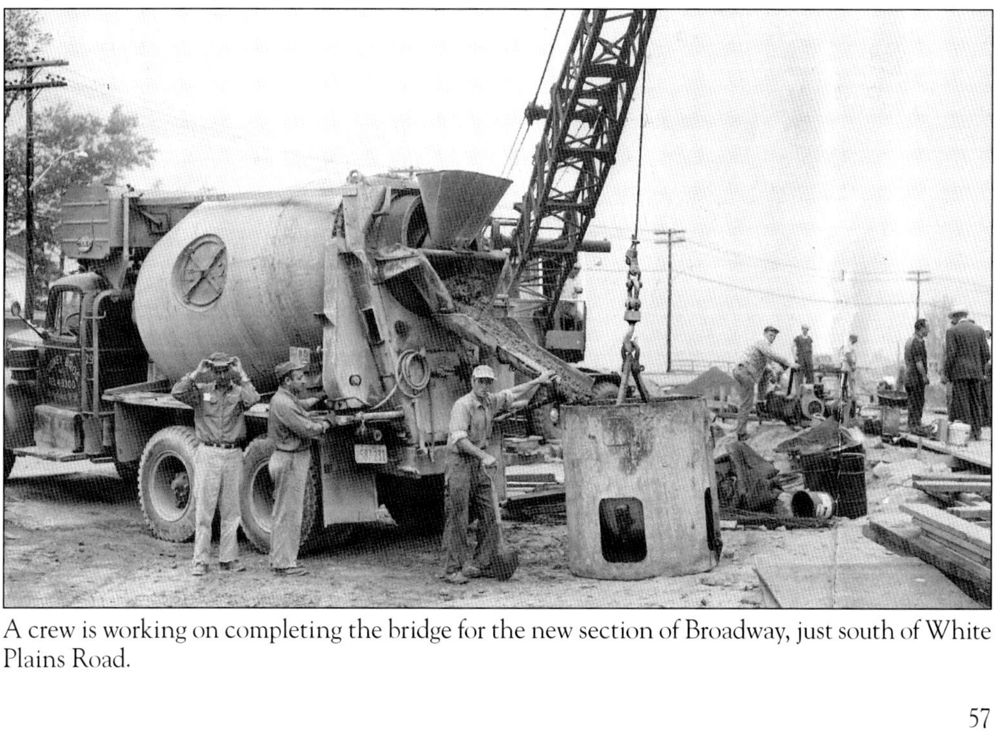

A crew is working on completing the bridge for the new section of Broadway, just south of White Plains Road.

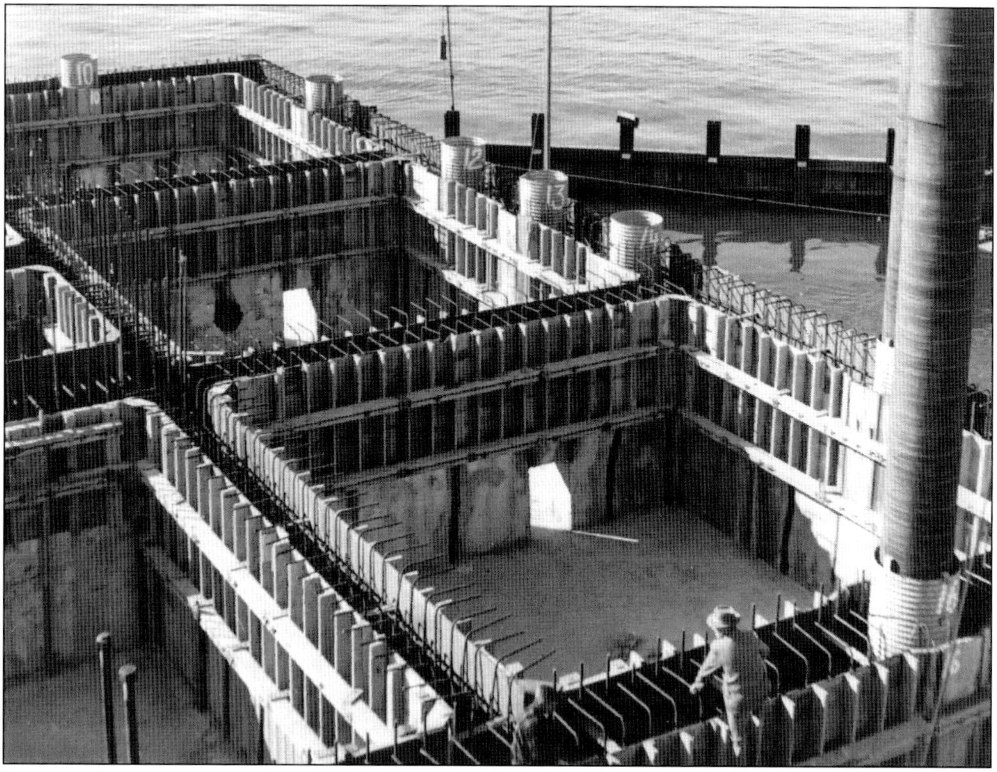

Because the site of the proposed bridge was located where bedrock lies too far beneath the river bottom to support piers for the main span, a new construction method developed during World War II was chosen for the final design. One of the features was the use of huge caissons (concrete watertight boxes) set on steel piles driven into the bedrock to support 70 percent of the weight of the bridge.

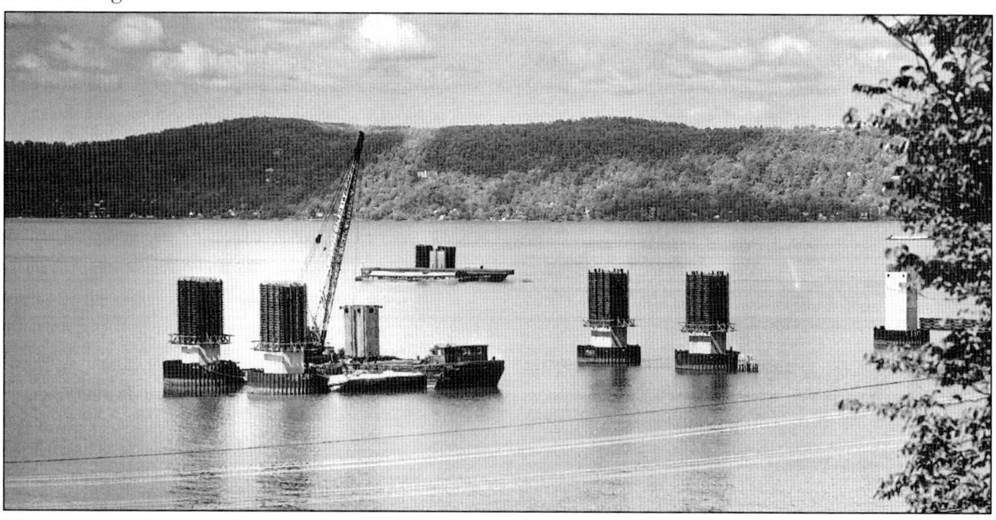

The caissons, built at Grasspoint near Haverstraw by Merritt-Chapman and Scott Corporation, were floated down the Hudson and sunk into position on specially prepared bases. Here piers of reinforced concrete await the placement of the steel-truss sections (also prefabricated in Haverstraw), which would support the final roadway.

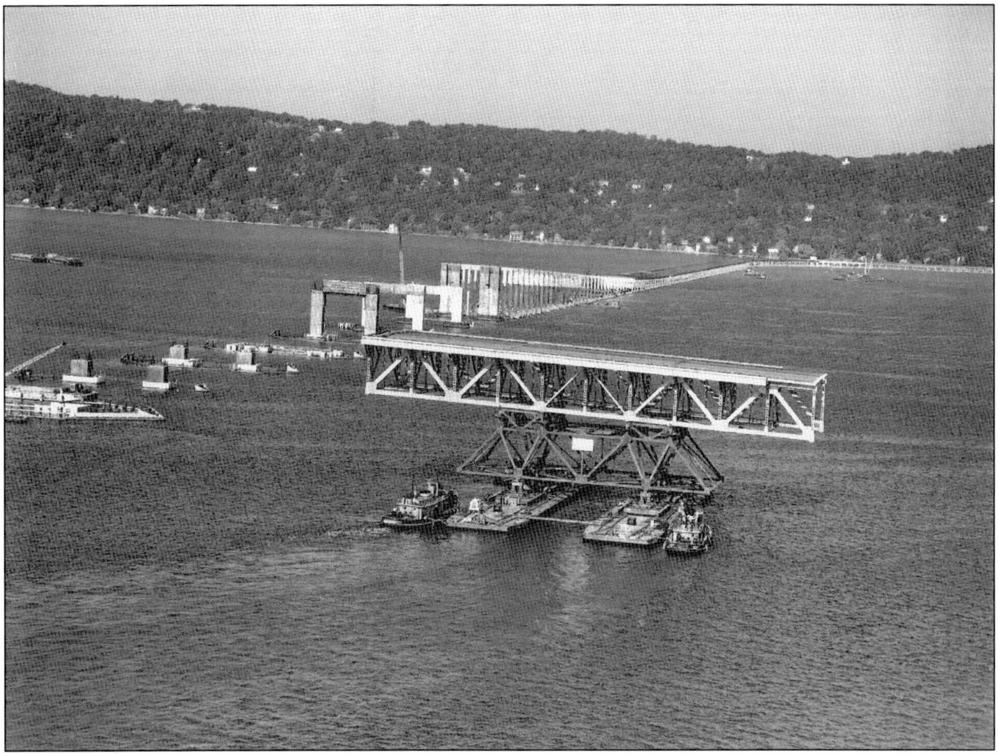

Exact tidal conditions were necessary as the trusses were floated downstream on barges and tugboats and then gently dropped into place by the receding tide.

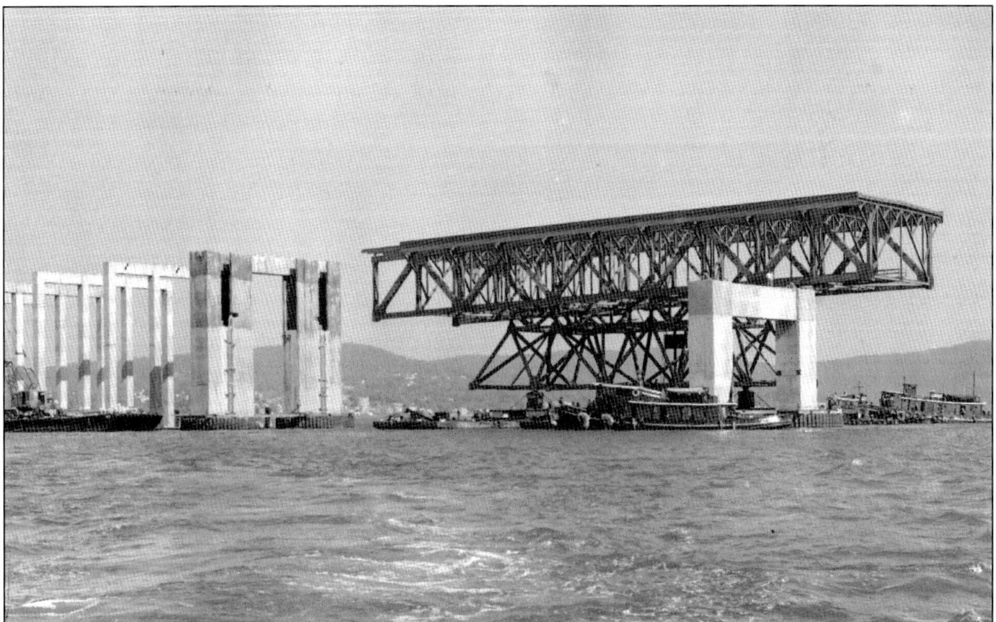

These dramatic pictures of the meticulous movement and placement of the bridge sections were taken by Catherine Peters McCaul, Tarrytown village clerk, over an extended period of time. Tugboats, barges, and numerous personnel were all vital parts of the construction process.

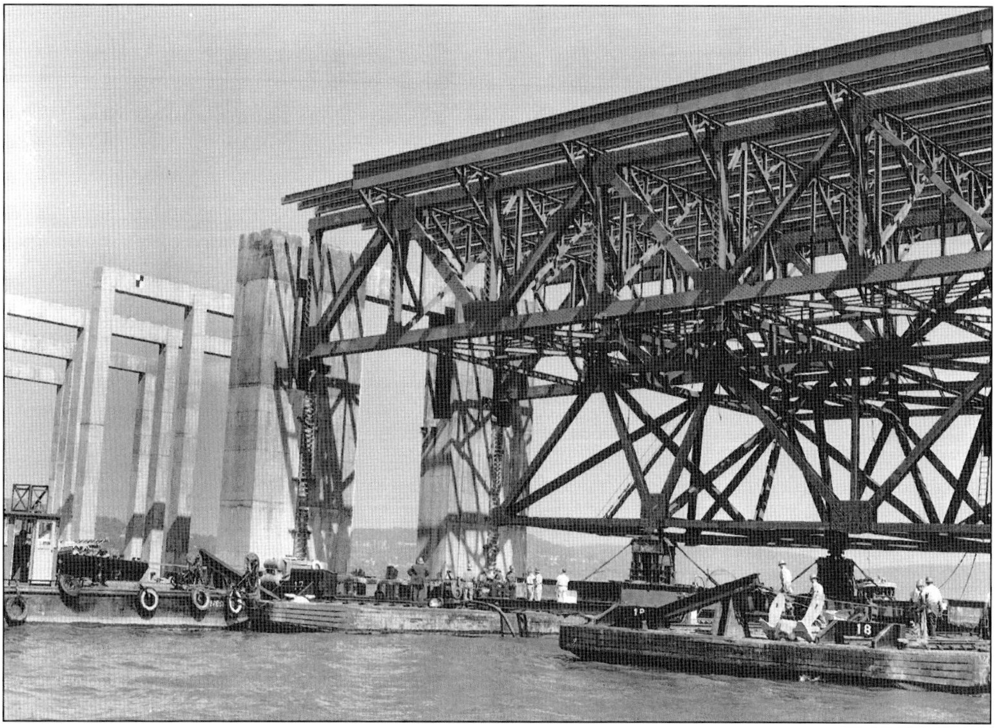

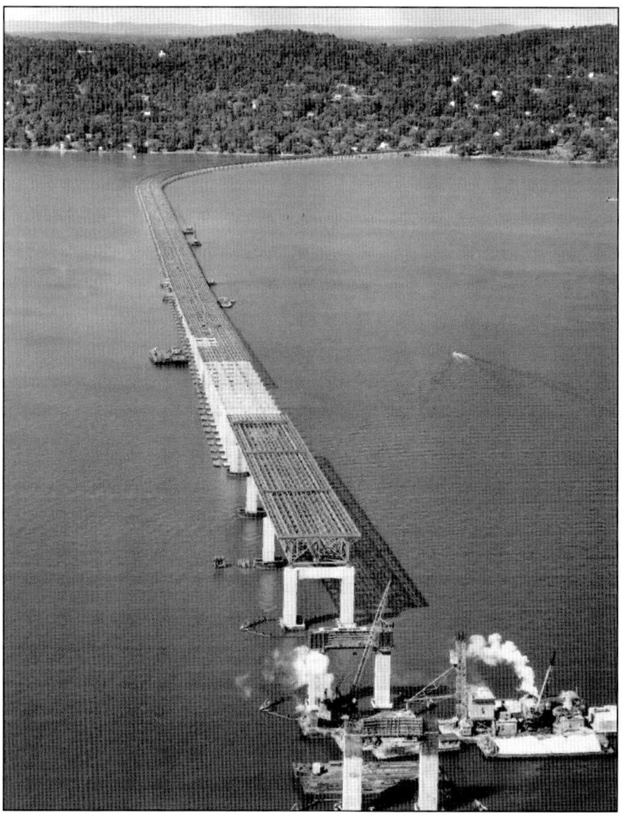

Scaffolding and huge steel trusses are being maneuvered into place by tugs and workers on the barges.

This photograph shows the curved causeway under construction. Contractors worked for a year to install underwater foundations for the structure with little visible above the surface except pilings and concrete supports.

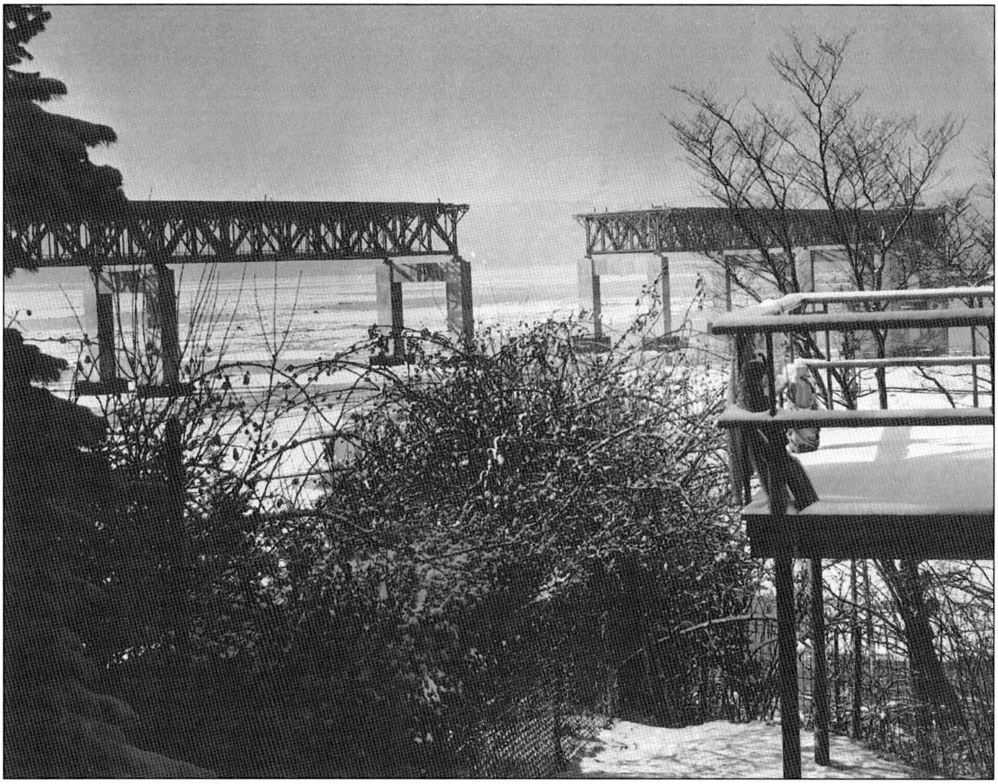

Viewed from the porch of a local residence, the new bridge is coming together piece by piece. Winter weather caused delays during construction, as heavy ice in the river threatened to damage the work already completed. The Coast Guard's icebreaker *Westwind* was assigned to break up the ice around the piers.

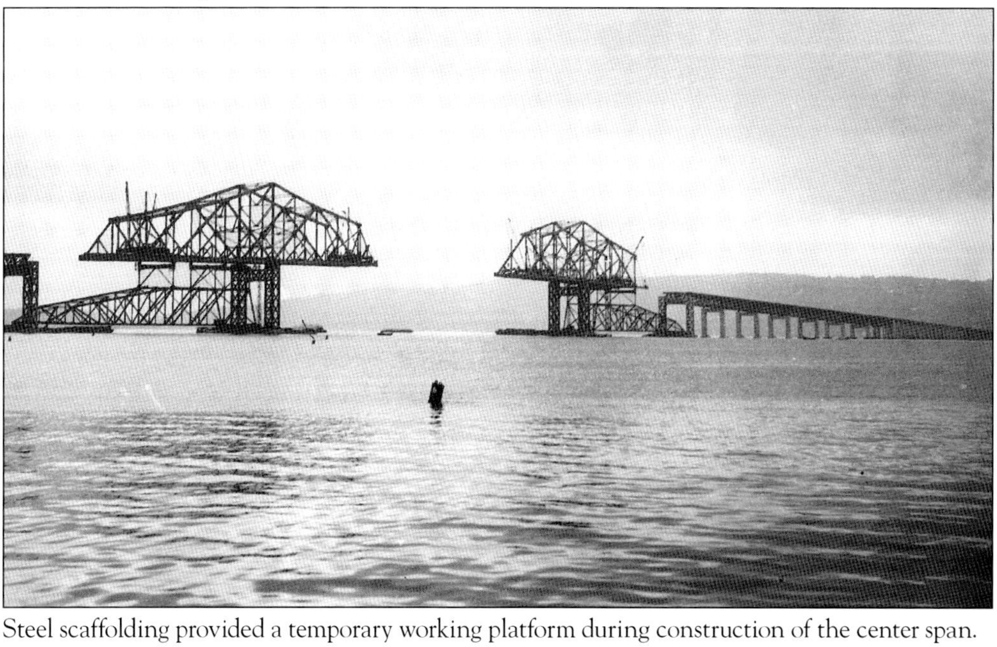

Steel scaffolding provided a temporary working platform during construction of the center span.

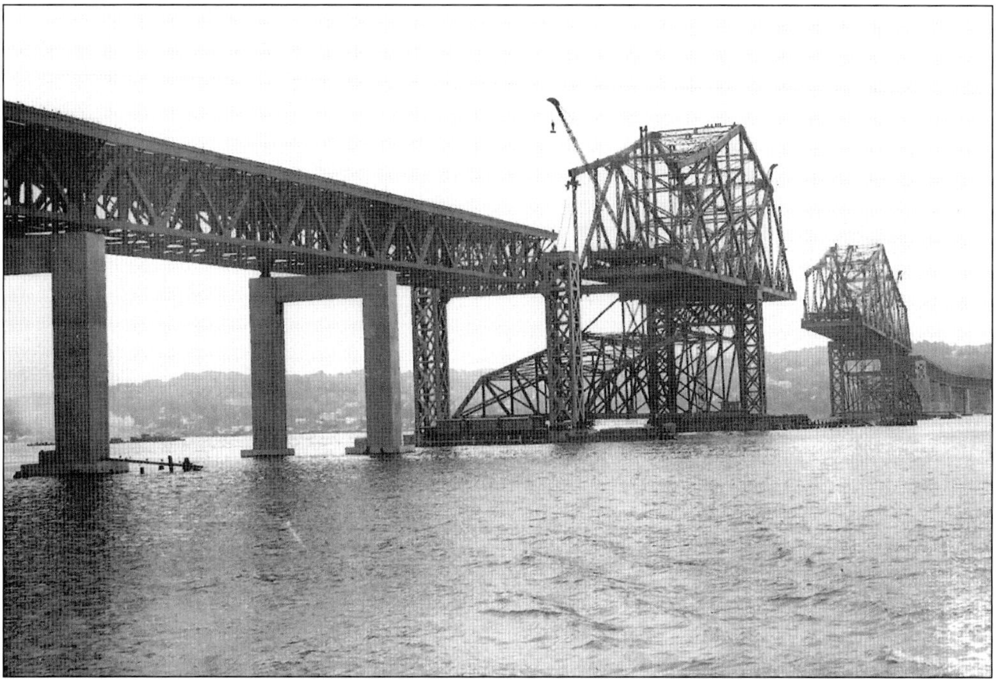

Two falsework sections were used for the main center span. They were among the largest ever created for use in bridge construction.

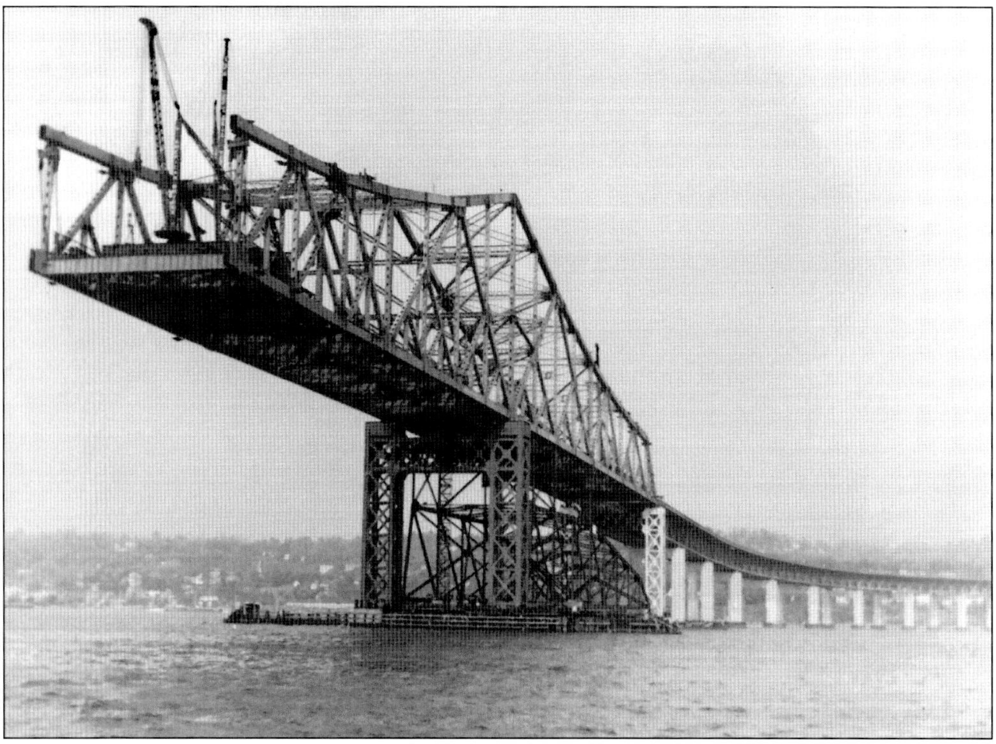

The cantilevered center span, shown near completion, would be 1,212 feet long and 138 feet above the river.

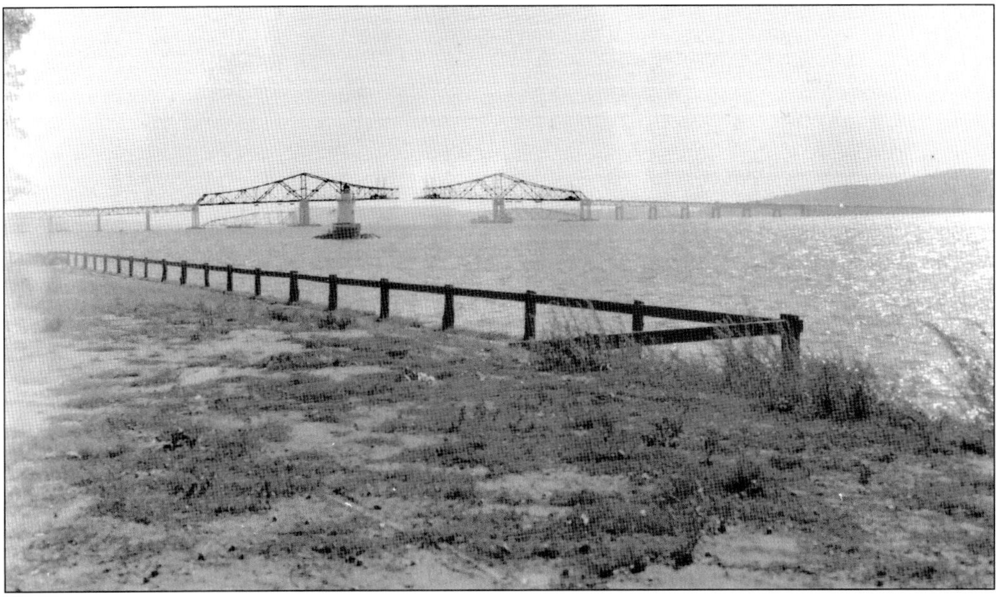

This view taken from Kingsland Point Park shows that only one section was needed to complete the 3-mile-long bridge. Construction had started in March 1952, and the final connection was made on September 29, 1955.

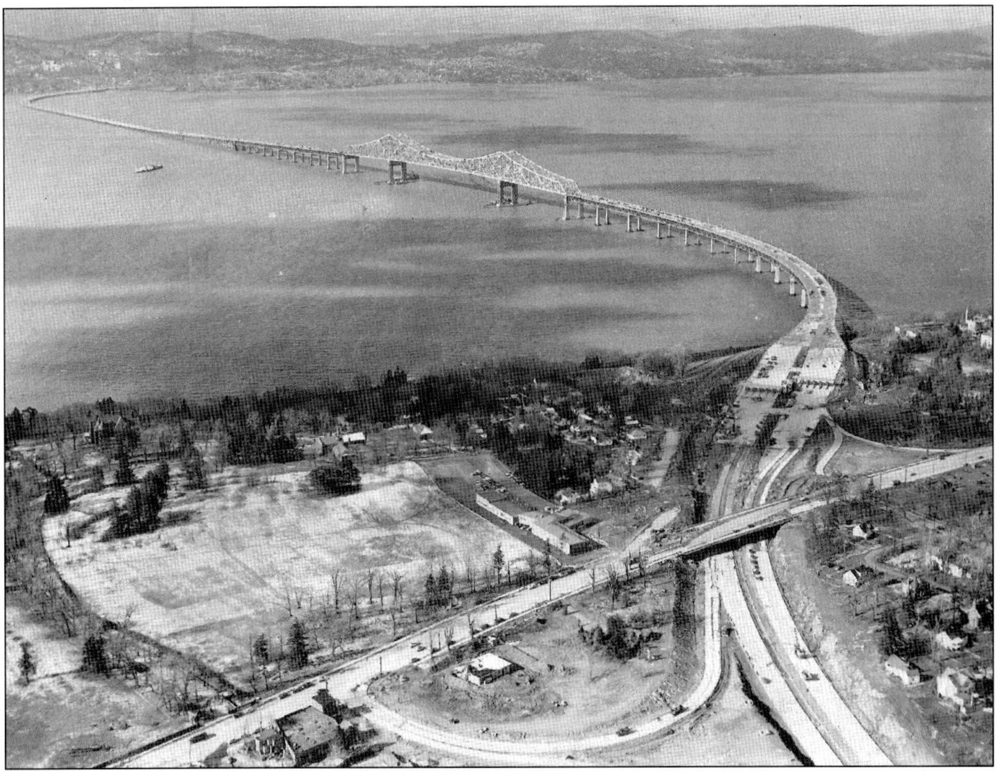

The toll plaza was one of the last components of the bridge to be constructed. Built at the eastern end, the plaza had 12 booths servicing both eastbound and westbound traffic lanes. The original toll for a single vehicle was 50¢, and the cost of a monthly commuter ticket was $10.

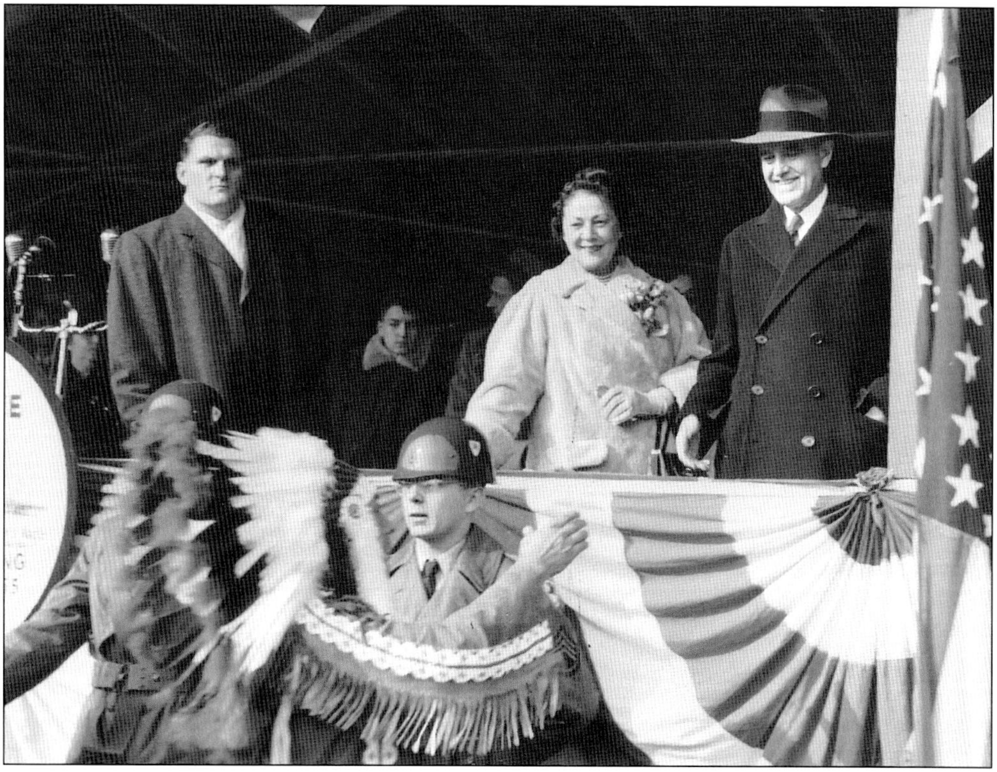

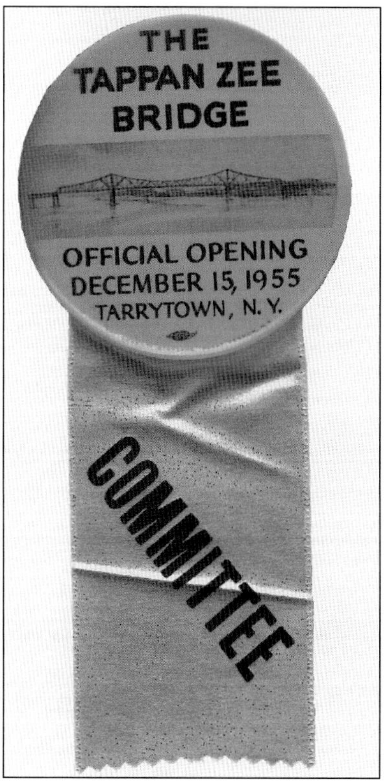


Although much of the planning and construction took place during the administration of Gov. Thomas E. Dewey, Gov. Averell Harriman (right) was in office when the bridge opened and presided over the official ceremony on December 15, 1955, with Tarrytown mayor Edward Vetrano (left).

At the ceremony, a commemorative button was given to the planning committee members, and it was announced that "with the completion of the great bridge across the Tappan Zee, the New York State Thruway now connects our two greatest port cities: Buffalo, far to the west, with its lines of trade reaching deep into the American Heartland, and New York City to the east, with its far-flung ties with the wide world."

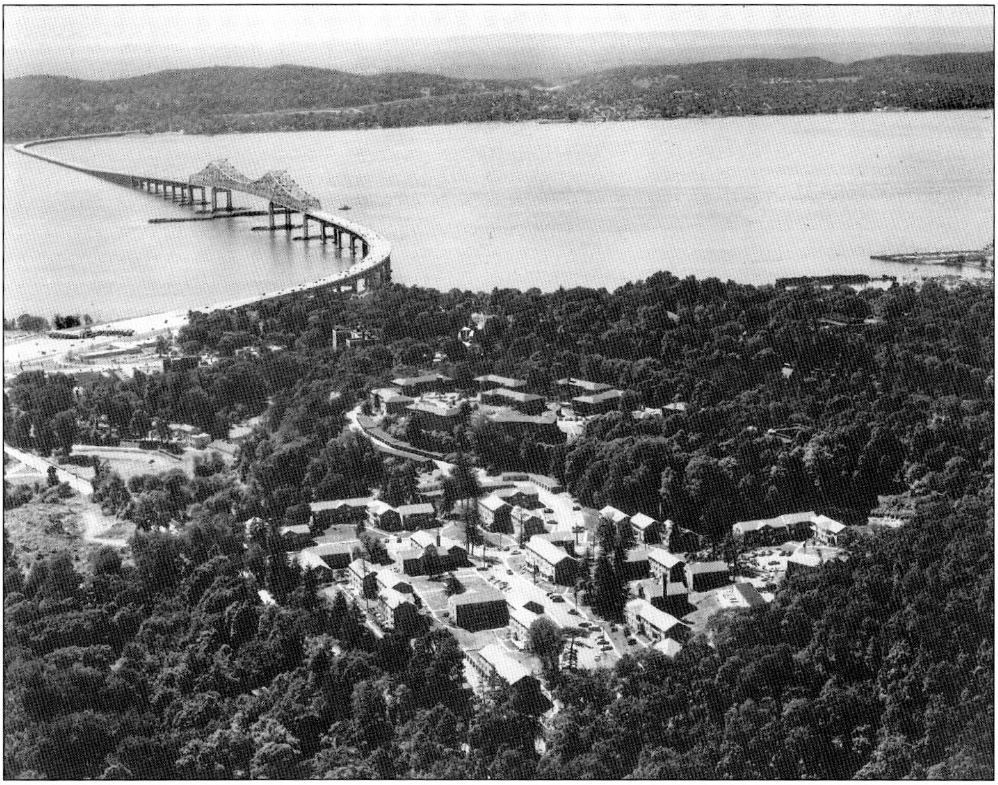

An aerial view of postwar residential development is shown with the Tappan Zee Bridge in the background.

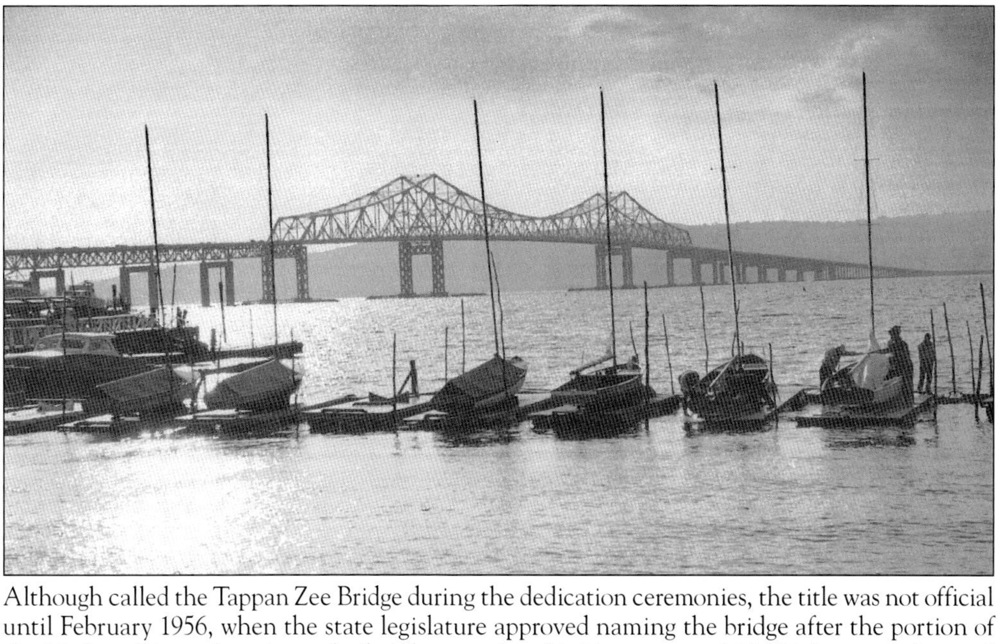

Although called the Tappan Zee Bridge during the dedication ceremonies, the title was not official until February 1956, when the state legislature approved naming the bridge after the portion of the Hudson River where it was built. The completed bridge measured 15,764 feet, and the total cost of construction was approximately $60 million.

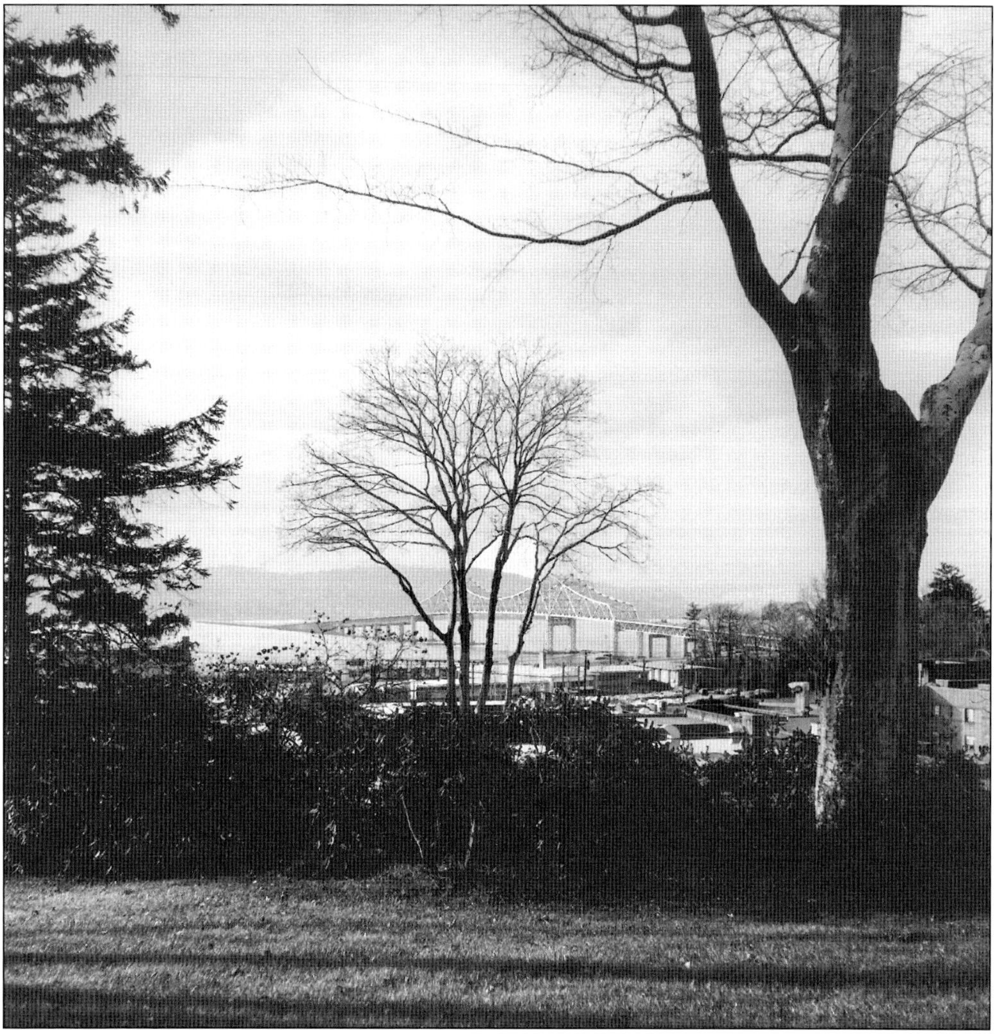

As the Tappan Zee Bridge grew older and more congested, upgrades and repairs were constantly required to maintain the roadway. The addition of the movable center divider and the decision to only collect tolls from eastbound vehicles marginally eased some of the congestion. By the end of the 20th century, commuters, politicians, and residents from the surrounding communities were debating the merits of building a replacement bridge in the same location.

# *Six*

# Personalities

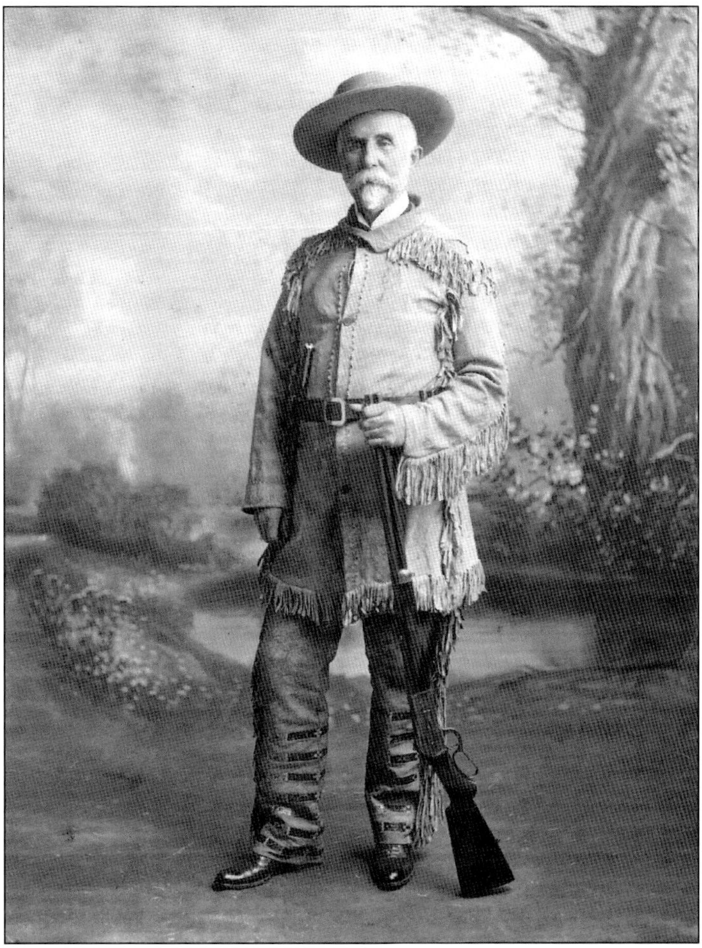

From the eccentric and flamboyant to the ordinary and reliable, here are a few local individuals who were unique among their neighbors. Alfred Weed lived in Tarrytown from the 1880s until his death in 1907. He had a secret workshop in the basement of his house, where barred windows and his faithful English setter protected his inventions. An avid traveler and outdoorsman, Weed is pictured in his traditional buckskin outfit.

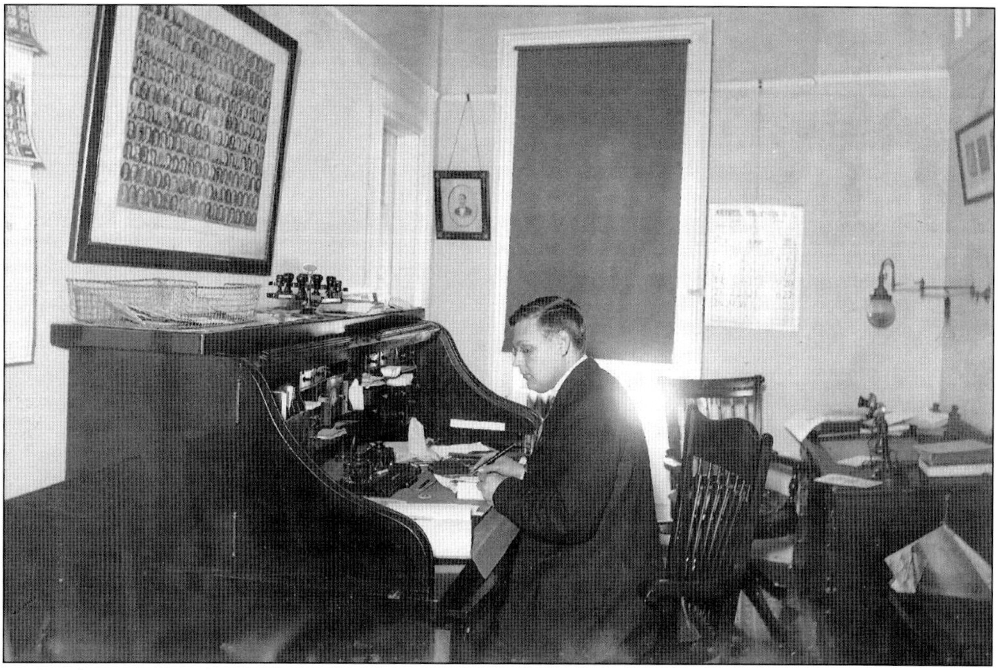

A third-generation lawyer, Ernest Griffin specialized in probate and real estate law. Griffin also served as a Tarrytown trustee in 1921, village president from 1922 to 1927, and trustee of the school board from 1936 until 1945. Motivated by his love of history, he was elected president of the Tarrytown Historical Society in 1931. One of his proudest achievements in life was the publishing of the three-volume history *Westchester County and its People*.

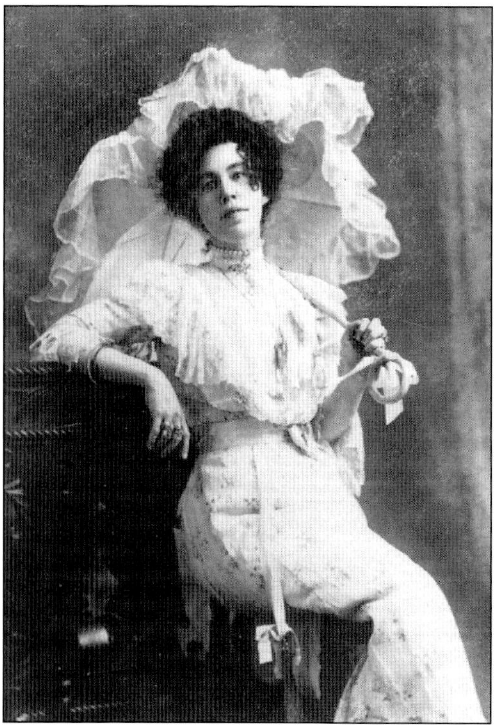

A dramatic poet and eccentric, Minna Odell began professionally publishing poems using the pen name Minna Irving when she was 15. During the early 20th century, she published hundreds of her poems in magazines and newspapers. In 1923, she was asked by the French government to create a poem for the grave of Pres. Theodore Roosevelt's son Quentin. Odell walked everywhere and was one of the first local women to wear heavy makeup in public.

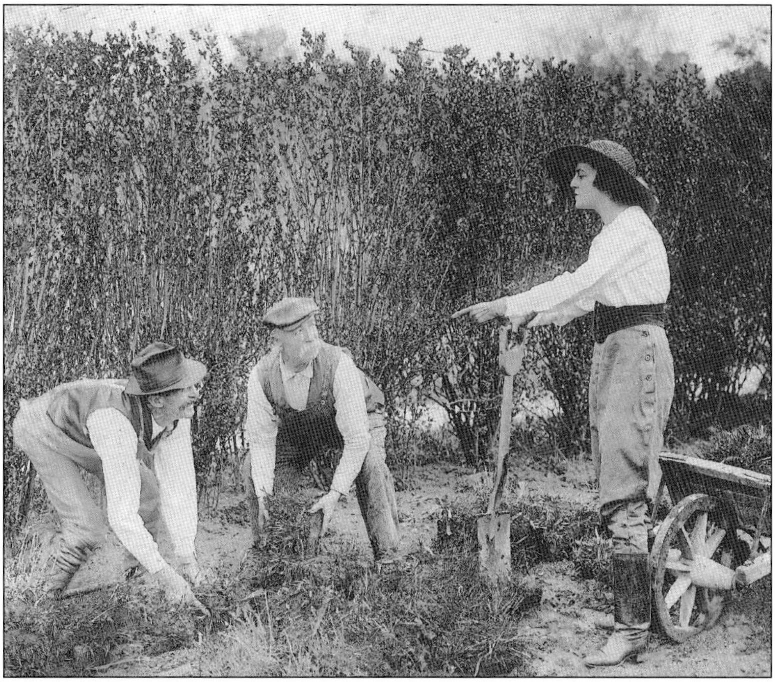

Known during the early 20th century as an actress and vaudeville star, Elsie Janis lived and entertained her famous friends at Philipse Castle from 1915 to 1935. During World War I, she was the first American entertainer to perform for the troops in France. Janis lost most of her money and her home in the stock market crash. She is pictured above posing with two of her estate workers.

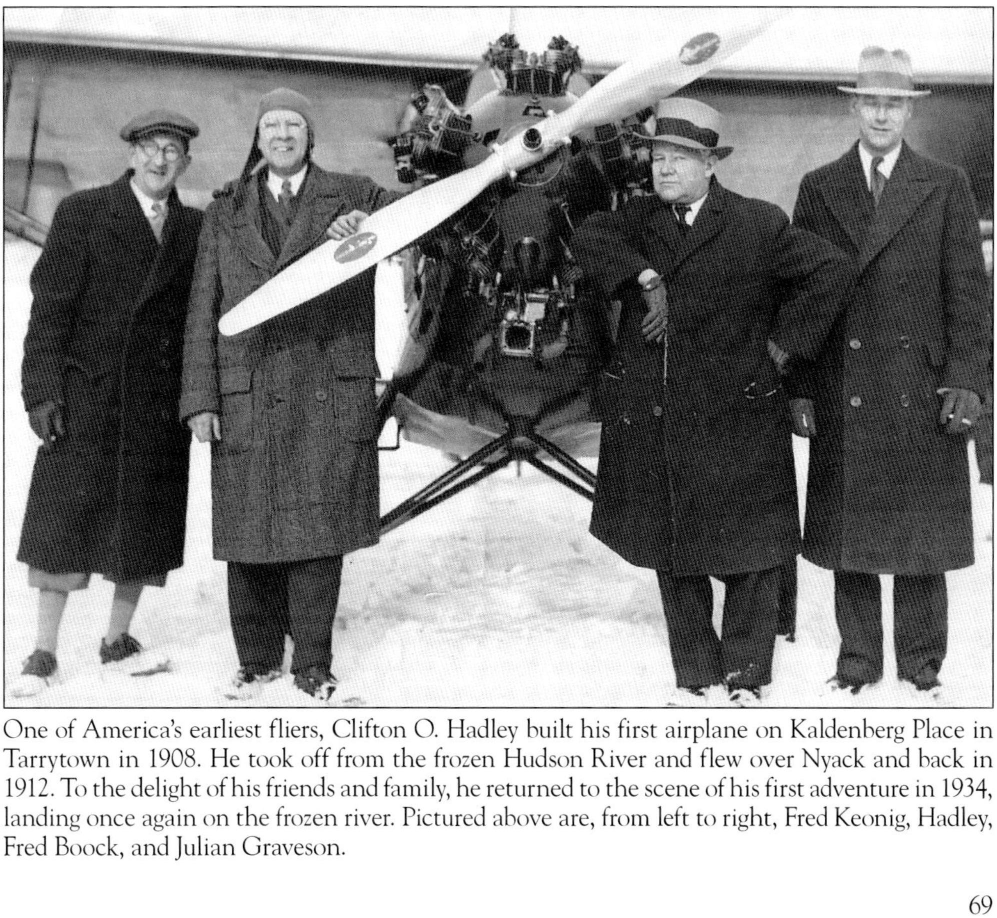

One of America's earliest fliers, Clifton O. Hadley built his first airplane on Kaldenberg Place in Tarrytown in 1908. He took off from the frozen Hudson River and flew over Nyack and back in 1912. To the delight of his friends and family, he returned to the scene of his first adventure in 1934, landing once again on the frozen river. Pictured above are, from left to right, Fred Keonig, Hadley, Fred Boock, and Julian Graveson.

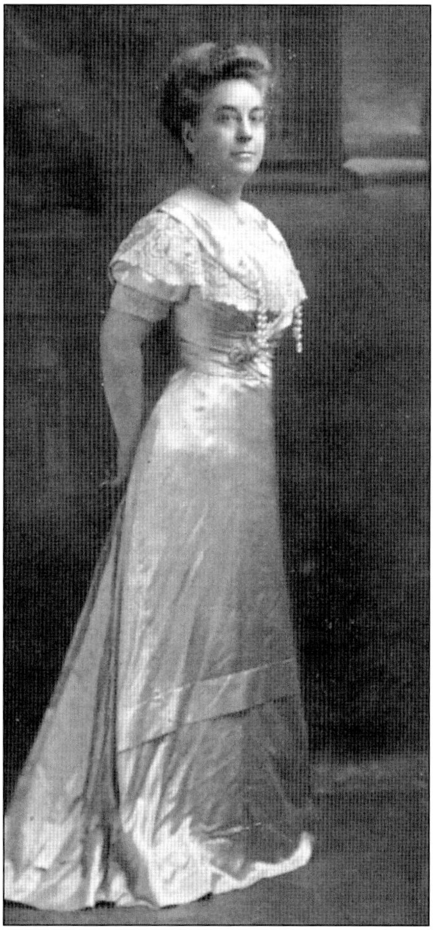

Cassity Mason purchased the former Herrick Castle in 1895 in order to open a fashionable girls school in Tarrytown. Her initial enrollment of 37 students eventually grew to over 100. The girls ranged in age from 7 to 25 and were taught to be independent and strong. Over the 38 years that Mason was the headmistress, her Castle School invited numerous guest lecturers including musician Rafael Joseffy and author Mark Twain.

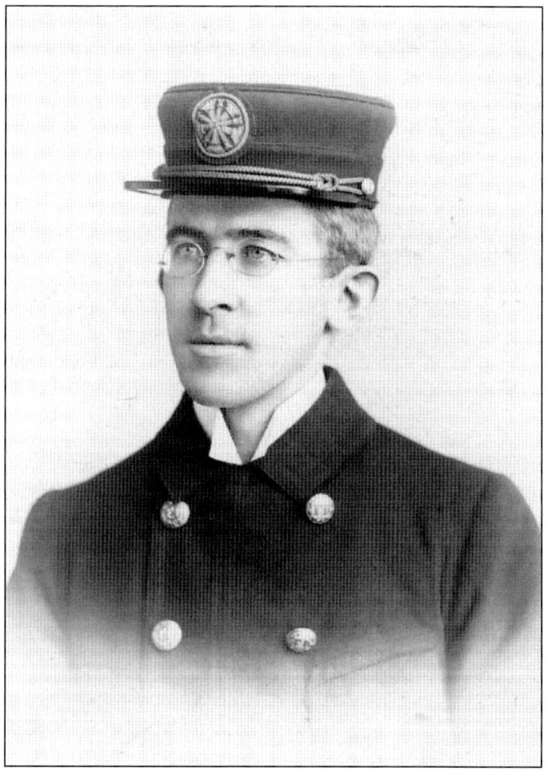

Known as Tarrytown's "first fireman and first citizen," John Gross was a successful merchant and five-term Tarrytown president. When he was 14 years old, he organized Jackson Engine Fire Company with 12 other young men. Gross was honored in 1941 at a testimonial dinner celebrating 60 years of service. When he died at the age of 98, he had served as a firefighter longer than any other person in the United States up to that time.

"I think I will build a library for our two villages if Tarrytown will provide the convenient site," Cornelia Blakemore Warner was often quoted as saying. She and her husband, Worcester, funded the construction of the Warner Library for Tarrytown and North Tarrytown. Worcester died in 1929, the year the project was completed. Cornelia continued her philanthropic work, providing funding for Patriots Park, Philipsburg Manor, and the Historical Society, Inc.

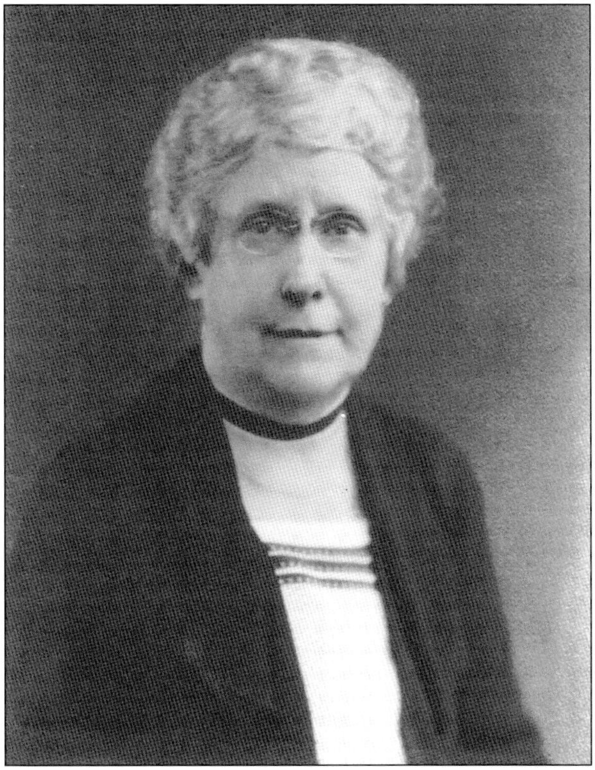

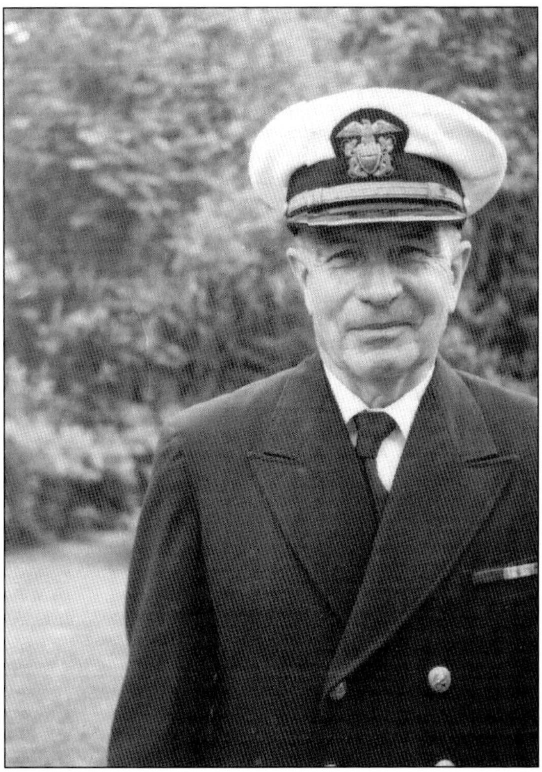

Born into a distinguished military family, Harry Storm served in the U.S. Navy from 1909 until 1945. While in the navy, he served on ships in the Atlantic and Pacific Fleets and participated in both world wars. After he retired, Storm gave a short speech during the ceremony at the end of every Memorial Day parade. He also shared entertaining military stories at community events until his death at age 98 in 1987.

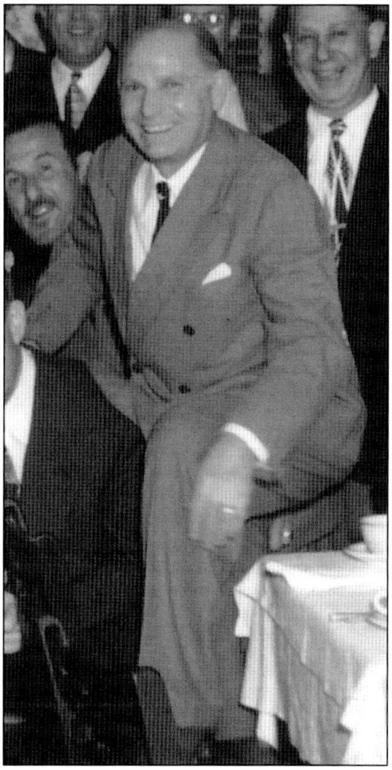

In Patriots Park there is a bench dedicated to Robert Goldblatt. He was a founder of Washington Irving Trust Bank, the chamber of commerce, and the Lions Club. After purchasing the Music Hall in 1925, Goldblatt operated it until his death in 1964. He donated the first ambulance to Phelps Memorial Hospital, provided funds for the World War I and II memorials, donated the Veterans Memorial Building, and made personal loans to needy individuals.

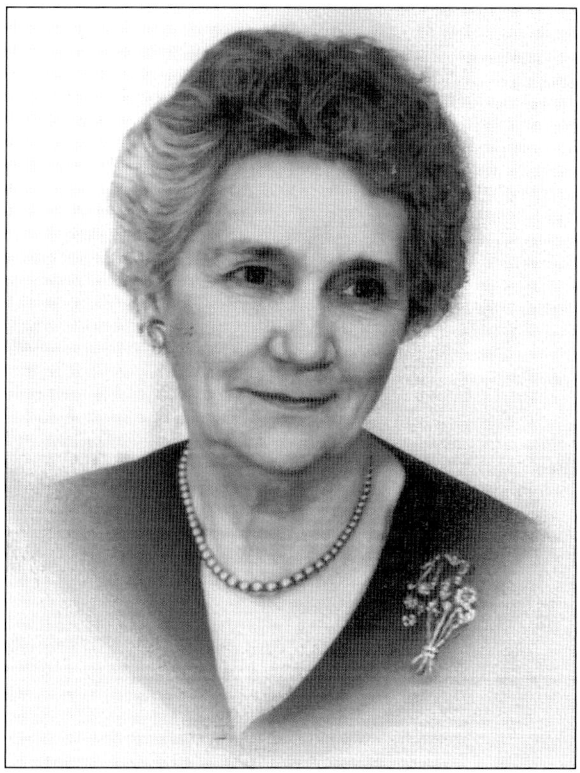

A transplanted southern belle, Sarah Case was involved in numerous civic and nonprofit organizations in the community. She was one of the founding members of the local chapter of the Daughters of the American Revolution. Case was also devoted to the preservation of local history, and after the Historical Society, Inc., purchased her Grove Street home in 1953, she became curator of the Jacob Odell House Museum until her retirement in 1969.

In 1914, Addie Jackson and her daughters, Virginia and Marie, were interested in volunteering for the American Red Cross. After discovering that the closest chapters were segregated, the Jackson women founded a new Tarrytown chapter. Only 15 years old at the time, Marie went on to serve as a volunteer for nearly 70 years. She was particularly involved in establishing several innovative programs to assist senior members of the community.

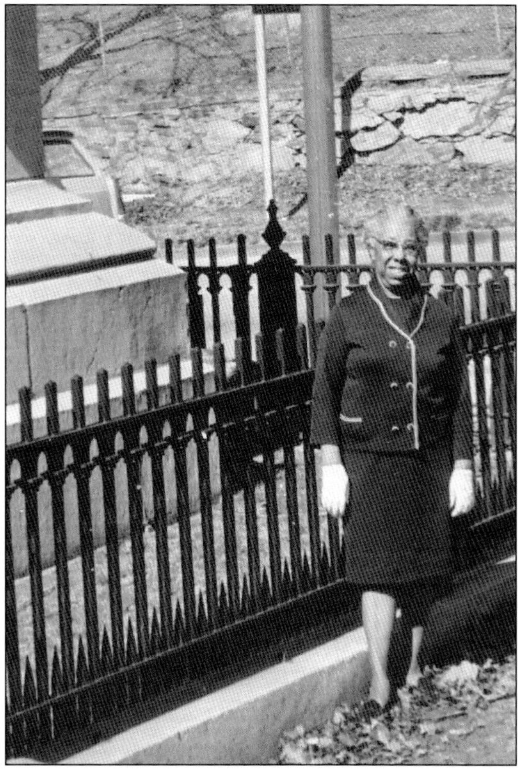

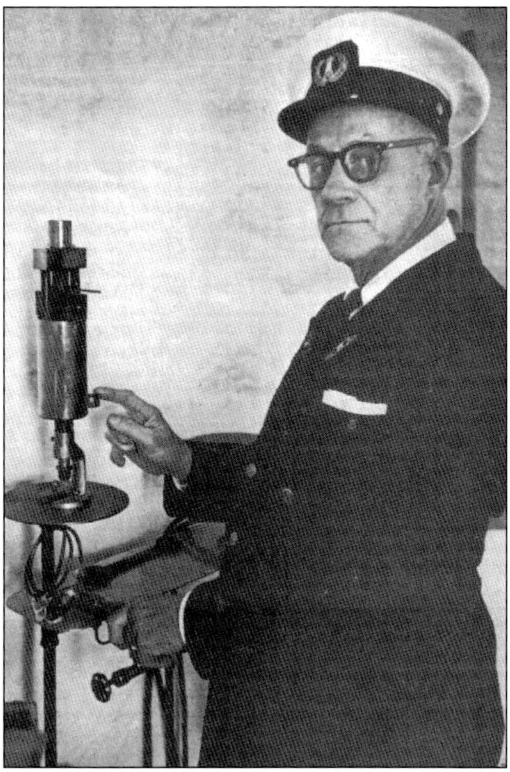

Located in the Hudson River off the shoreline in North Tarrytown (now Sleepy Hollow), the Tarrytown Lighthouse was home to several lighthouse keepers during the 20th century. The last civilian keeper, prior to the Coast Guard taking over the station in 1954, was Laureat LeClerc. For 11 years, LeClerc and his family lived in the lighthouse and took a boat back and forth for food, supplies, and trips to school.

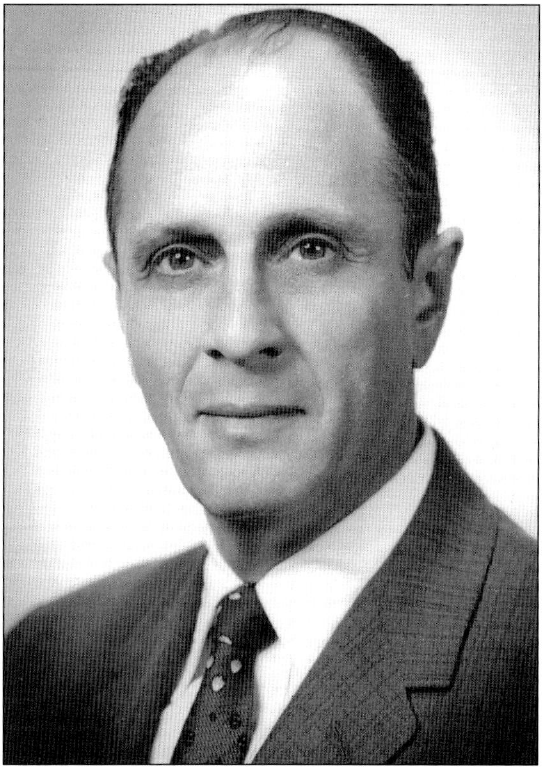

Dedicated to community service, Morrie Slifkin began his law career in Tarrytown in 1935. He presided over the Tarrytown village court, was appointed a Westchester family court judge, and eventually served as a state supreme court justice from 1969 until 1986, all while volunteering for numerous nonprofit organizations. From 1959 to 1963, Slifkin also appeared on the CBS show *The Verdict Is Yours*, the first television courtroom show to use an actual judge.

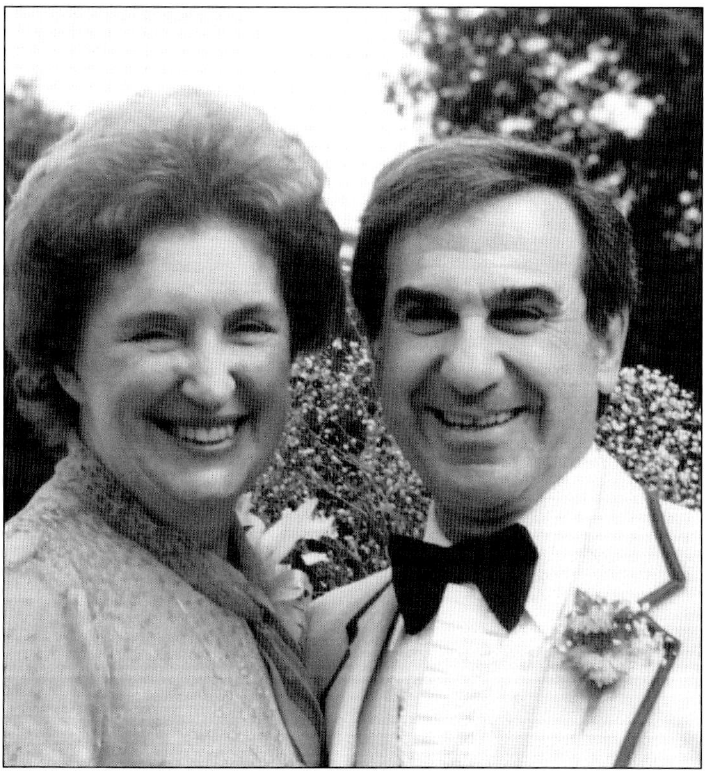

After moving to the area in the early 1950s, Armond and Elizabeth Mascia became involved in numerous children's organizations. A local pediatrician, Mandy supported the founding of Phelps Memorial Hospital and served on the school board. A proponent of affordable child care, Libby was one of the founders of the Day Care Center of the Tarrytowns, later renamed the Elizabeth Mascia Child Care Center. They were honored as the communities' first Couple of the Year in 1981.

Born in Tarrytown in 1935, John Keels has had a significant impact upon the local community in his role as founder and director of the Community Opportunity Center. Keels founded the center in 1965, and he and his wife, Bertie, worked together to create a variety of social programs. Throughout the last quarter of the 20th century, Keels overcame numerous financial and political obstacles to keep the center's doors open.

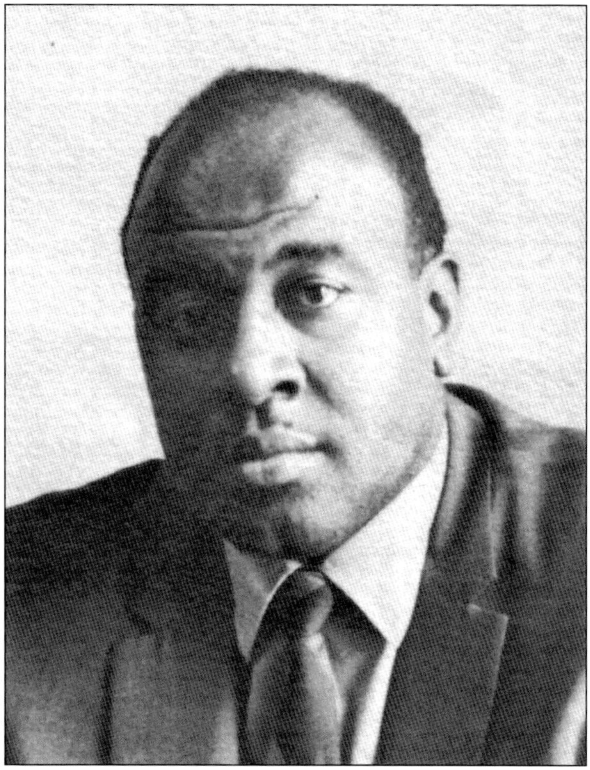

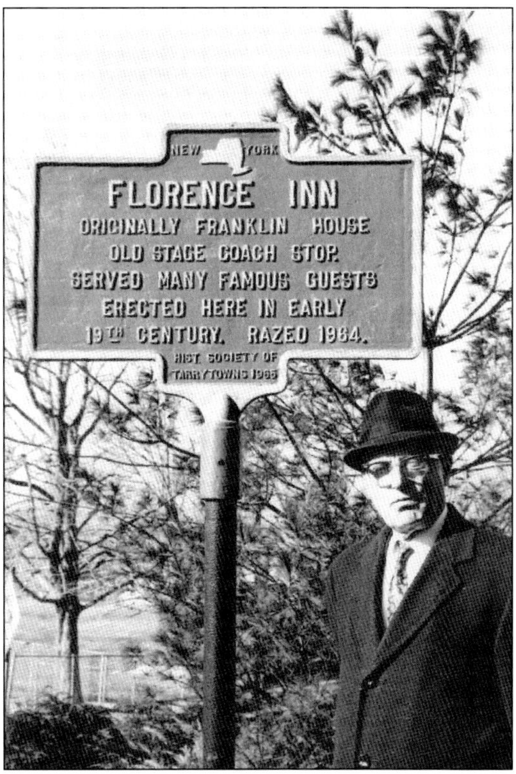


Christopher Lennox lived in Tarrytown from 1919 until his death at age 99 in 1997. A local real estate broker, he served as president of both the Friends of the Warner Library and the Historical Society, Inc. In 1963, Lennox was appointed as the executive director of the Sleepy Hollow Urban Renewal Program. He was also instrumental in placing New York State landmark signs locally and getting the lighthouse designated as a historical monument.

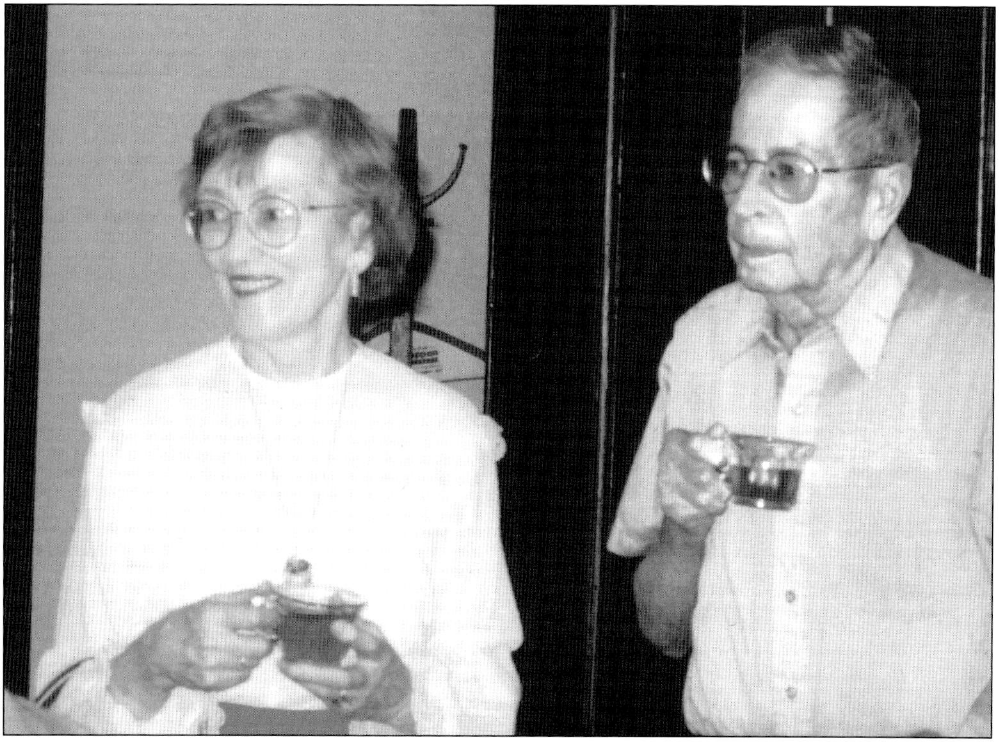

Totally committed to the study of history, Lucille and Theodore Hutchinson were advocates for the Old Dutch Burying Ground, coauthors of the *Centennial History of North Tarrytown*, and North Tarrytown village historians. They were also active in the Literacy Volunteers of the Tarrytowns for 47 years. Ted taught English and physics in the public schools, and Lucille volunteered as map curator for the Historical Society, Inc.

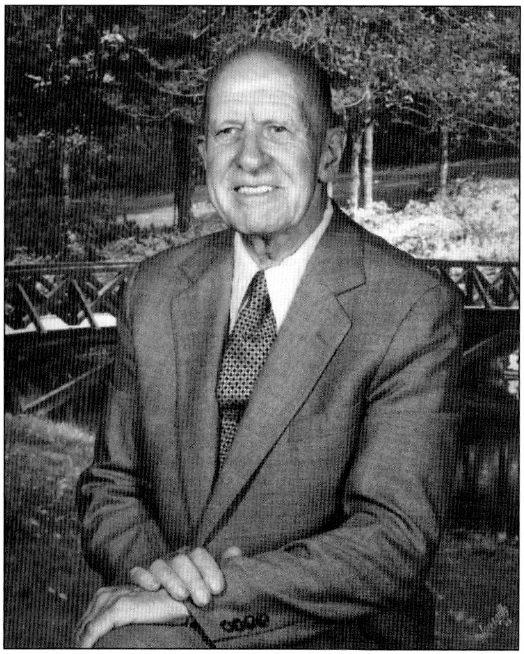

Born in 1900, William Gross (Wally Buxton) spent a good part of his life collecting and writing historical essays and stories about Tarrytown and Sleepy Hollow. He was best known as the "Combing the Villages" columnist for the *Tarrytown Daily News*, now the *Journal News*. He served as Tarrytown's village historian until his death in 1996 and wrote the definitive local history reference book the *History of the Tarrytowns* with Jeff Canning.

# *Seven*

# Businesses Coming and Going

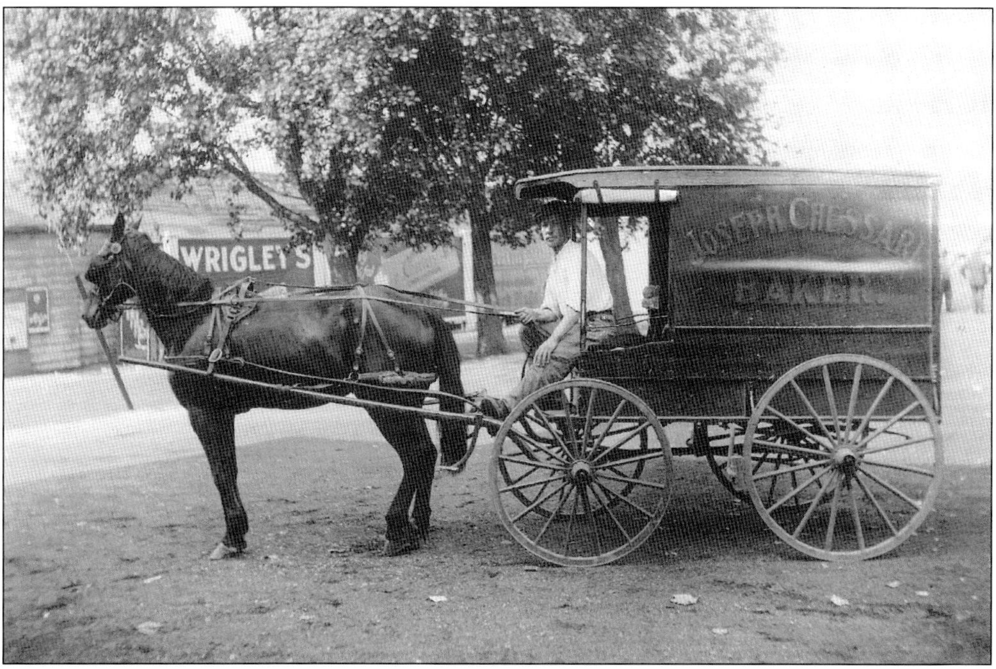


Throughout the 20th century, the villages had a mix of small retail shops, markets, family trades, manufacturing concerns, and large national companies. The changing business landscape mirrored the rest of America, as commercial concerns appeared and disappeared during the move from the industrial to the information age. Joseph Chessari, a baker on Cedar Street, continued to use his old horse-drawn delivery wagon well into the 1920s.

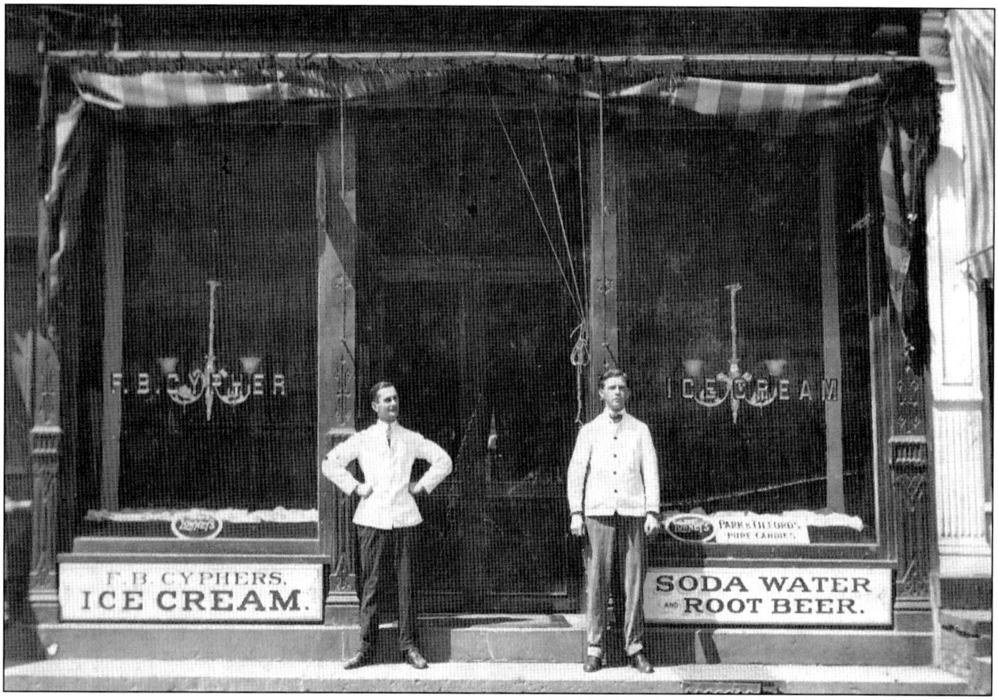


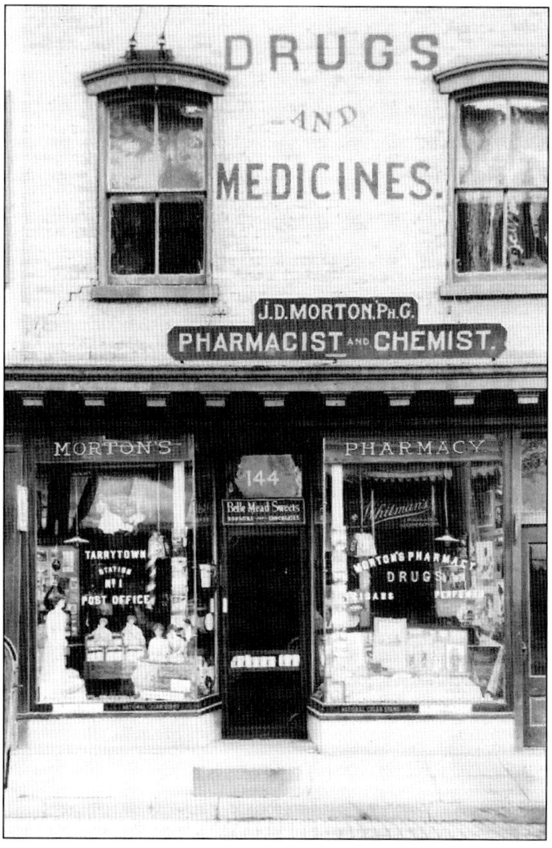


Francis Burdette Cypher opened a small ice cream shop and confectionery on lower Main Street in 1878. By the early 1900s, F. B. Cypher's had become nationally famous for brewing high-quality root beer. He had numerous offers from large companies who wanted to buy his recipe, but he refused all inquiries. Cypher's busy shop was open during the summer months until he died suddenly in 1916, and his famous recipe was lost forever.

Jay D. Morton operated his drugstore at 144 Main Street in Tarrytown. The building also served for a short time as the Tarrytown Post Office. The photograph at left was taken around 1915.

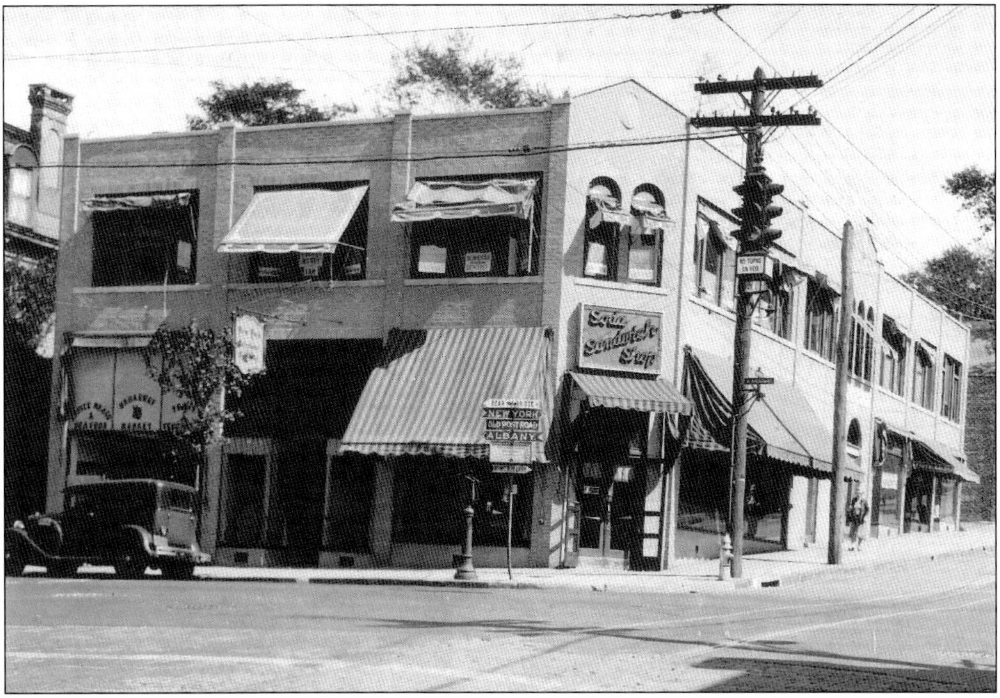


This photograph shows the building on the corner of Neperan Road and North Broadway on November 17, 1929. At that time, occupants included the Sandwich Shop, Dr. Harvey Rosenthal (dentist), the New York Telephone Company, the Broadway Market, and the Tarrytown Post Office. Main Street, shown in the foreground, was paved with yellow bricks.

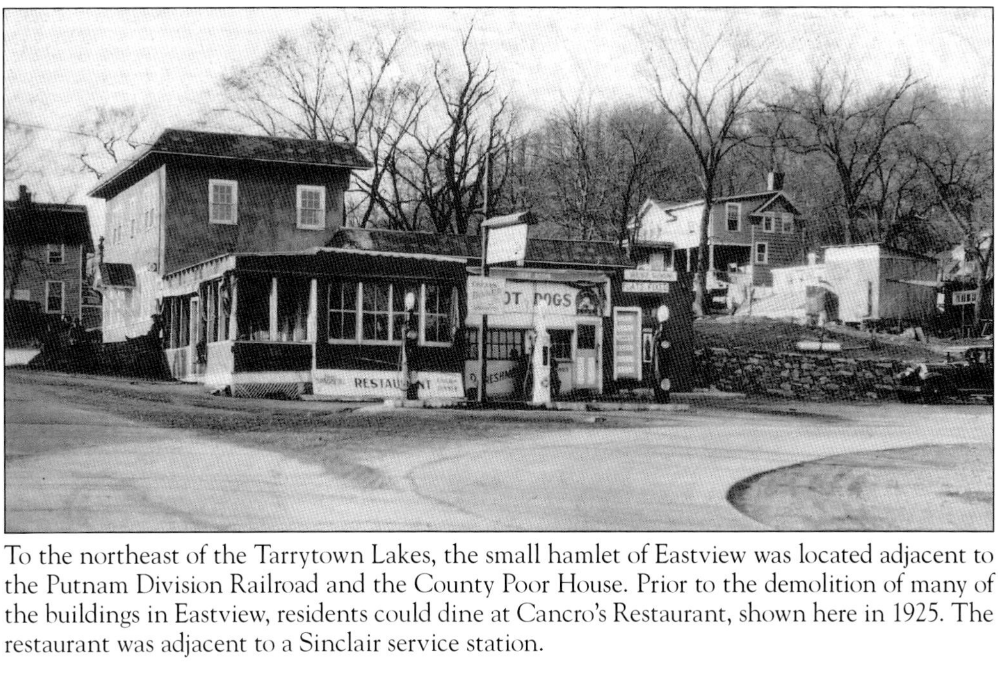

To the northeast of the Tarrytown Lakes, the small hamlet of Eastview was located adjacent to the Putnam Division Railroad and the County Poor House. Prior to the demolition of many of the buildings in Eastview, residents could dine at Cancro's Restaurant, shown here in 1925. The restaurant was adjacent to a Sinclair service station.

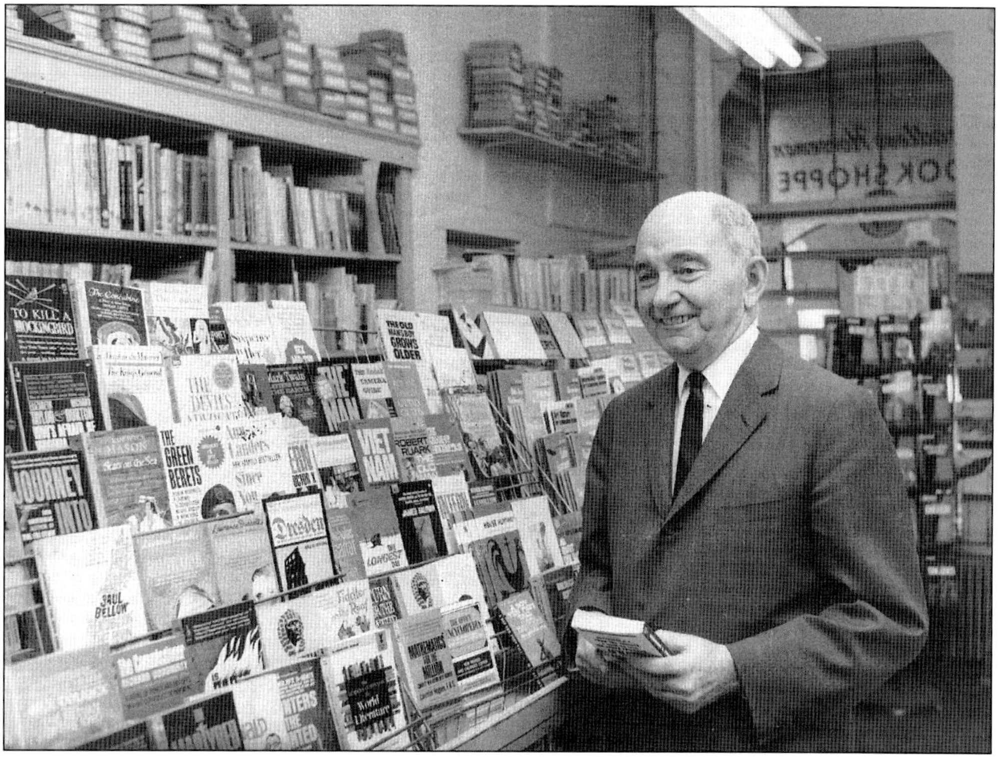


Fred V. Peters operated the Headless Horseman Book Shoppe at 23 Main Street from 1934 until he retired in 1967. He was a leader in Scouting for 50 years and received all of the top awards from the National Boy Scouts of America. After the store closed, Peters pursued his love of photography.

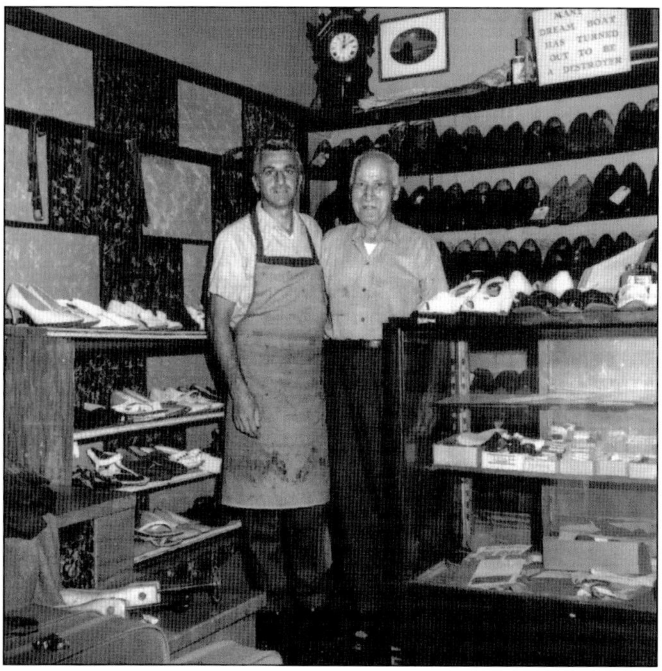


The villages had several small shoe repair shops during the 20th century. This photograph shows Louis Dolcetti in his Main Street shop with his father, Michael.

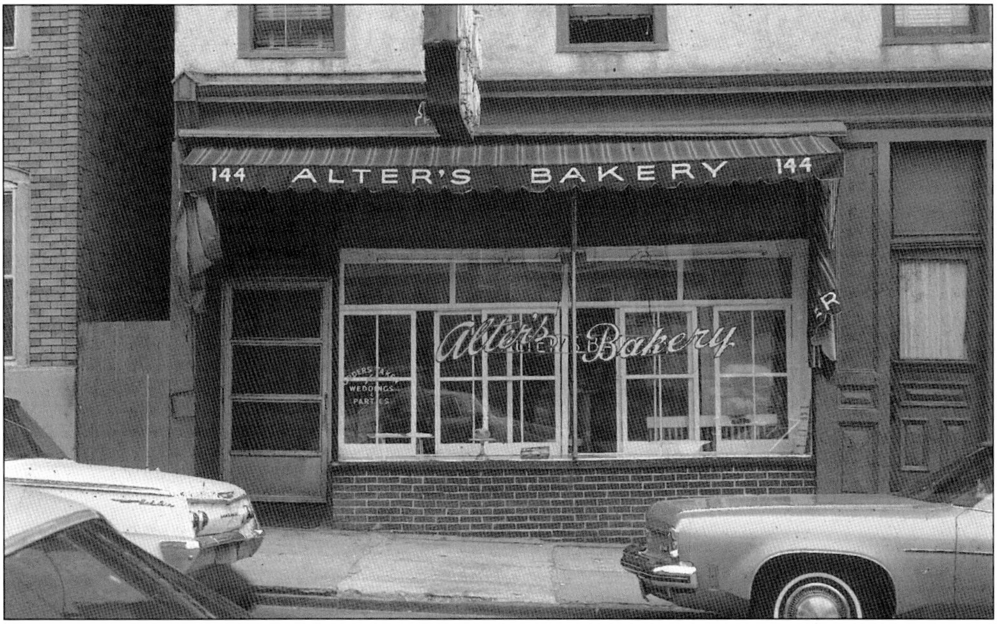


Ruth and Abraham Alter, immigrants from Poland, moved to Tarrytown in 1928. After working in a bakery on Orchard Street, the Alters opened their first shop on lower Cortlandt Street in North Tarrytown. The couple moved to a new shop at 144 Cortlandt Street in 1949. Over the next 40 years, the family-owned bakery continued to utilize old-style techniques and bake in the large brick-lined, coal-heated oven located in the basement.

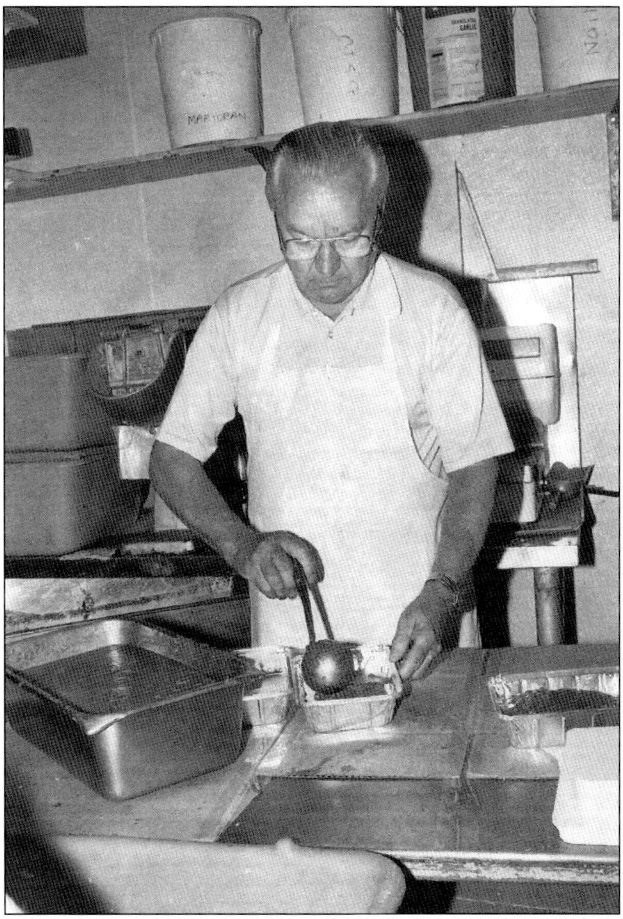

Mario Brauna had opened his Greene County Importing Corporation on Cortlandt Street prior to 1952. Brauna, famous for his homemade pasta, moved his operation to 44 Beekman Avenue. At this location, he sold imported Italian groceries, combination wedges, and homemade Italian specialties. Pictured here in 1982, Brauna is packaging his pasta sauce for sale.

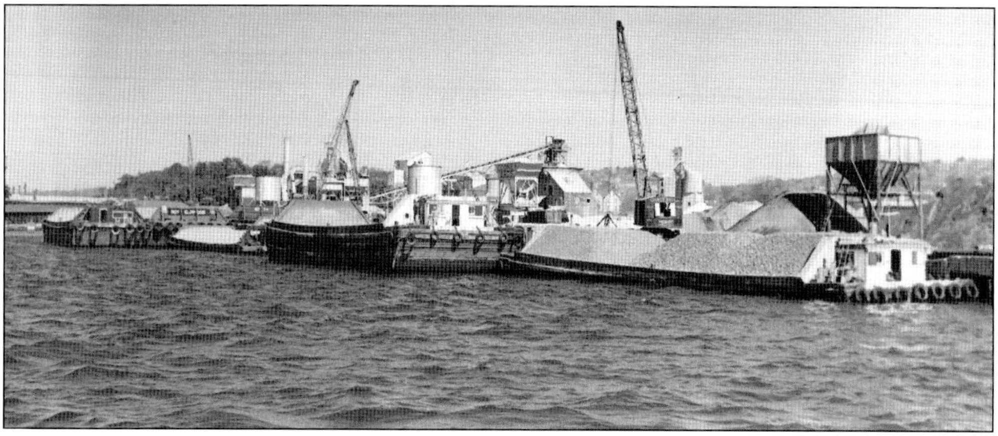

Cooney Brothers County Asphalt Construction Company was located along the waterfront in Tarrytown for over 75 years. As the American love affair with the open road grew, three generations of the Cooney family provided crushed stone, concrete, blacktop, and other necessary material for an always-expanding network of roadways.

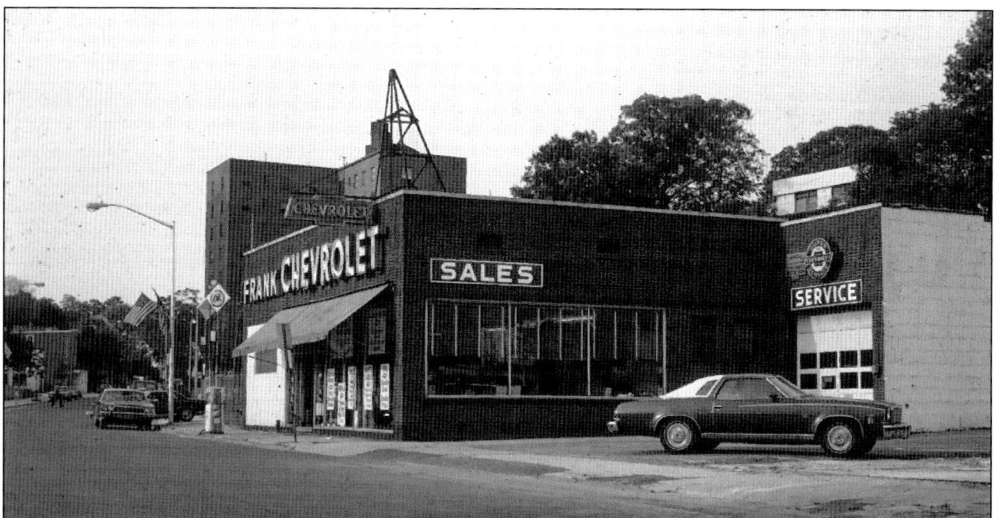


From the 1920s until the 1950s, the local authorized Chevrolet dealership was Cawood Motors on Valley Street. Chester Cawood sold the franchise to Frank Chevrolet Corporation, and the dealership operated at 96 Valley Street throughout the rest of the century.

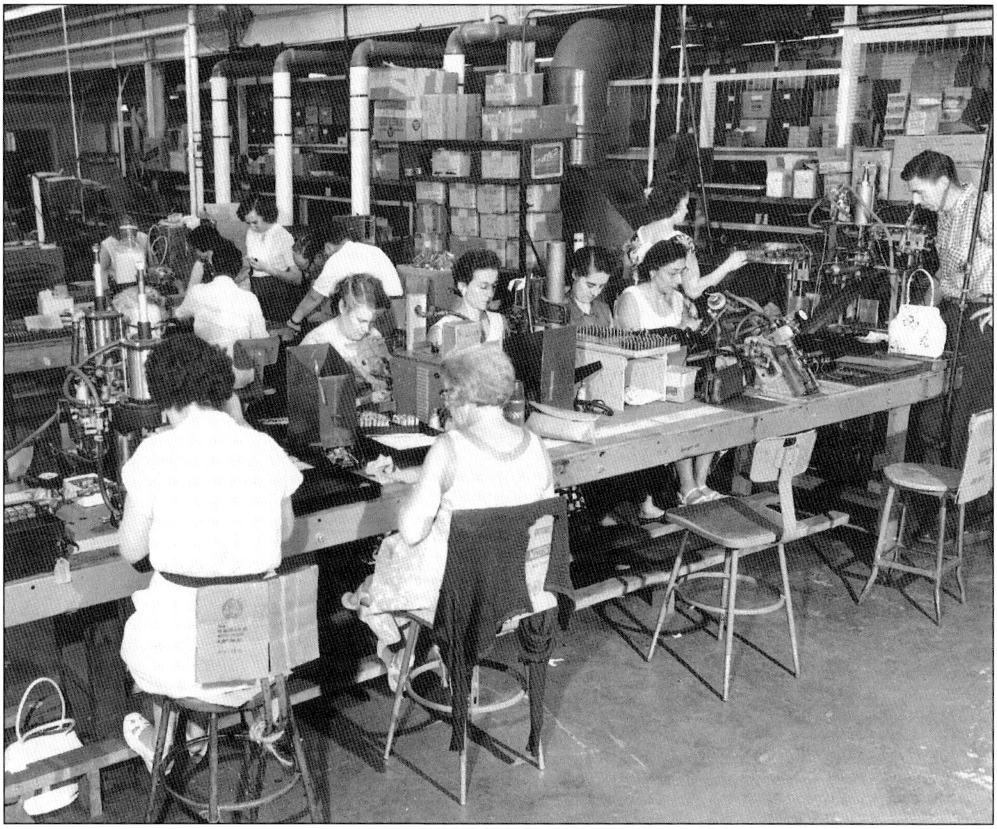

P. R. Mallory and Company opened a battery plant on Elm Street in North Tarrytown in 1946. For almost 40 years, the plant operated under a number of different corporate owners, with the last being Duracell. These women are working in the battery assembly room in the 1950s. A reduction of defense contracts for lithium sulfur dioxide batteries utilized in military equipment precipitated the final closure of the plant in December 1984.

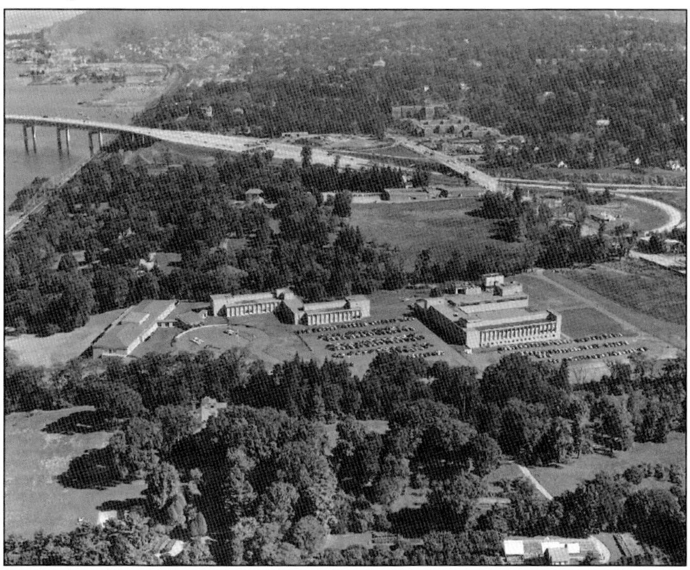

General Foods Corporation purchased the Evelyn Lehman estate near the south end of Tarrytown for its technical center, which opened in 1957. After purchasing an additional 35-acres, General Foods cosponsored the Requa Archaeology Project at a site on the expanded property during the 1970s and 1980s. Kraft Foods merged with Philip Morris's General Foods Unit in 1989 and became Kraft General Foods.

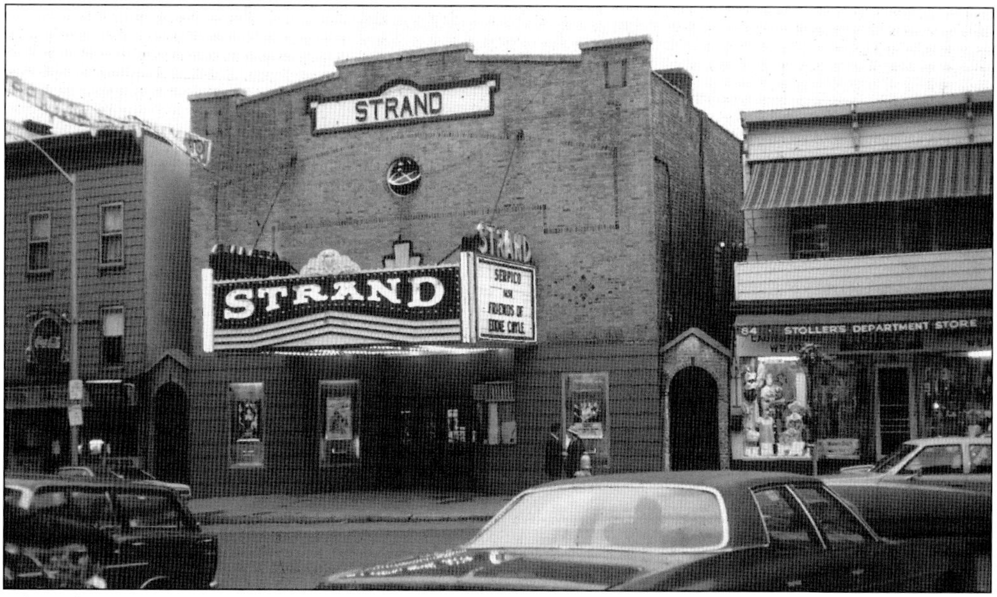


Edward Pollack opened the Strand Theater on Beekman Avenue in North Tarrytown on October 7, 1915. Advertised as "fireproof," the 450-seat venue showed popular films until it first closed in 1961. For the next two decades, the Strand had a series of owners who tried to keep it open to the public; however, the theater could not compete with large multiscreen cinemas that opened all over the county.

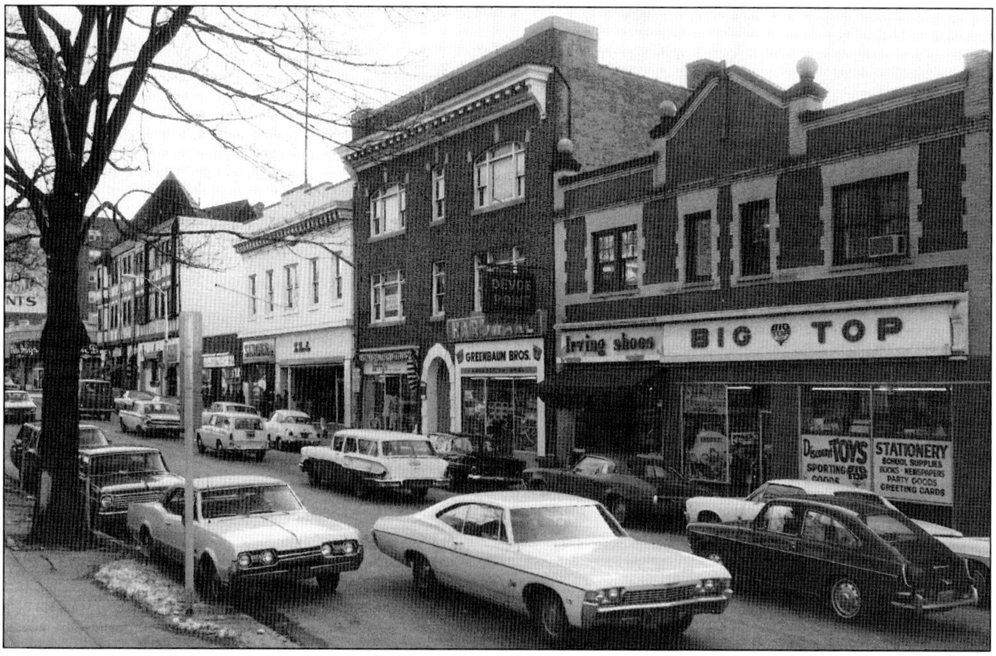


This photograph shows several stores on Broadway in the early 1970s. Big Top, located at 21 North Broadway, was a favorite toy store from 1972 until 1982, when the business found it could not compete with larger chain stores. Irving Shoes, in the same building, offered "footwear for everyone in the family." Greenbaum Brothers Hardware Store, once located on Orchard Street, moved to the Fulling Building on Broadway after a fire destroyed its store in 1964.

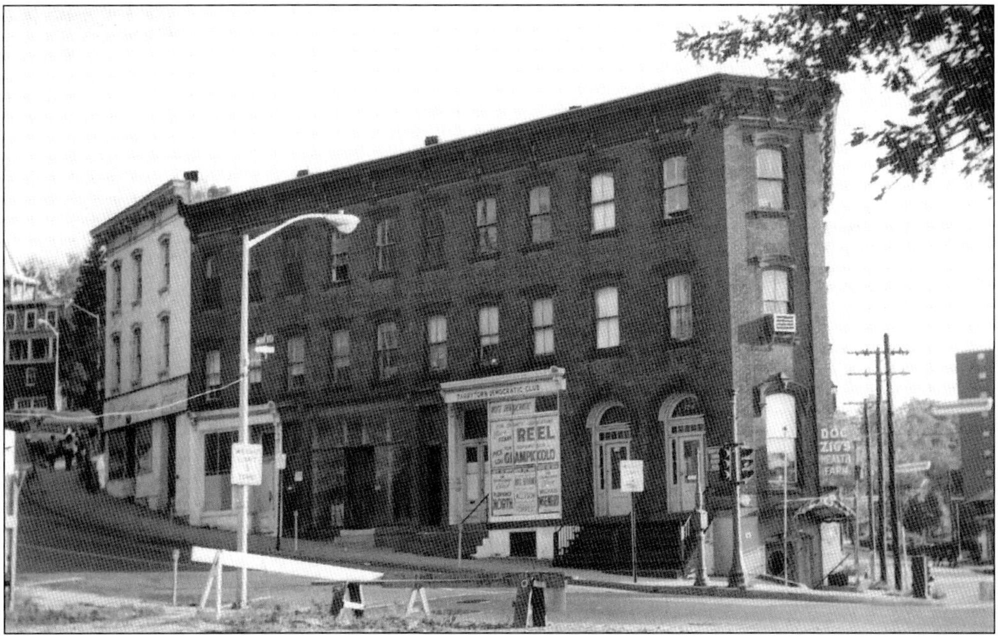


Doc Zig's Health Farm was a local watering hole located on lower Main Street in the Griffin Building. The building was across from the southern end of Orchard Street and was demolished during the urban renewal project in the 1960s. It also housed the Tarrytown Democratic Club.

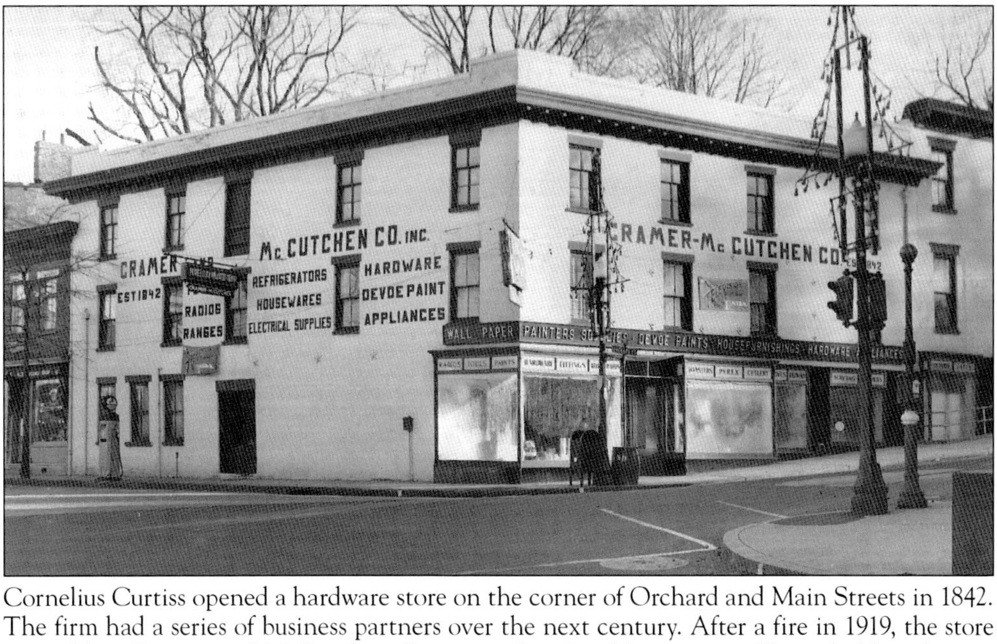


Cornelius Curtiss opened a hardware store on the corner of Orchard and Main Streets in 1842. The firm had a series of business partners over the next century. After a fire in 1919, the store was sold to Cramer and McCutchen Company, Inc. It sold a variety of household appliances and repair supplies. In addition, a flag outside of the establishment touted the availability of televisions for consumers.

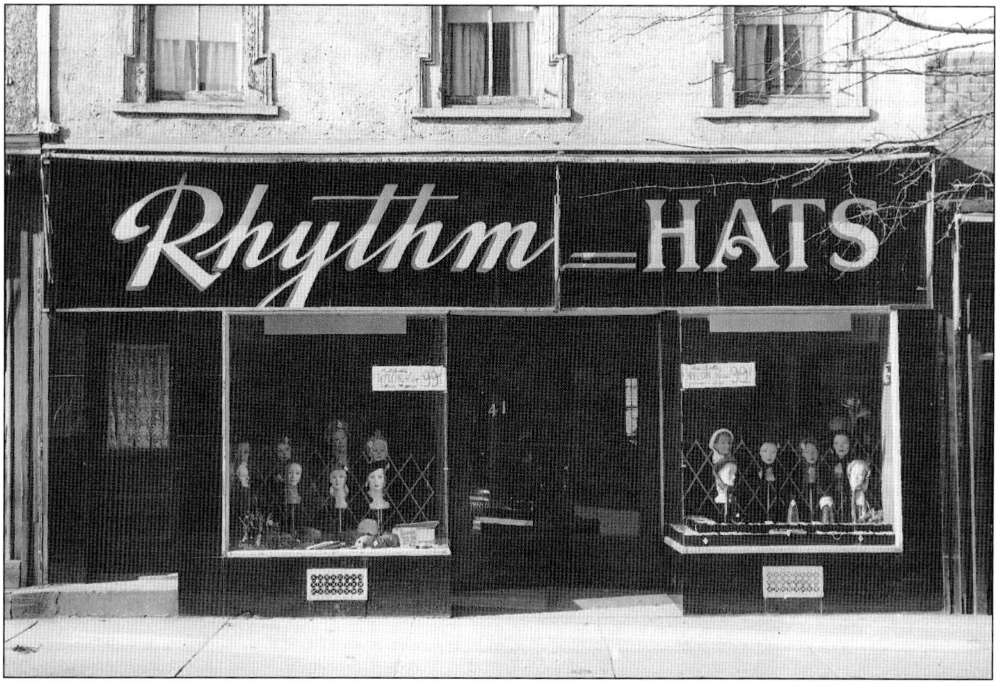


Orchard Street was the central business district for the villages throughout most of the 20th century. In the late 1960s, the entire street was demolished as part of the large urban renewal project. Rhythm Hats was one of the many popular shops on Orchard Street. At the same time that the buildings were torn down, exclusive hat stores for women were going out of style.

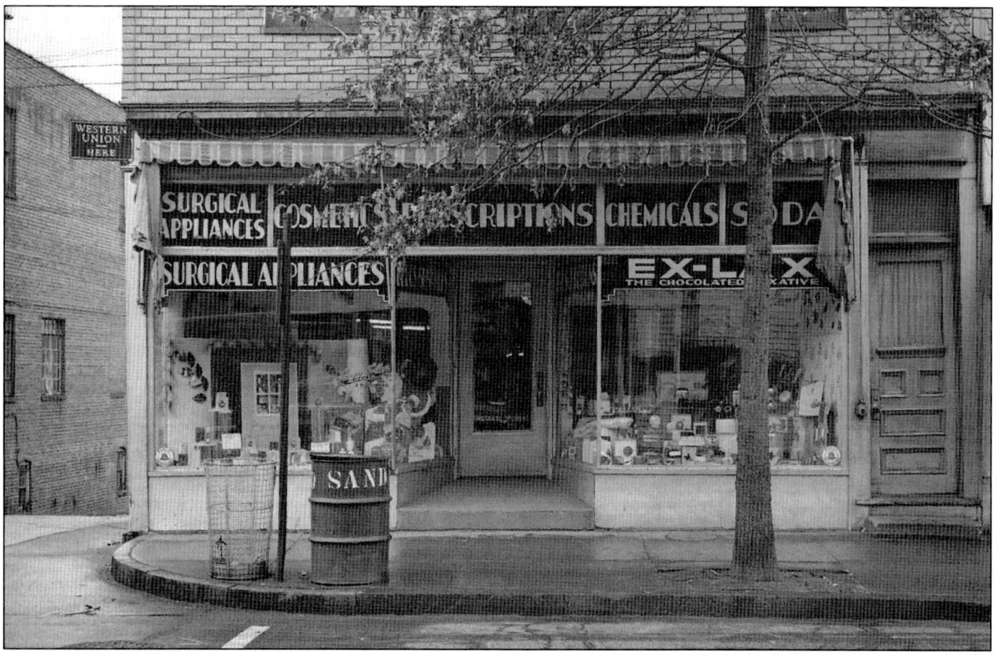


Alvin Biloon opened the Sleepy Hollow Pharmacy on Orchard Street in 1933. This establishment filled medical prescriptions and offered a variety of surgical appliances to customers. Alvin's son Stanley took over the business in 1961 and operated it until the building was demolished in 1966.

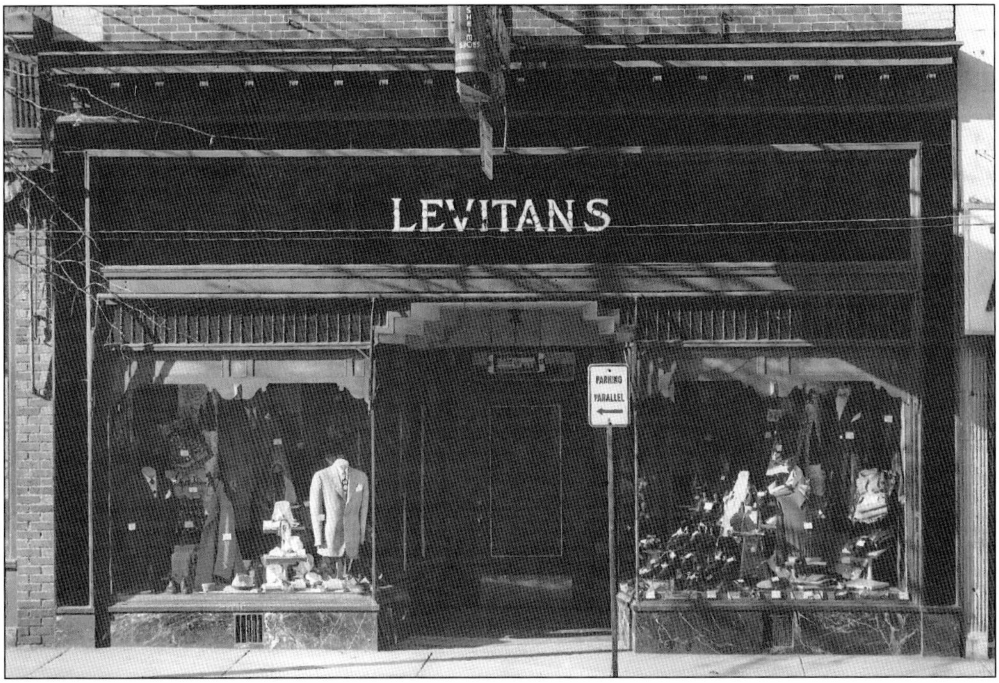


Another favorite establishment on Orchard Street was Levitan's clothing shop. Levitan's had a marble, granite, and brick facade, a Spanish-tile entrance, and an original stamped-metal ceiling. The store sold all kinds of menswear, from hats to shoes and all manner of accessories.

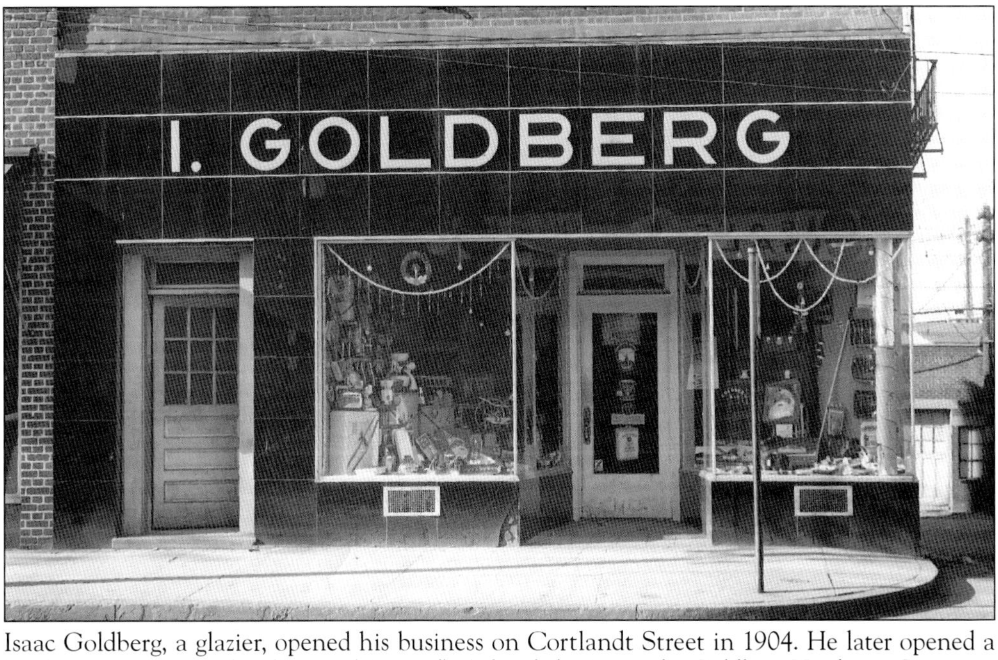


Isaac Goldberg, a glazier, opened his business on Cortlandt Street in 1904. He later opened a hardware store on Orchard Street (pictured). A family business, the Goldberg Hardware Company remained on Orchard until urban renewal in the 1960s. On January 28, 1966, the *Daily News* reported that Goldberg Hardware would be moving to the Andrews Building at 63 Main Street, where it remained throughout the rest of the century.

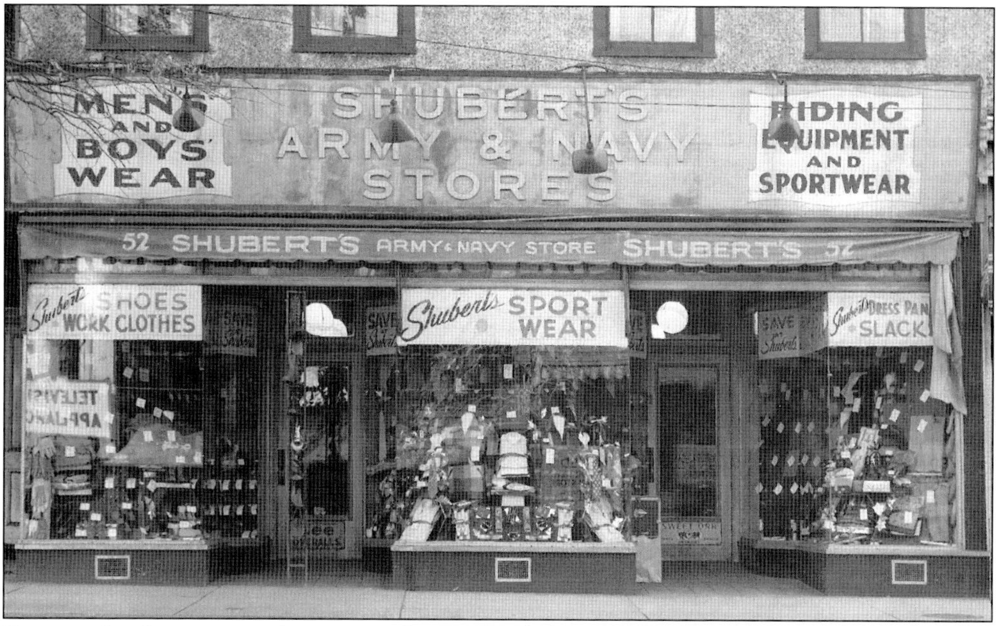


Prior to the downtown urban renewal project, Shubert's Army and Navy Store was located at 52 Orchard Street. The business sold "men's and boys' wear" of all kinds, including riding equipment and sportswear. When the buildings on Orchard Street were razed, Shubert's moved to 19 Main Street.

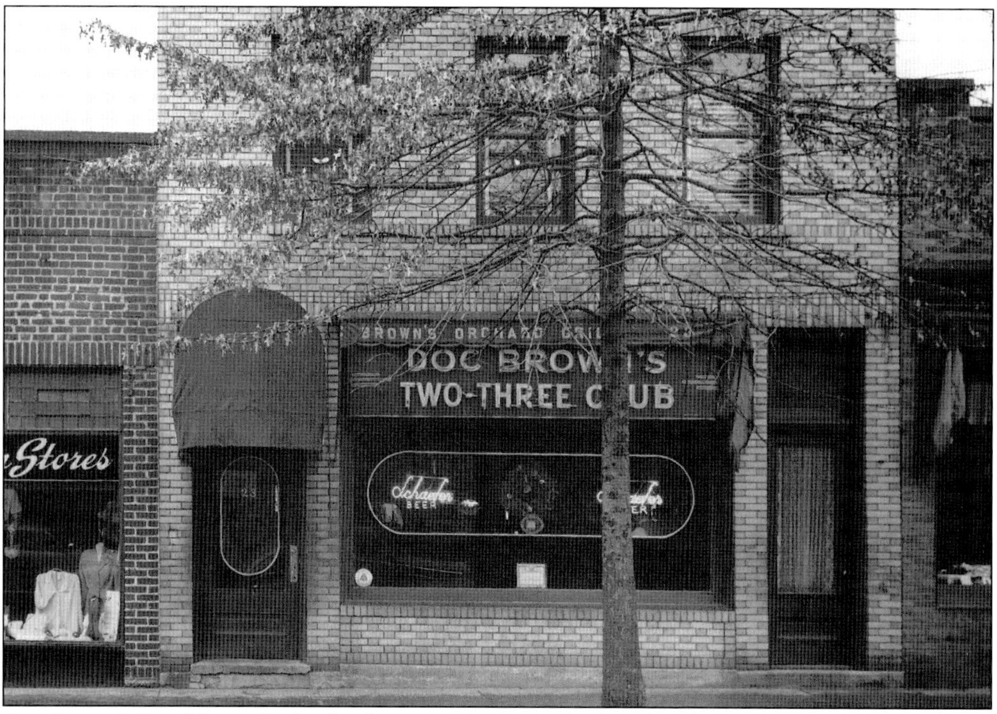


Doc Brown's Two-Three Club, also known as Brown's Orchard Grill, was located at 23 Orchard Street. The bar and grill was a member of the National Tavern Association and served a variety of spirits and pub food.

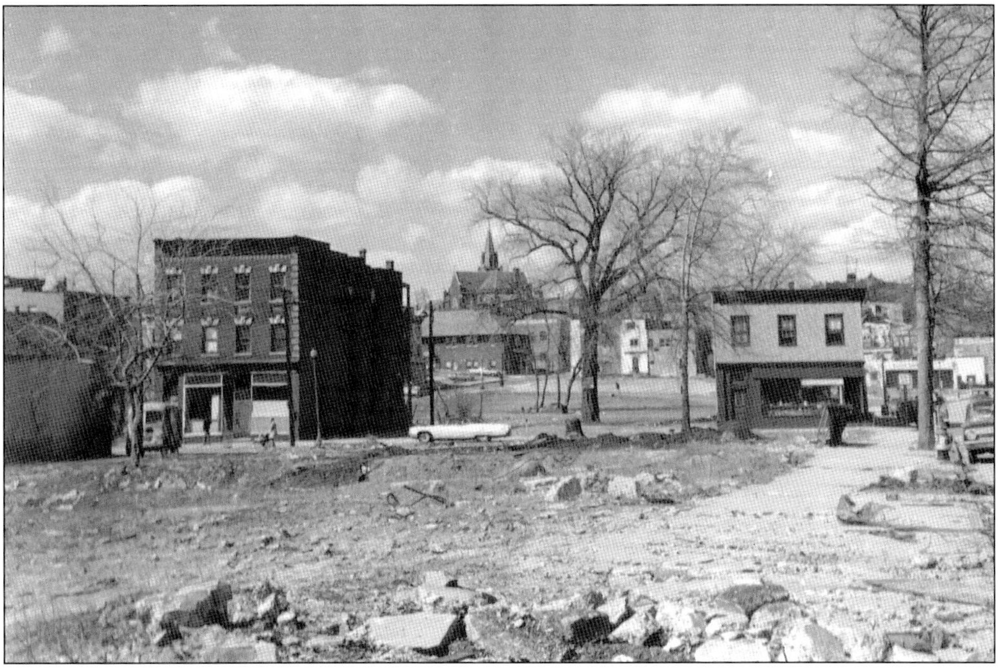

The demolition of the buildings on Orchard Street and some of the surrounding roads cut a dramatic path through the heart of the commercial district. This photograph was taken during demolition.

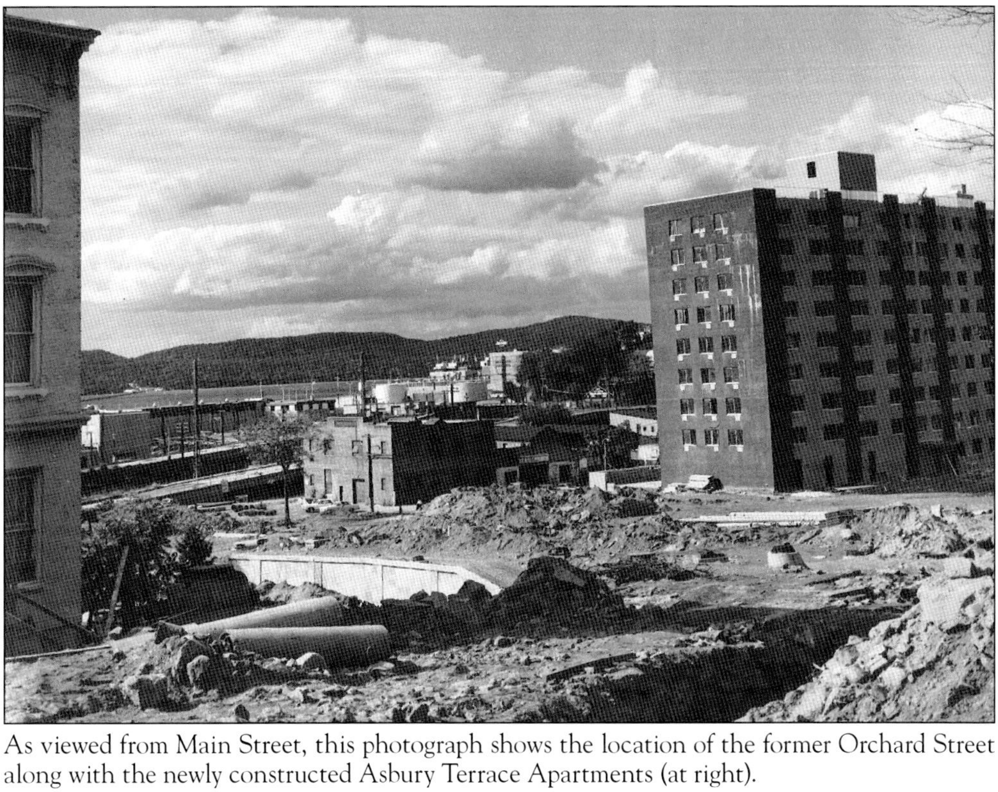

As viewed from Main Street, this photograph shows the location of the former Orchard Street along with the newly constructed Asbury Terrace Apartments (at right).

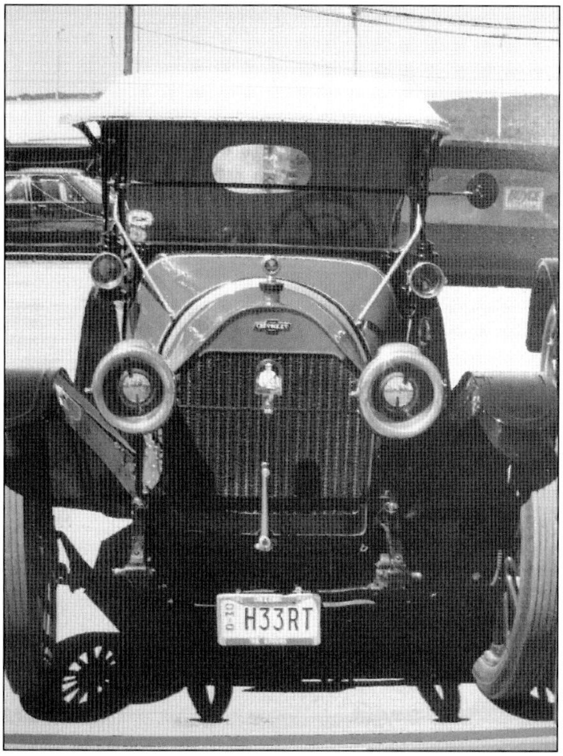


For most of the 20th century, the General Motors Corporation (GM) was the backbone of the local economy and the largest single employer in the villages. When William Durant and Louis Chevrolet purchased the old Maxwell plant in North Tarrytown for the Chevrolet Motor Company in 1914, they paid $267,000. Pictured here, this 1915 Chevrolet Model 490, which cost $490, was one of 4,902 built at the plant that year.

Hard work and long hours on the assembly line was a way of life for the workers at the GM Chevrolet plant in North Tarrytown. By the end of 1937, the plant had assembled over 2 million vehicles. In the years leading up to World War II, the majority of the workers were men, shown here in this photograph of a company picnic in 1938.

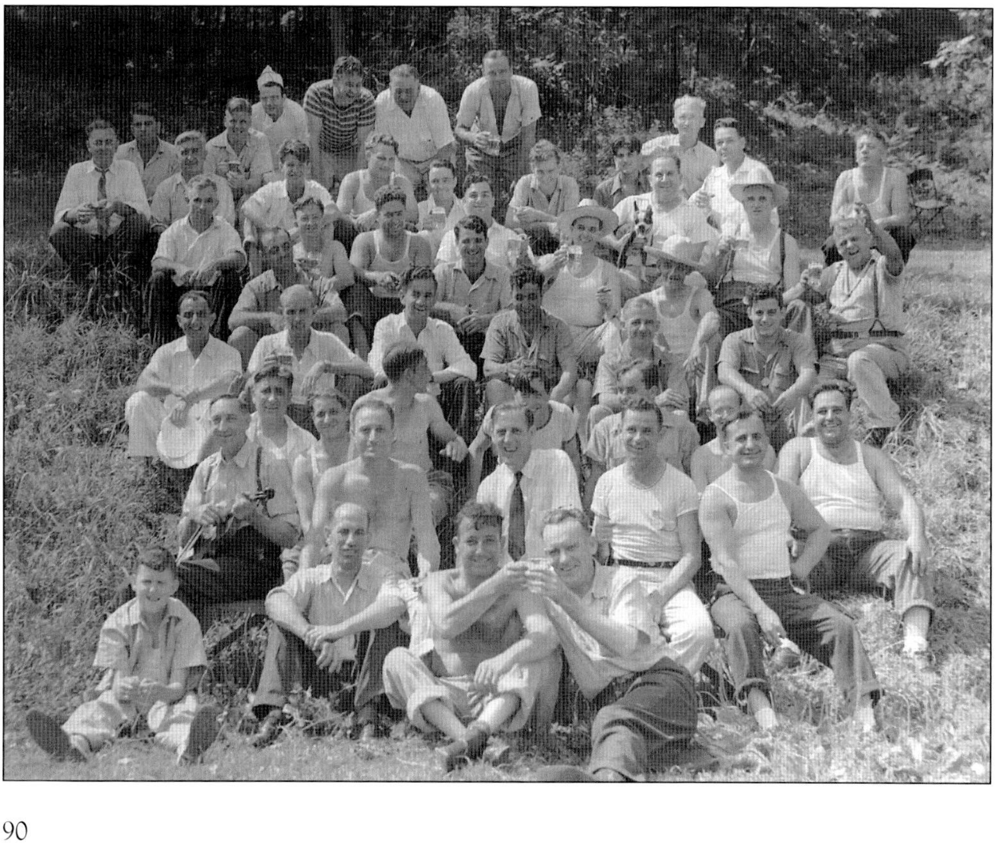

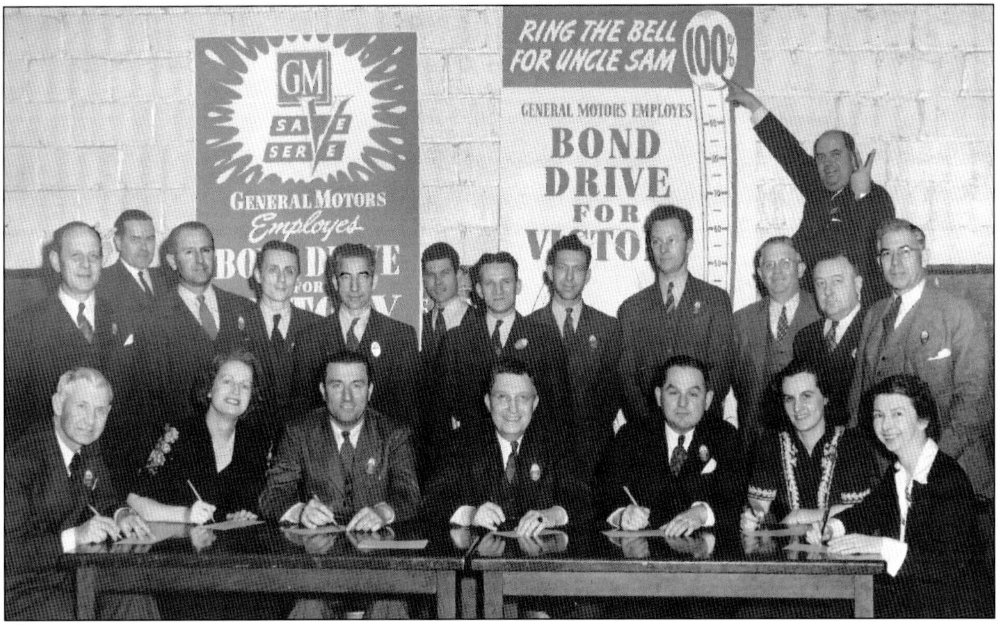


After the bombing of Pearl Harbor in 1941, employees of the GM plant participated in bond drives to support the war effort. The plant office employees are shown above at the 1941 Bond Drive for Victory kickoff. While Chevrolet was producing military trucks and other equipment for the army, ordinary citizens dug into their pockets to purchase stamps and bonds in support of the United States of America.

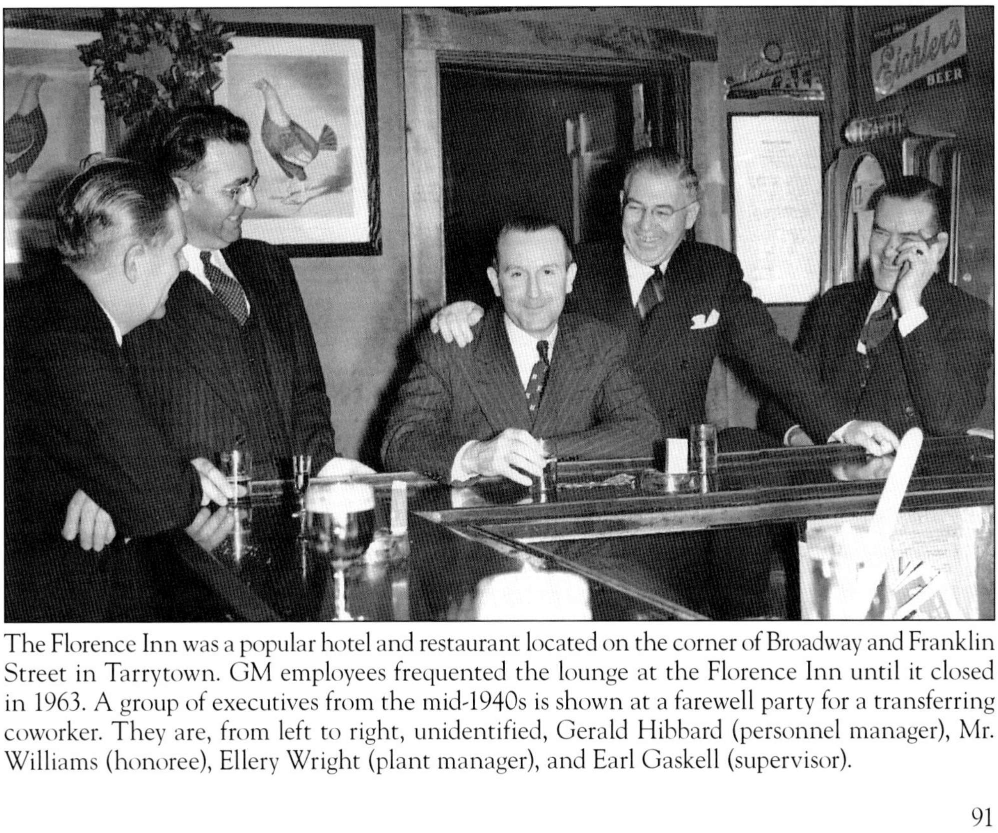


The Florence Inn was a popular hotel and restaurant located on the corner of Broadway and Franklin Street in Tarrytown. GM employees frequented the lounge at the Florence Inn until it closed in 1963. A group of executives from the mid-1940s is shown at a farewell party for a transferring coworker. They are, from left to right, unidentified, Gerald Hibbard (personnel manager), Mr. Williams (honoree), Ellery Wright (plant manager), and Earl Gaskell (supervisor).

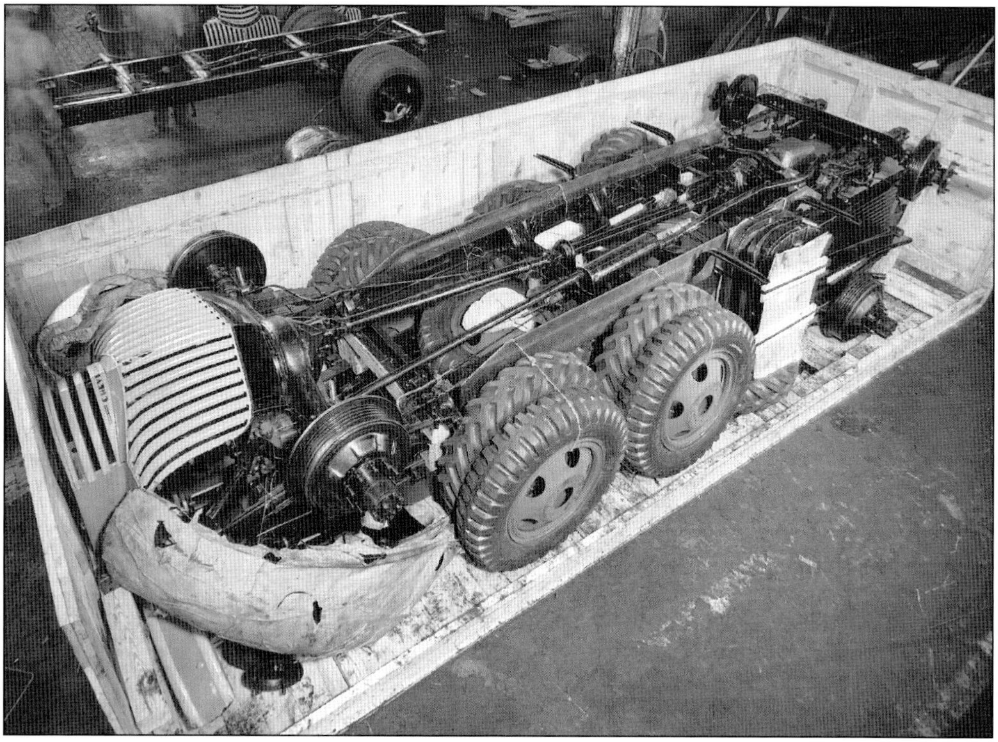

In 1939, production of military vehicles increased when the assembly of lend-lease units was allotted to the plant. Normally one assembly line was devoted to passenger car production, a second line was used for trucks, and a third line for boxed units for export. During the early part of the decade, military units were assembled on the truck line, and the former passenger car line was utilized for boxing vehicles for export.

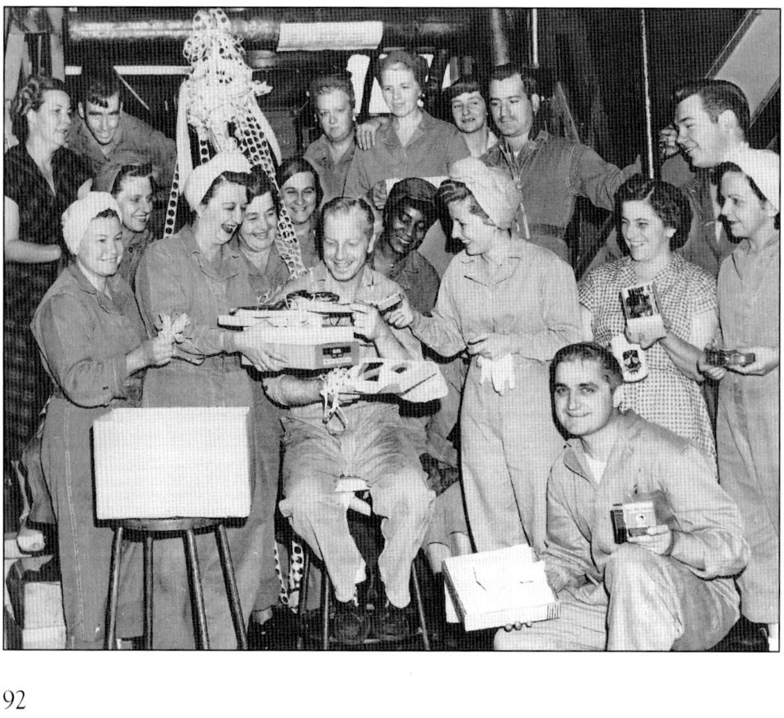

At the height of wartime output, large numbers of women were recruited to work on the assembly line. Shown here at an impromptu party for a coworker are several of General Motors Eastern Aircraft Division's own versions of Rosie the Riverter.

In January 1942, GM established the Eastern Aircraft Division, with a contract to assemble planes jointly with the Grumman Corporation. GM would produce wings, cabins, canopies, and motor mounts for the Avenger, a navy plane designed by Grumman. The former Fisher Body facility was converted to wartime production in August, and by October, the first set of wings was shipped to the Trenton plant for final assembly.

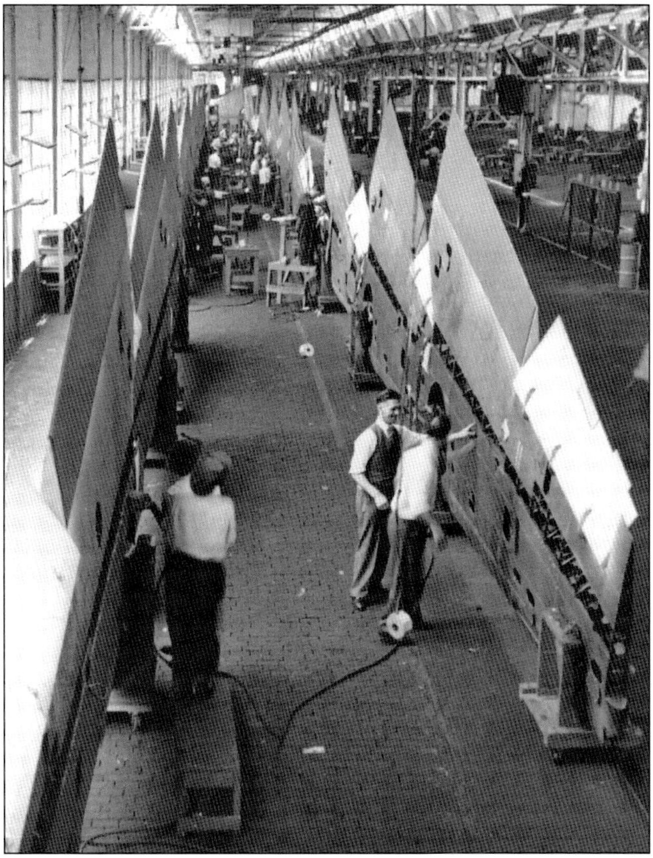

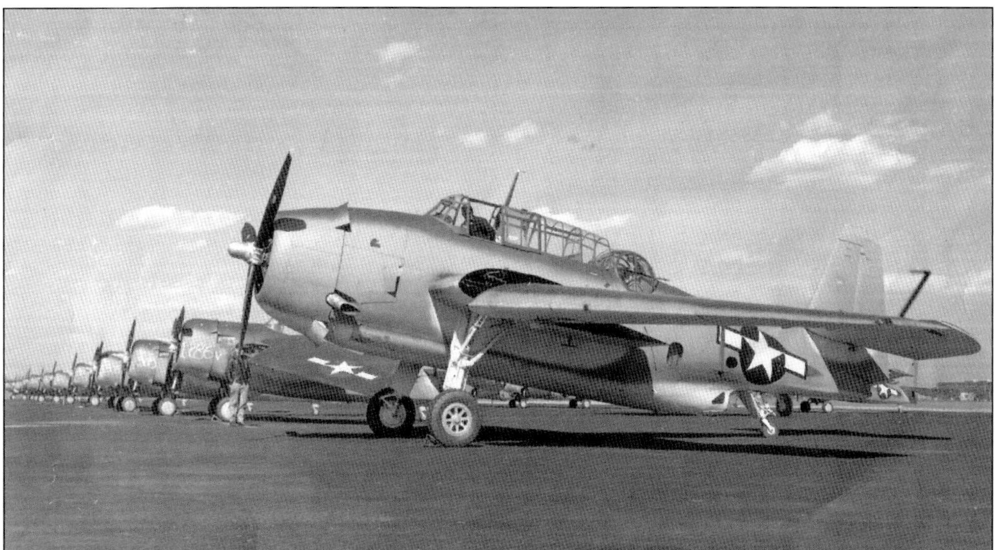

In mid-1943, the Chevrolet plant began assembling Avenger wings and parts as well. The next year, Grumman stopped building the Avenger, and the navy turned all production over to the GM facilities in Trenton, Baltimore, Bloomfield, Linden, and North Tarrytown. Here assembled planes are ready for inspection.

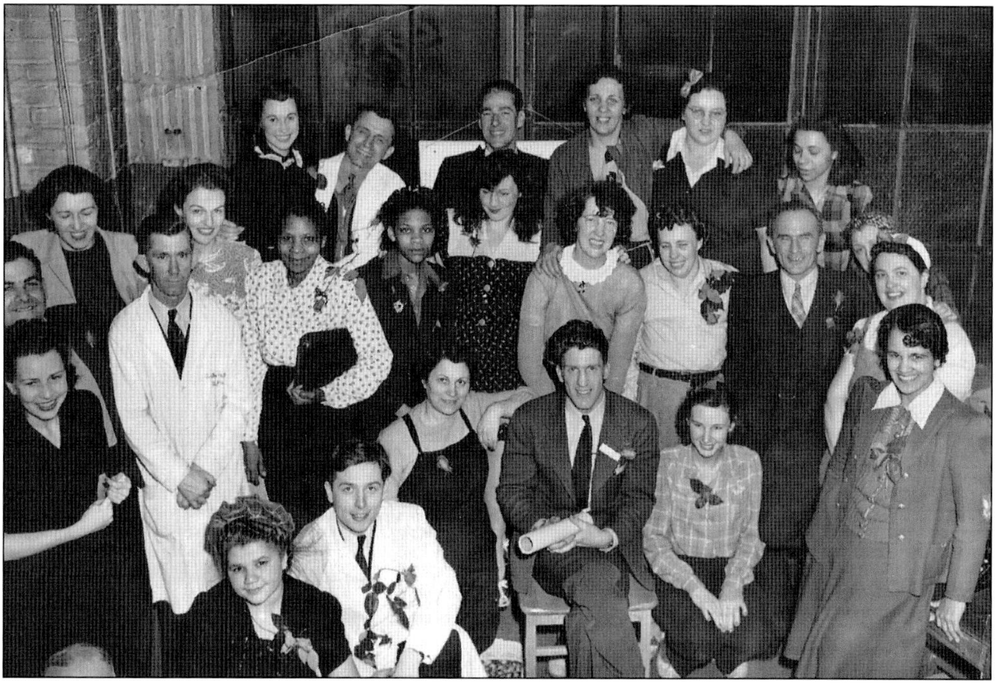

Although conversion of the physical plant occurred quickly, the challenge was to educate personnel. Engineer Leonard Abraham taught classes at the Cawood Motors dealership to train employees how to work aluminum and use the drill press to assemble the 10,000 parts that made up the Avenger. Training in aircraft production was a major undertaking for the engineering staff. By the spring of 1943, more than 2,900 workers, mostly women, had been hired.

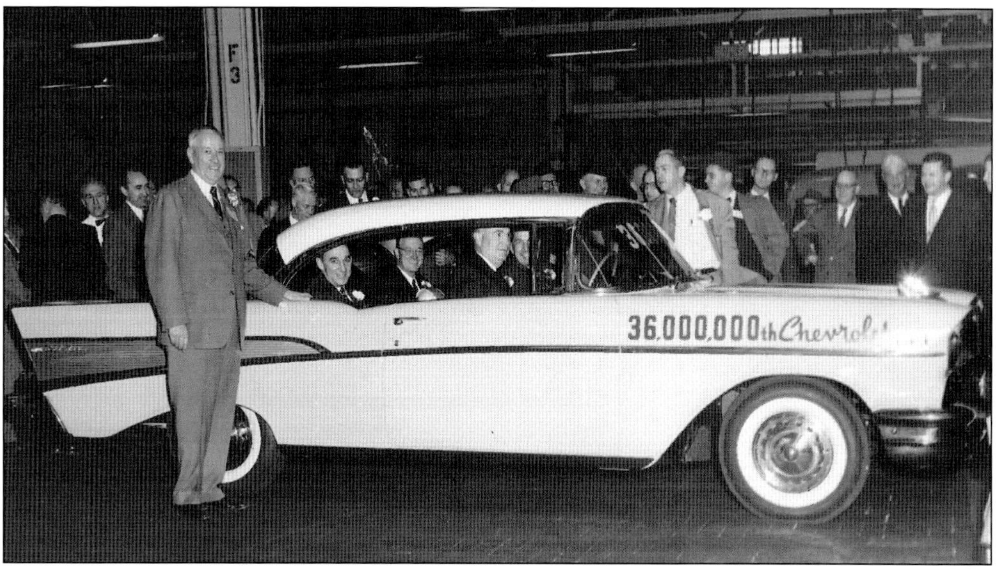


At the end of the war, GM quickly resumed domestic production. In September 1946, the first peacetime cars and trucks looked identical to prewar models. A sporty new model, the Bel Air, was introduced in 1950, and by November 28, 1956, the "36,000,000th Chevrolet," a 1957 Bel Air Coupe, rolled off the assembly line. Walter B. Brownlie, manager of the Chevrolet Tarrytown Assembly Division is standing on the left.

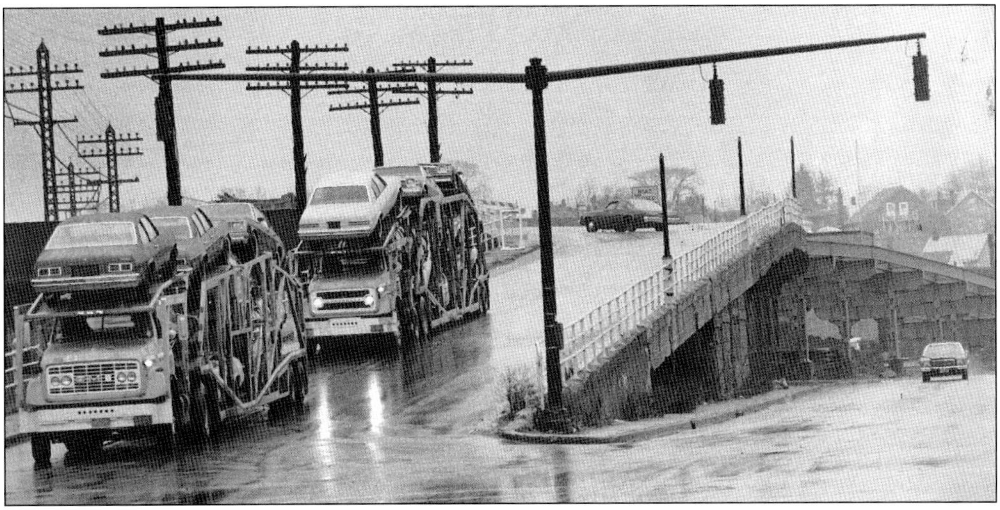

The first Anchor Motor trucks came to Tarrytown in 1924 with flatbeds that could carry three cars. They made a huge difference, since cars no longer had to be driven individually to nearby automobile dealers. Shown crossing the H-Bridge in Tarrytown during the 1970s, Anchor Motor trucks were carrying at least six cars.

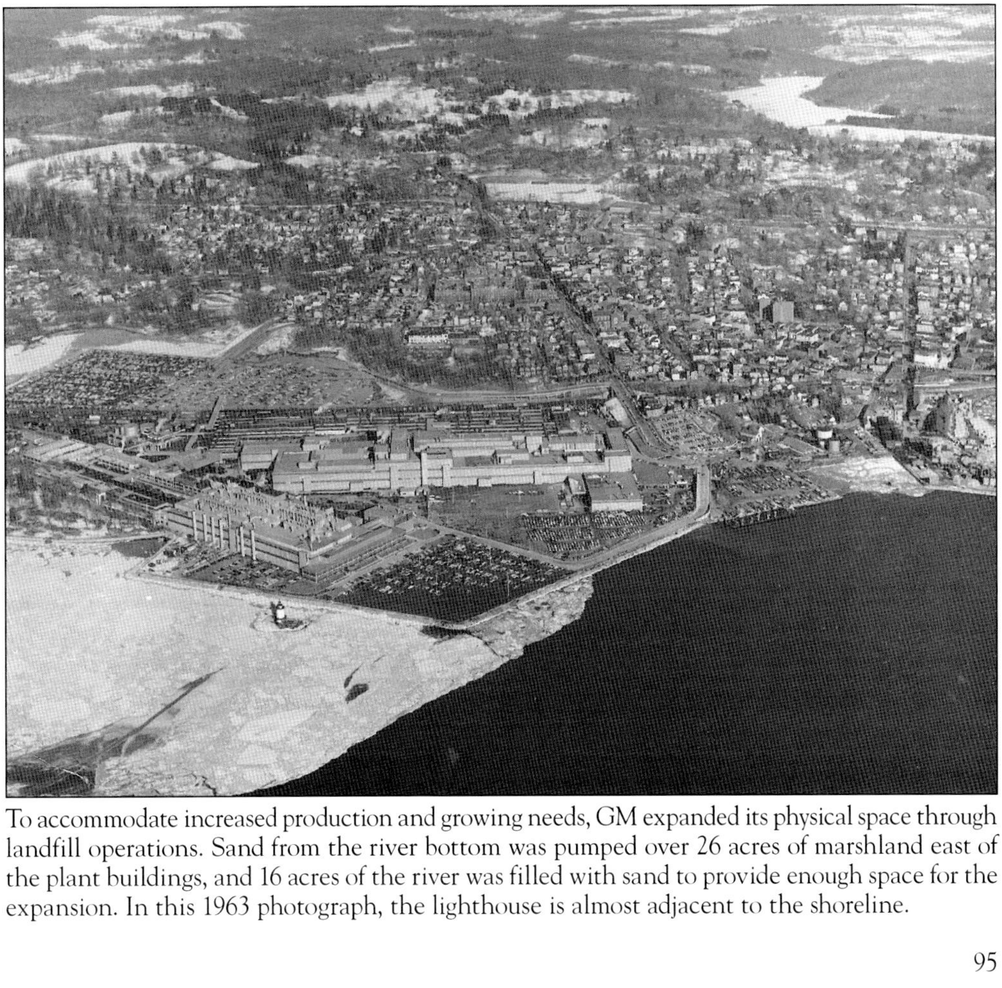

To accommodate increased production and growing needs, GM expanded its physical space through landfill operations. Sand from the river bottom was pumped over 26 acres of marshland east of the plant buildings, and 16 acres of the river was filled with sand to provide enough space for the expansion. In this 1963 photograph, the lighthouse is almost adjacent to the shoreline.

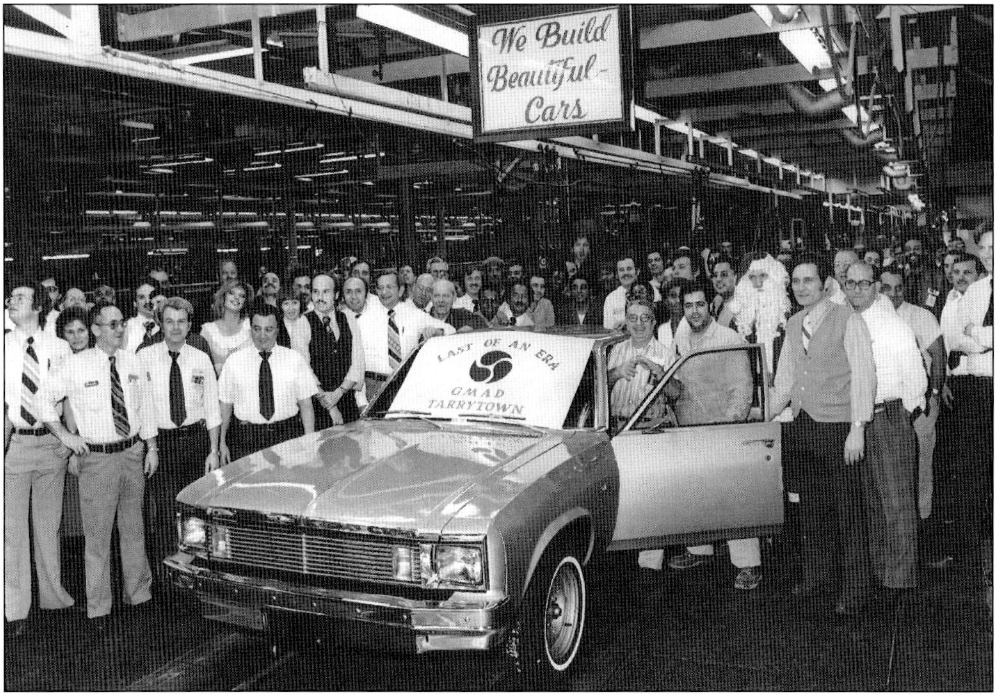

In 1971, the plant ended 55 years of light-duty truck production as its 1,545,738th and last truck came off the line. During the 1970s, changes were also taking place in the automobile industry due to rising gas prices. On December 22, 1978, GM workers celebrated the assembly of the last Chevrolet Nova, one of the most popular cars ever made at the plant.

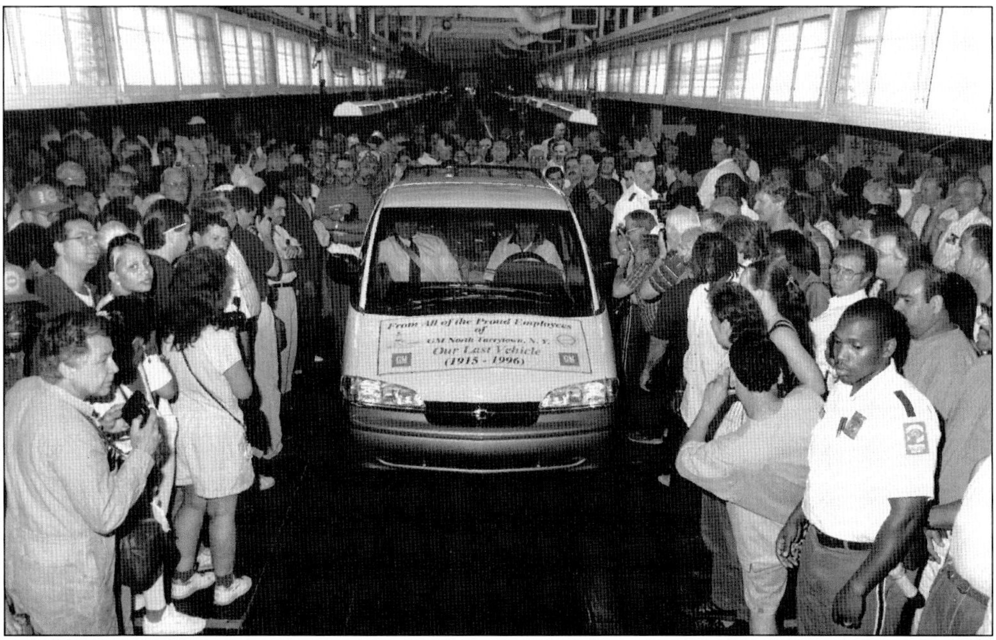

The first model APV minivans, originally built in 1989, were the last cars to be produced at the plant. In 1996, GM elected to close the facility, ending almost 100 years of automobile manufacturing on the property and losing 3,458 jobs.

# *Eight*

# A Century of Fashion

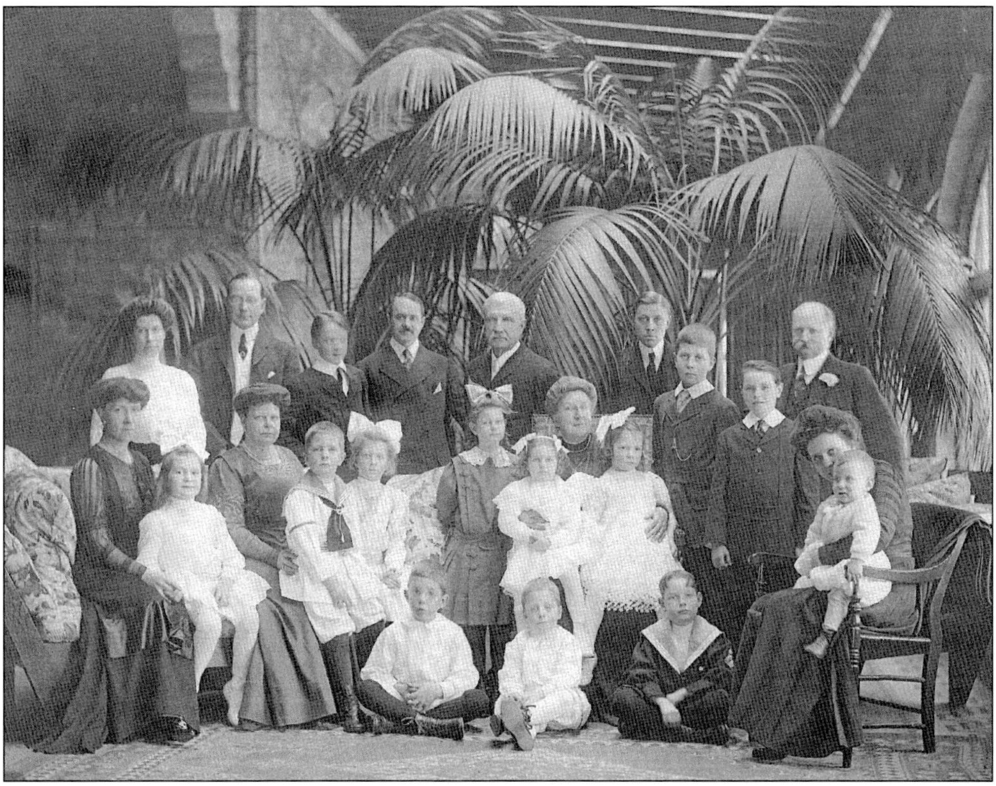

Popular clothing styles changed rapidly during the 20th century. From long white tea dresses to miniskirts and from knickers to casual pants, the photographs in this chapter depict some of the fashion trends of the century. Edward Coles, a local photographer in the first decade of the century, captured the William Rockefeller family wearing clothing that combined the modest, confining styles of the past with the shorter, flowing styles of the new century.

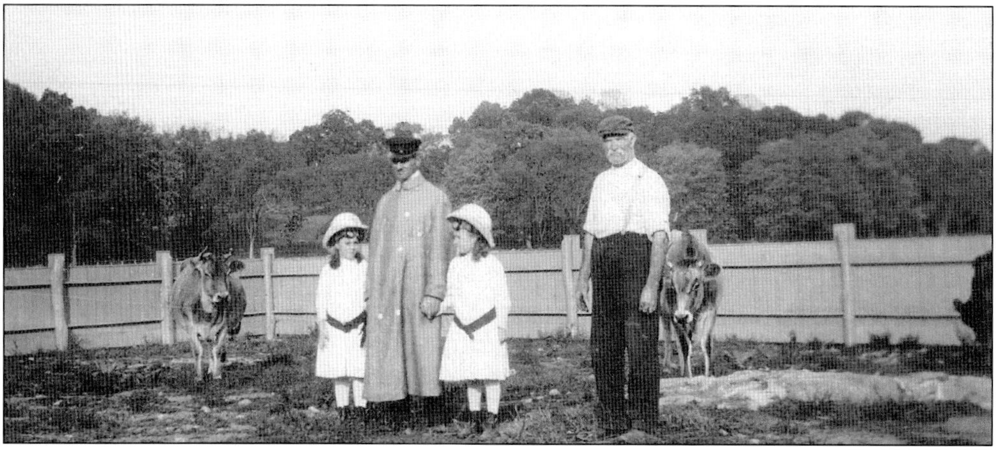

This photograph shows the two young daughters of Frank Gould with the family chauffeur on an outing during the first decade of the 20th century. The young girls are wearing white cotton frocks with silk ribbon belts and safari hats. The chauffeur is wearing a typical linen driving coat and cap. Driving coats, or dusters, were popular in the early part of the century, when most roads were still unpaved.

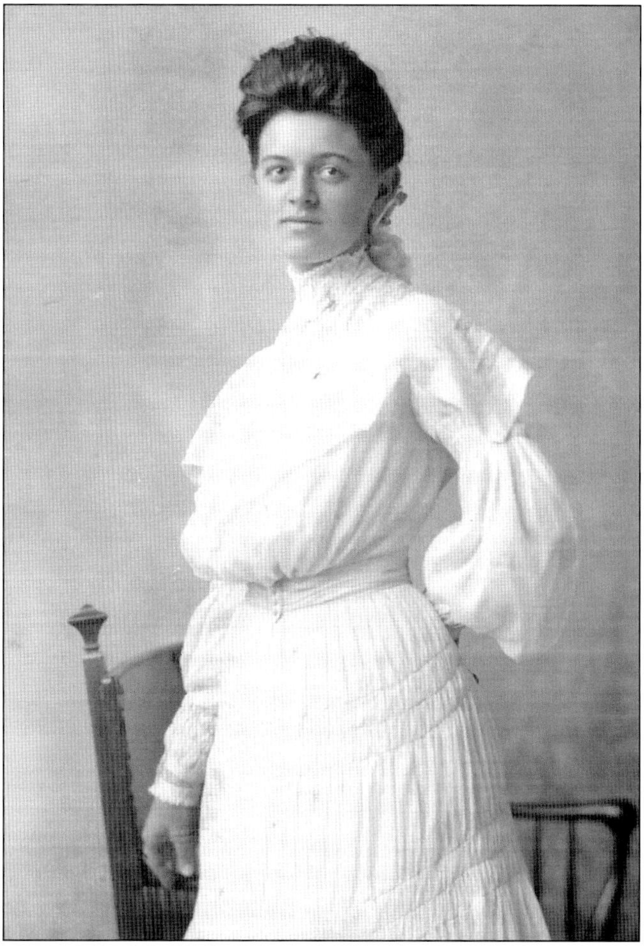

Florence Danielson is wearing a fashionable S-shaped Edwardian-day dress typical of the early 1900s. Women wore corsets under these dresses that were characterized by ornate high-necked, "pigeon-drooped" blouses and bell-shaped skirts.

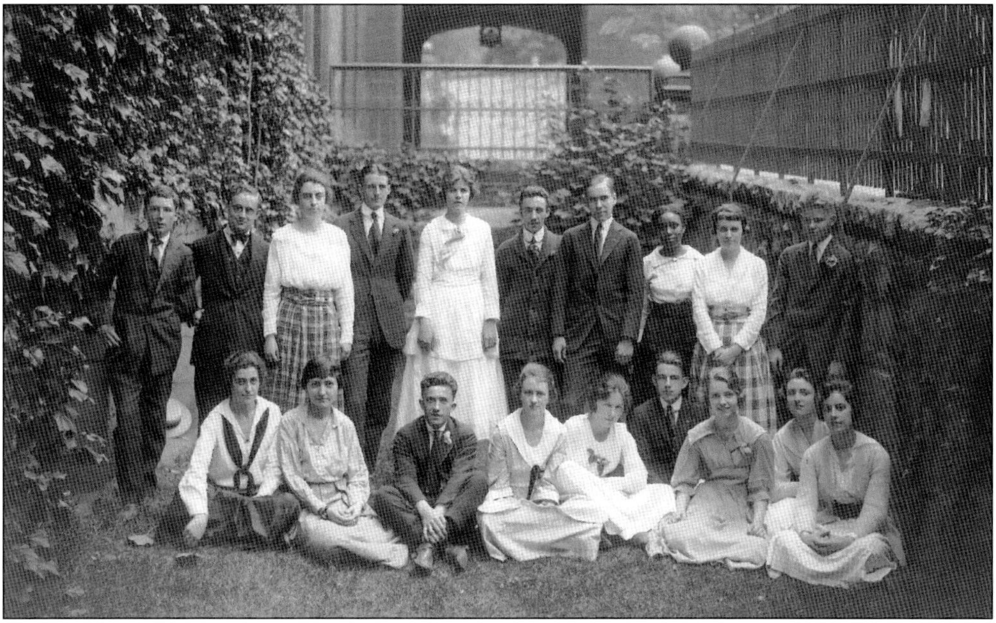

By 1919, women no longer wore corsets, and clothing was much looser for both sexes. Above is the graduating class of 1919 outside of Washington Irving High School. Class members are, from left to right, (first row) Martha Allan, Betty Wood, Milton Cartoon, Virginia Hawes, Margaret Melly, Lewis Palmer, Agnes Peters, Helen Murray, and Irene Martin; (second row) John Hanrahan, Morton Kantrowitz, Julia Bacon, Edward Broome, Fabian Bushel, Robert Poillon, Henry Miller, Jennie Dean, Katharine Spencer, and Percy Johnson.

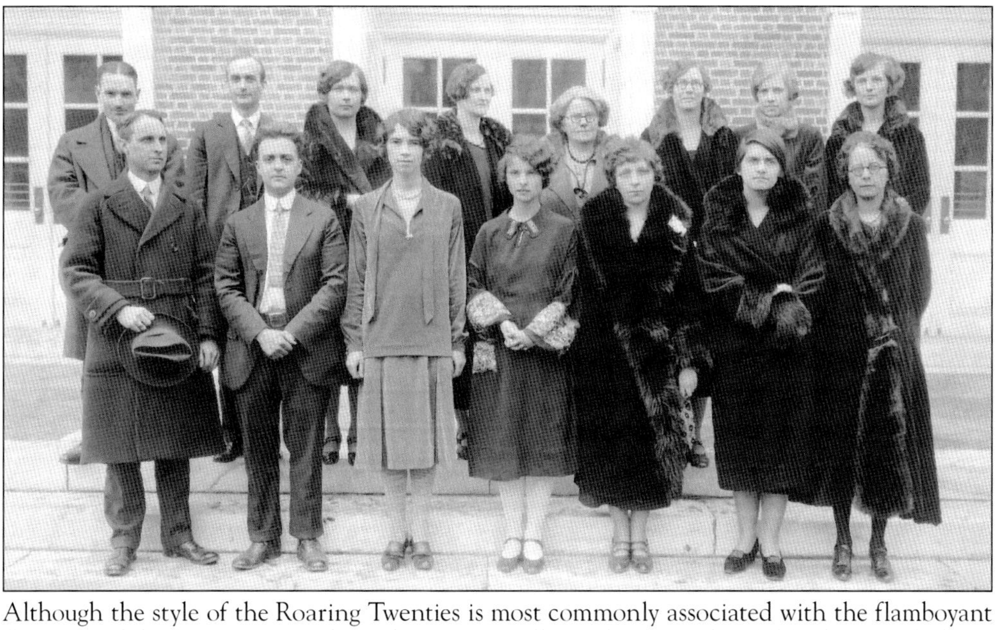

Although the style of the Roaring Twenties is most commonly associated with the flamboyant flappers and their escorts, everyday styles were actually much more sedate. This photograph shows the faculty at the new Washington Irving High School in 1926. Dresses were calf length with long or drooping waists. The 1920s saw the introduction of baggier suit pants for men, first worn by Oxford students and introduced to America in 1925.

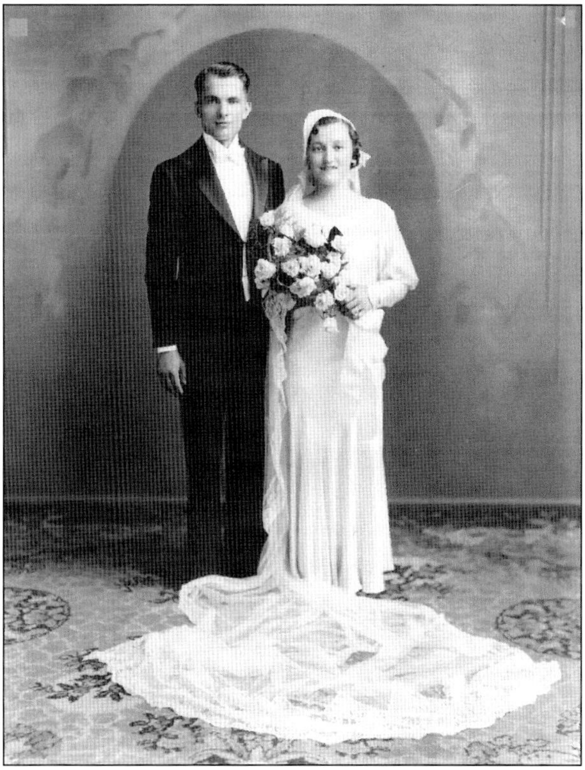

During the 1920s and 1930s, wedding attire reflected the fashion of the day, while maintaining the traditional long white dress. When Mary Yankovich married Peter Petcoff of Tarrytown on September 3, 1933, she wore a straight, unconstructed satin gown. Her veil, held in place by a cap, was also the train and is shown draped in front of the bride.

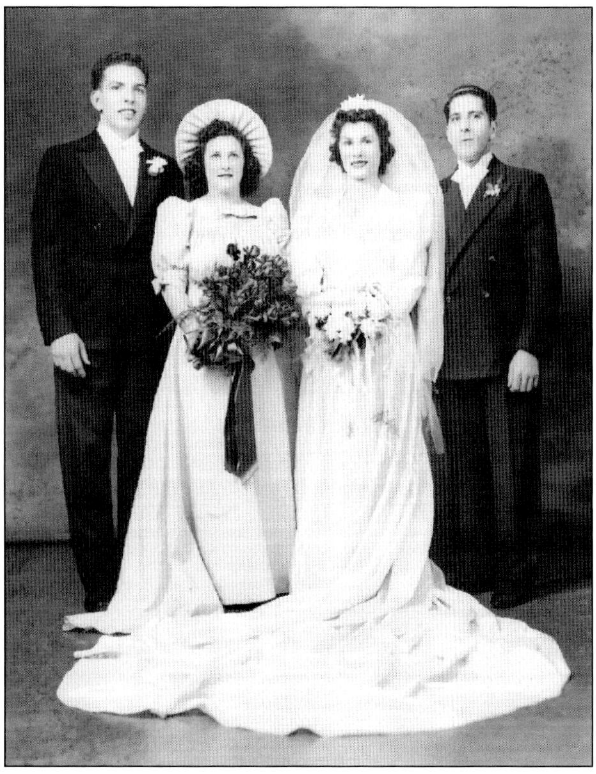

Shown in a traditional wedding photograph are, from left to right, best man John Cavalieri, maid of honor Sadie Mocciare, bride Sadie Cavalieri, and groom James Tonietti. The bride is wearing a long flowing gown with refined Gibson girl sleeves and a sweeping train, fashionable from 1939 to 1942. The couple married December 1, 1940, at Immaculate Conception Church. Posed studio portraits were standard until after the Second World War, when candid photographs became popular.

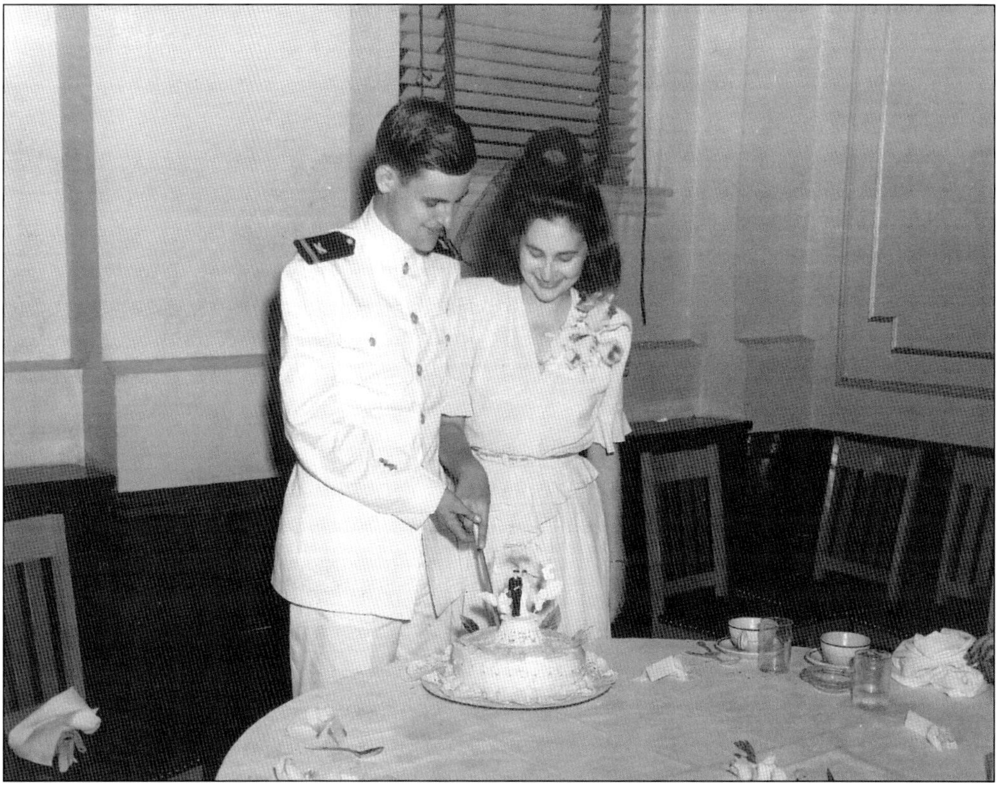

When George and Peggy Case married in June 1944 during the war, the long white wedding dress had all but disappeared. Men wore their uniforms, and women tended to wear a suit or a simple dress with a floral corsage pinned to the lapel.

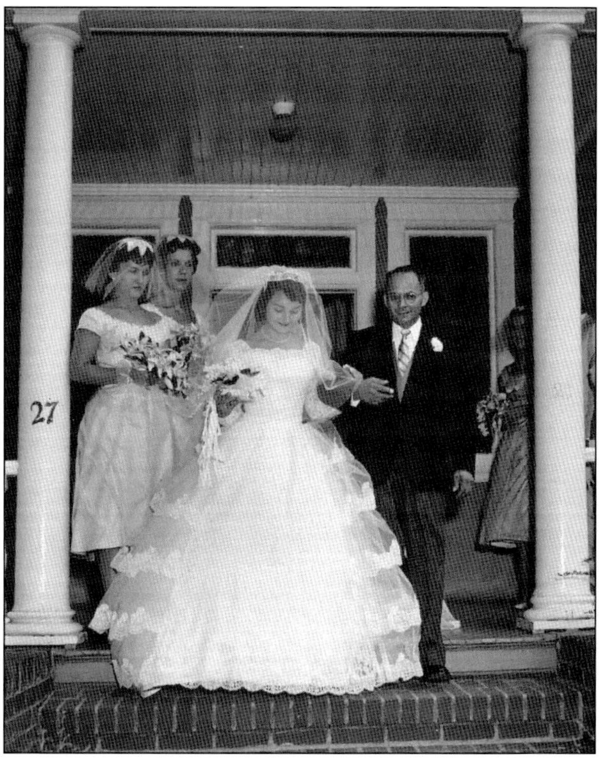


After the war, it was back to long gowns in luxurious fabrics for weddings. Beverly Petcoff, shown on her porch with her father and bridesmaids, wore a tiered gown of white satin and lace decorated with seed pearls. When she married John Jansen at St. Theresa's Church on August 22, 1959, the photography industry had evolved into a new candid style that captured the wedding as it was unfolding and recorded the entire event.

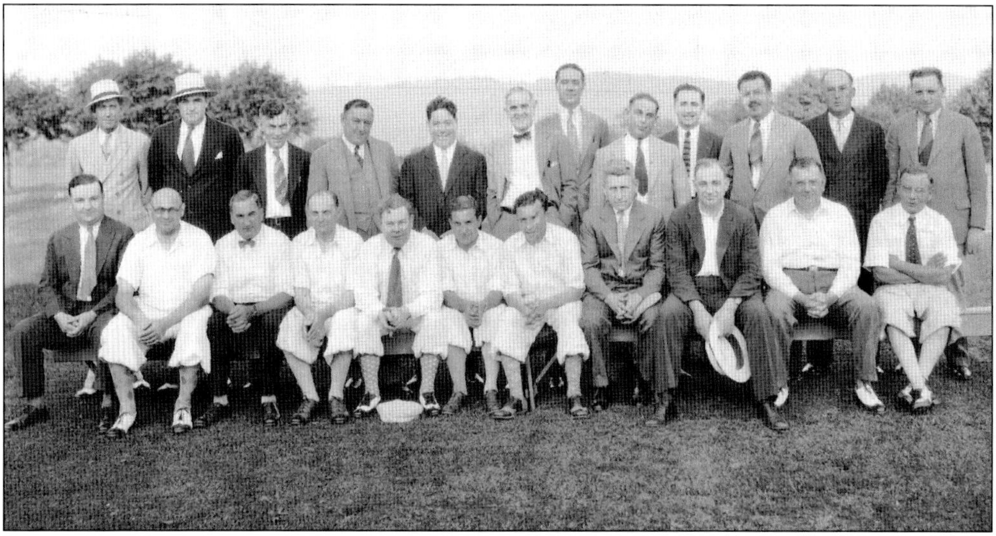

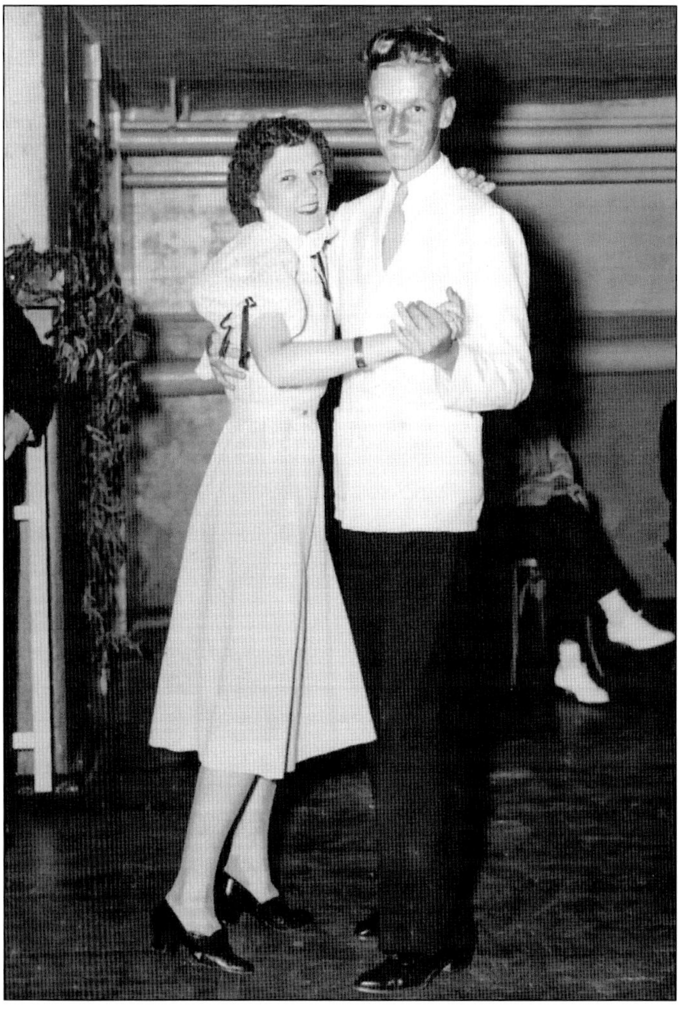

After the stock market crash, tailors endeavored to create causal inexpensive suits that projected the image of a man with a large torso and squared shoulders, as worn by some men in this photograph of a Lions Club outing in 1932. Several of the men attending the outing are wearing knickerbockers, or knickers, the most popular type of casual wear at the time.

Sylvia Page and Frank Stewart are shown at a YMCA dance in 1937. White jackets, instead of black suits, became popular in the 1930s as a way for men to dress formally in the warmer months. Ruffled high-waisted dresses that extended to mid-calf became the style for women in the mid-1930s.

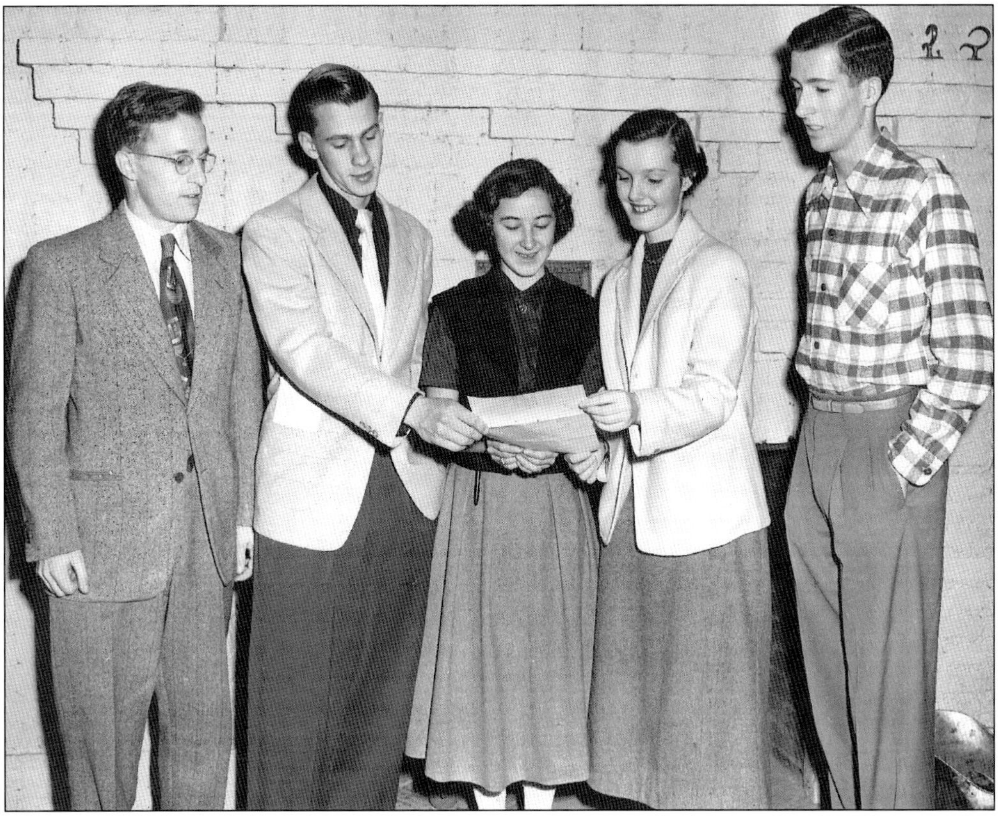

After World War II, styles reflected the postwar emphasis on the business world. The suits that women started wearing in the 1930s became less tailored by 1950, with skirts that hung straight from the waist to below the knee. Although men's suits were less structured than earlier, men continued to wear heavy fabrics. Pictured here are students from the class of 1951. They are, from left to right, unidentified, Frank Poli, Harriet Nichols, Patricia Cudney, and Robert Harmon.

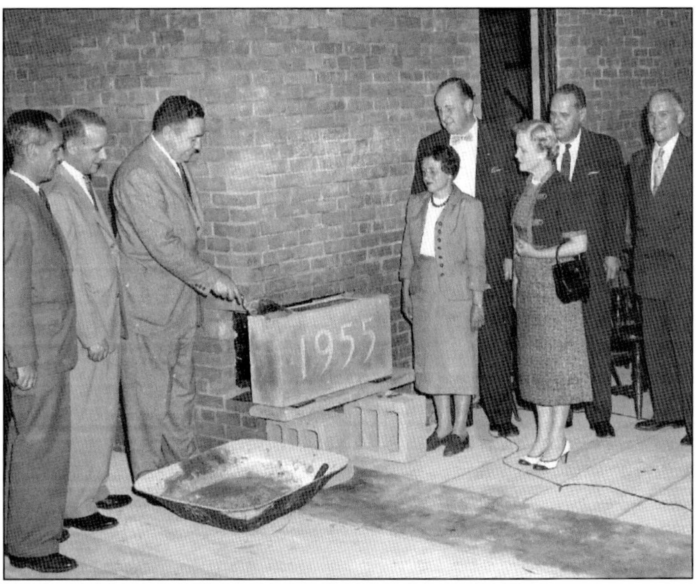


In the mid-1950s, both men and women wore suits to official events. Starched white shirts and shorter single-breasted suit jackets were popular for men. For women, skirts were straighter, without any obvious pleating. Pictured at the cornerstone dedication for Tappan Hill School in 1955 are, from left to right, Hugh Harten, Fred Cotter, Arthur Deverill, Dr. Rose Nelson, Byron Sweet, Jean Girard, Raymond Kroggel, and Norton Wilde.

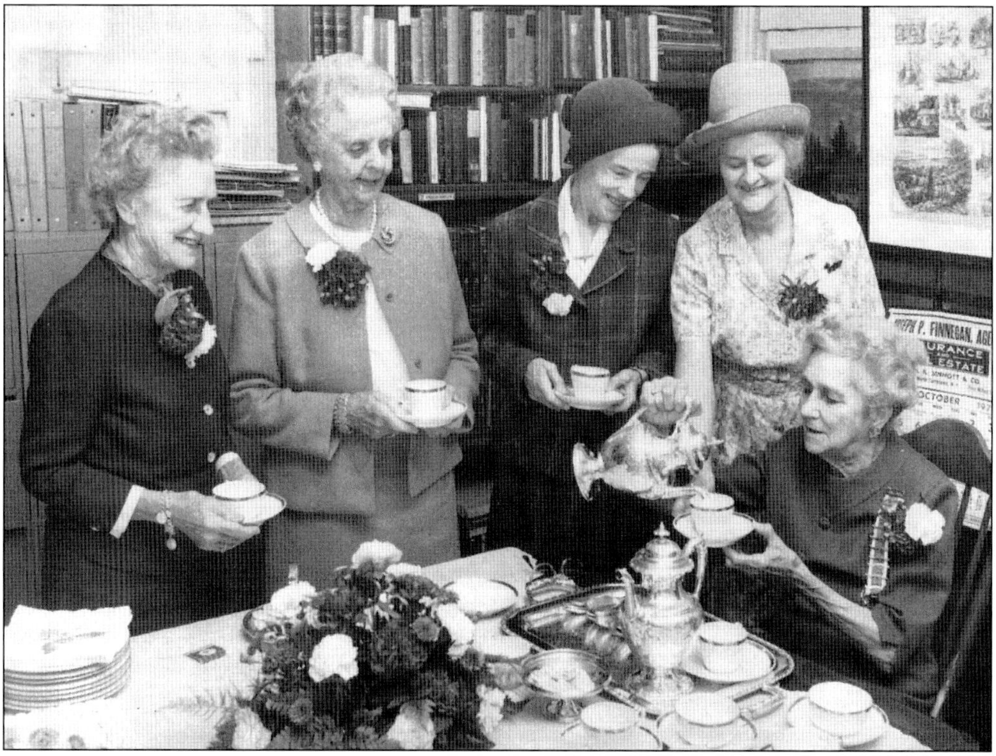

By the 1970s, formal afternoon tea parties attended by ladies in smart suits and hats were becoming rare. Pictured here from left to right, Sadie Husted, Elizabeth MacDonald, Edith Suydan, Catherine Suydan, and Sarah Case (pouring tea) are keeping the fine old tradition alive at the Tarrytown Chapter of the Daughters of the American Revolution 45th anniversary tea.

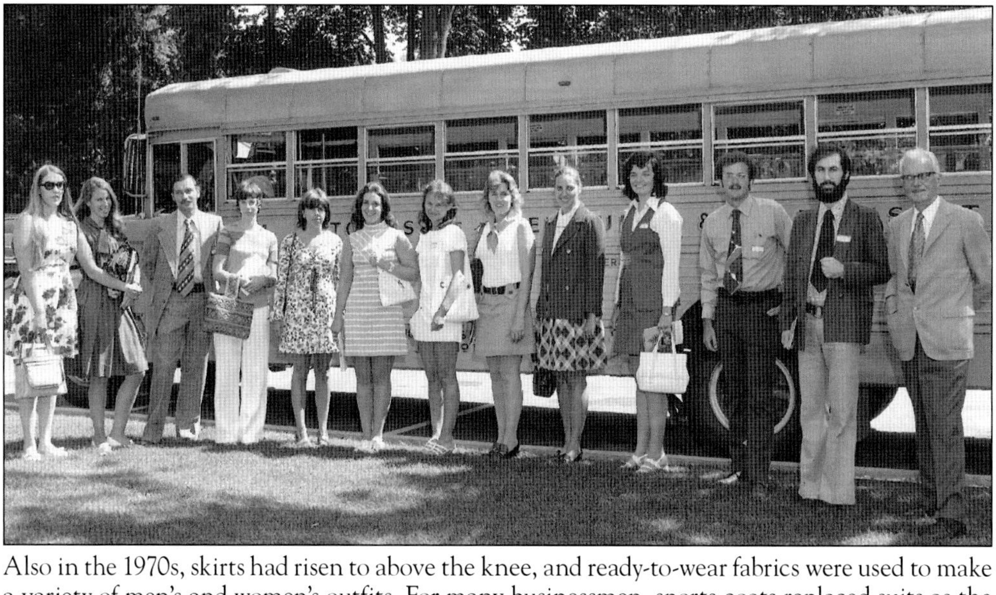

Also in the 1970s, skirts had risen to above the knee, and ready-to-wear fabrics were used to make a variety of men's and women's outfits. For many businessmen, sports coats replaced suits as the popular choice for work attire. Teachers, newly hired by the Public Schools of the Tarrytowns, are shown above touring the villages in 1974.

# *Nine*

# The Growing Population

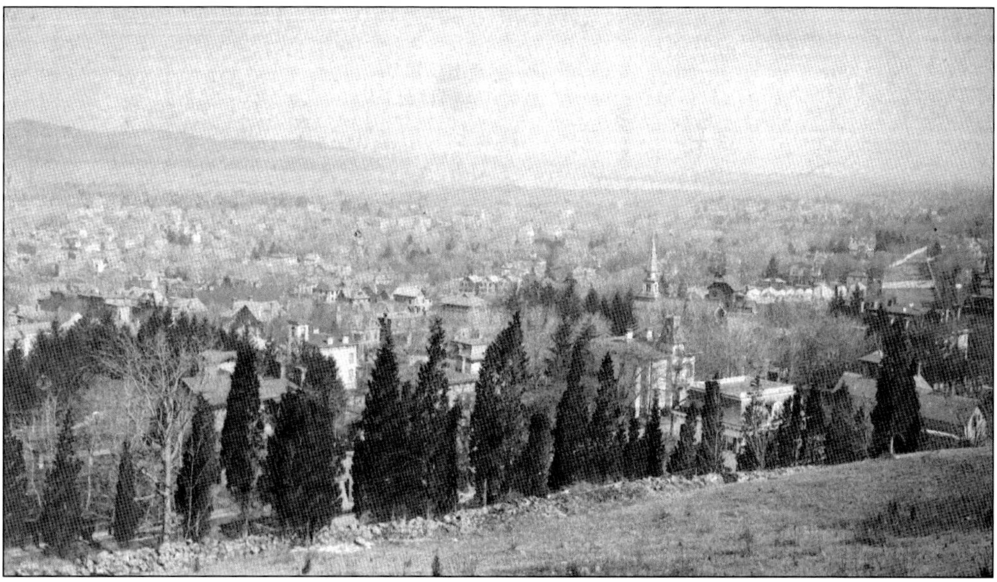

The story of the growing population in the villages is also the story of the residential development within a community that supported a steady influx of various immigrant groups. Historically, the heritage of local residents was Dutch, English, French Huguenot, and African. The 19th century saw an influx of immigrants from Ireland and Eastern Europe. At the onset of the 20th century, the population of both villages was just over 9,000.

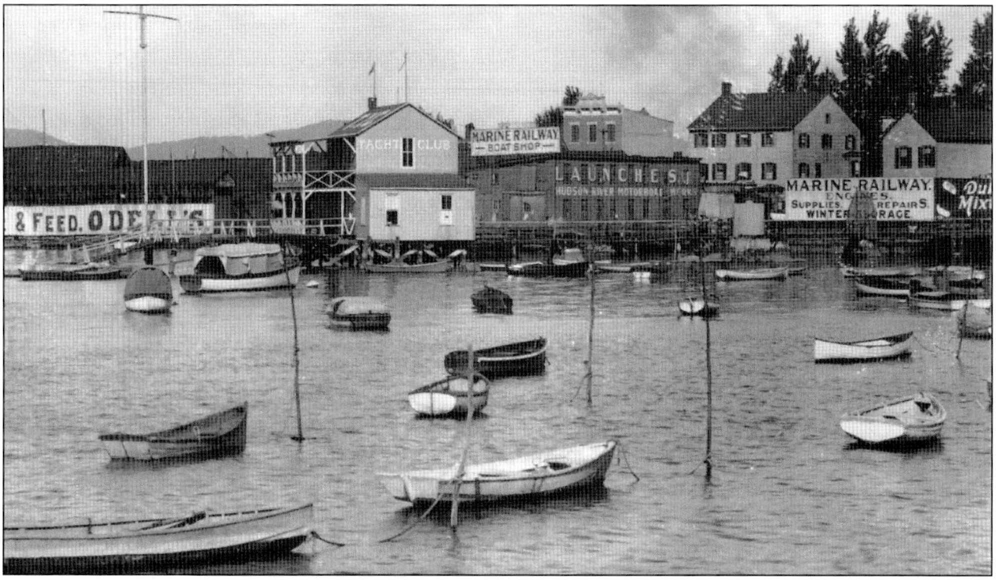


The gently sloping waterfront and abundant raw materials along the Hudson River made the location of the two villages attractive for settlement from the 17th through the 19th centuries. By the beginning of the 20th century, the riverfront was a bustling location where commerce, industry, and residential properties stood side by side. Residential development, which started at the waterfront, slowly moved eastward until it reached the village borders by the end of the century.

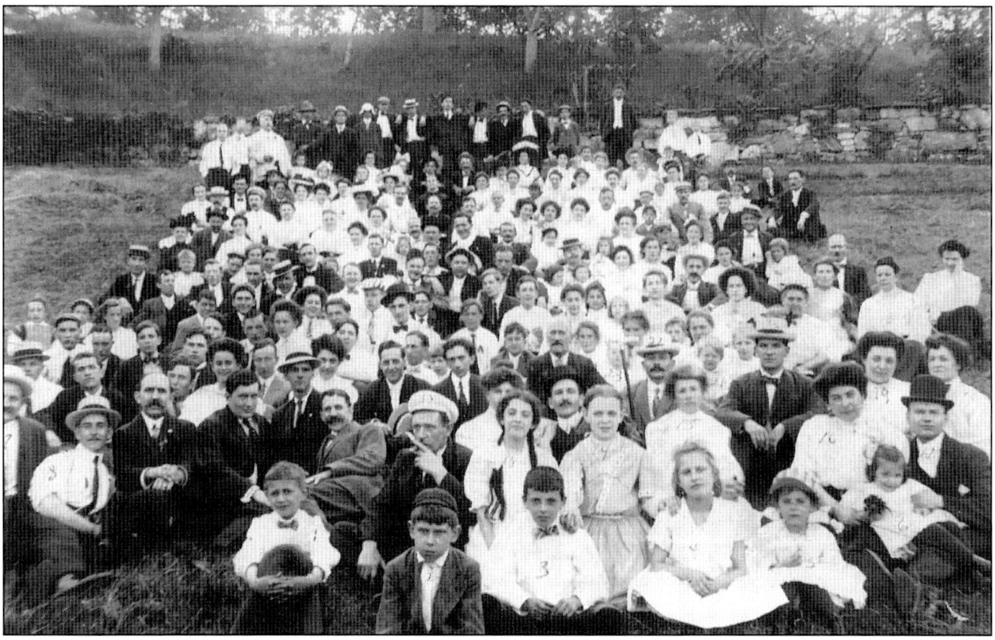

During the first decade of the 20th century, the Tarrytowns were advantageous destinations for the waves of immigrants that were coming to New York. Newcomers made connections with their countrymen, and jobs were available. While working to fit into the country, many of these new Americans also maintained ties to their cultural heritage through clubs and religious institutions. The German Picnic was an annual event, shown here in 1908.

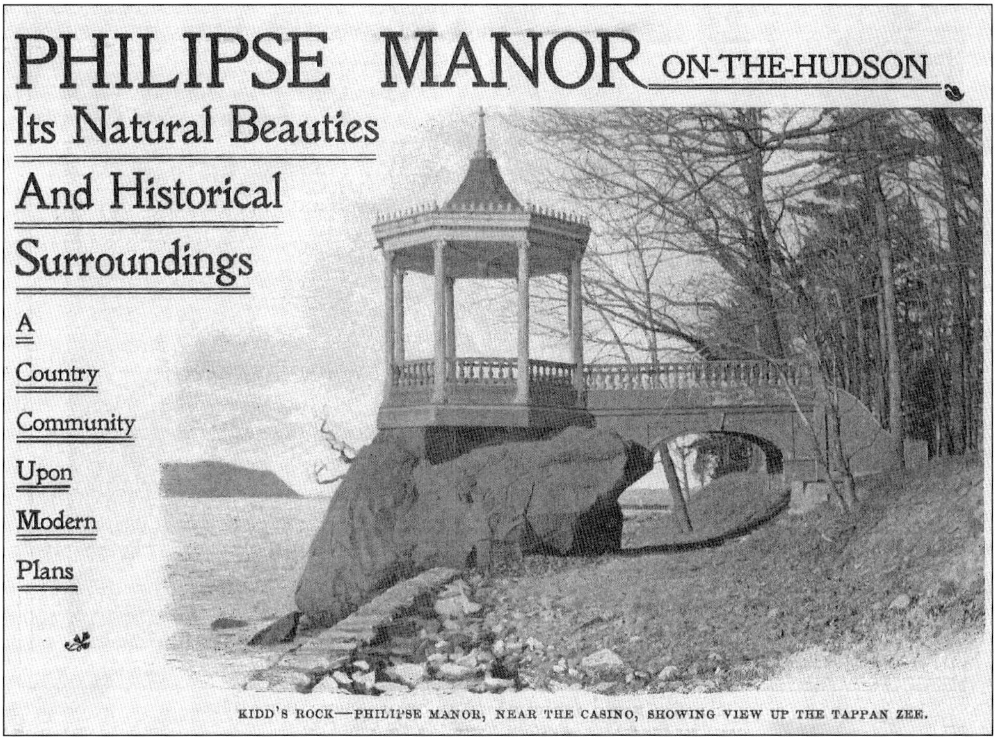


A 1903 Philipse Manor brochure describes a beautiful community with river views, easy access to New York City, and a lack of mosquitoes. Construction of 20 Philipse Manor houses began in 1909. A train station was built in 1912, and development continued through the 1920s. By 1939, there were 200 families in Philipse Manor, and by the end of the century, that number had grown to more than 300.

Division Street was named for the dividing line between the two villages where the road is located. Small two- and three-story structures were constructed during the first quarter of the 20th century. Italian and Slavic immigrants who arrived between 1900 and 1925 soon filled these buildings. Large estates and the automobile factory provided jobs for many of these new residents. By 1920, the population of the two villages had reached 11,834.

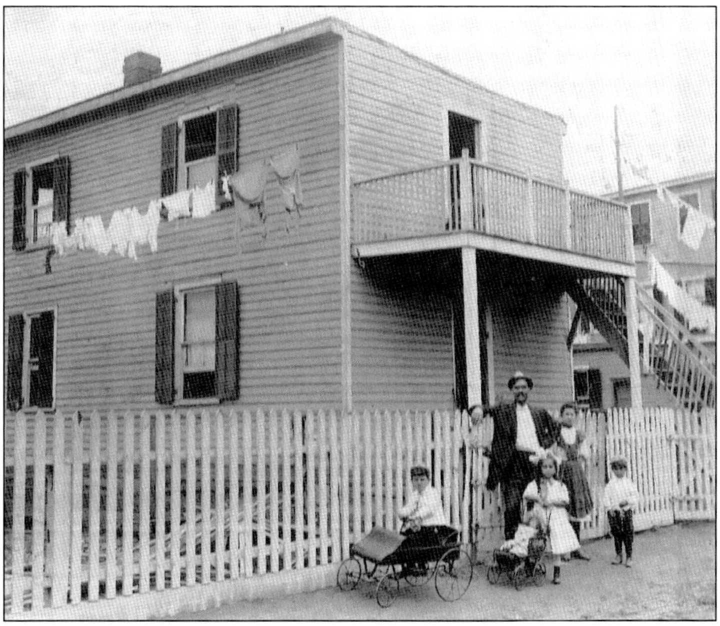

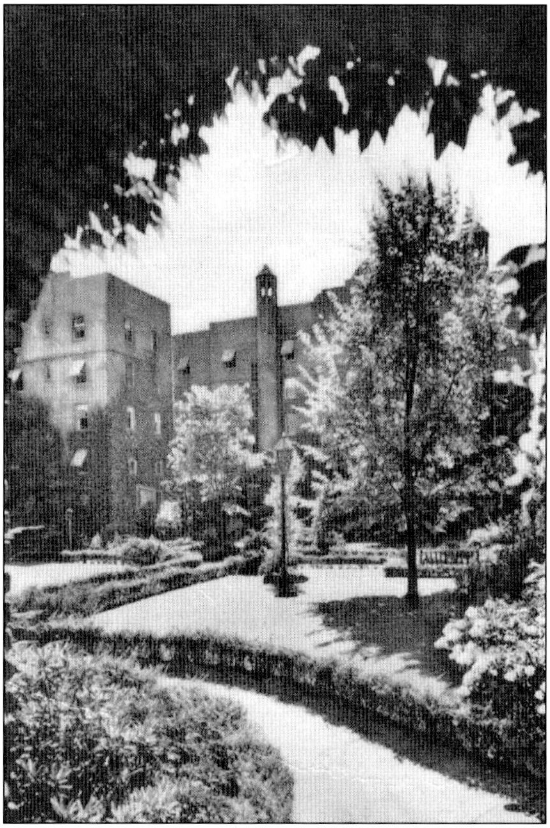

With the population growing to 14,258 by 1930, John D. Rockefeller helped relieve the housing shortage by funding the Van Tassel Apartments in North Tarrytown in 1929. Conveniently located within walking distance of the Chevrolet and Fisher Body companies, it included 241 apartments, a large central garden, a playground, an auditorium, and free bus service to the trains. During the depressed 1930s, the original cooperative ownership plan could not succeed, and the apartments became rental units.

The neighborhood of Pennybridge, named after the historical toll collected at Sheldon Brook, is located at the south end of Tarrytown. During the 19th century, skilled craftsmen and nearby estate workers settled this area. The population of the villages had grown to 15,678 by 1940. Between 1930 and 1950, new residents were drawn to the rural character and open areas that were still present in Pennybridge.

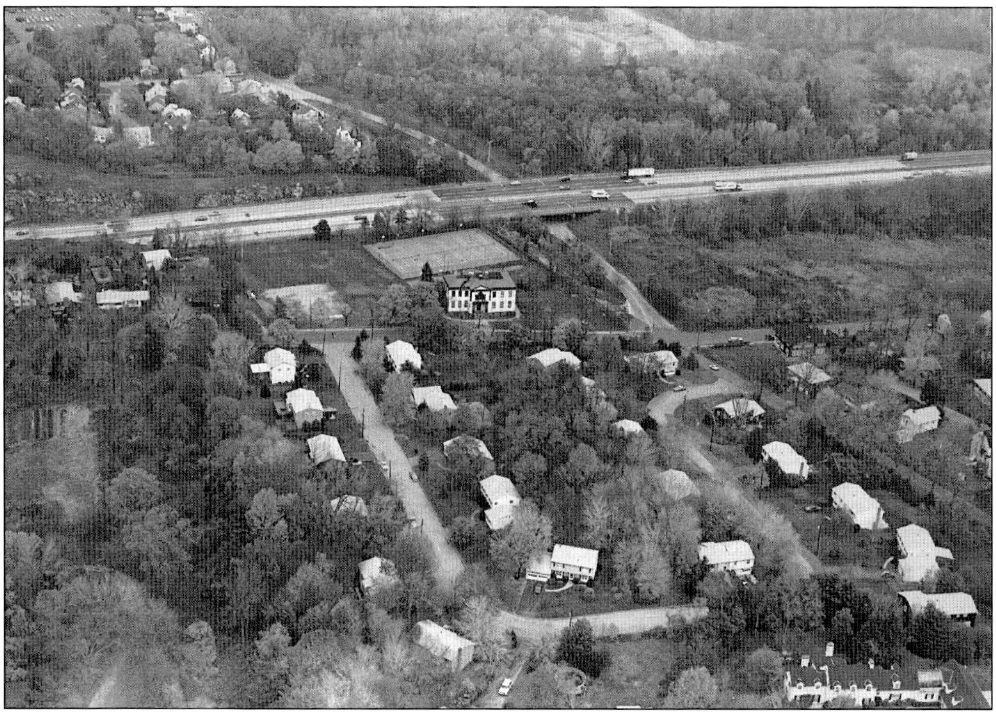

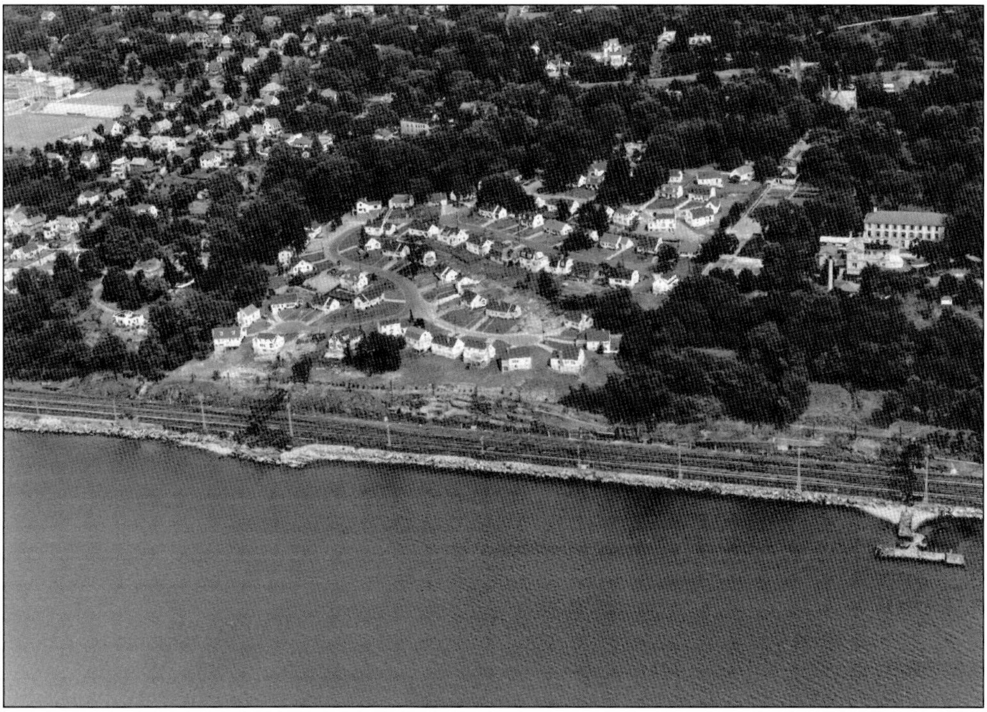

Proximity to New York City with commuter access via the Hudson River Railroad encouraged suburban residential development during the 20th century. Before and after World War II, residential developments such as Tappan Landing became a necessity for the growing population, which had increased to 17,669 by 1950.

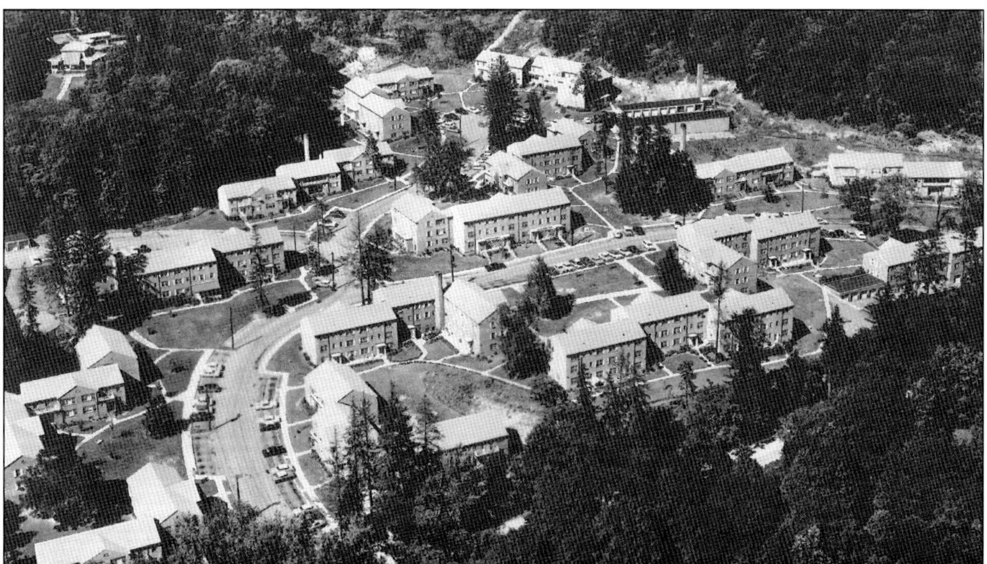

Sleepy Hollow Gardens Apartments, located adjacent to the White Plains Road, was a planned development during the postwar construction boom. The New York City developers of the complex initially offered small investors preferred stock as limited partners in the corporation.

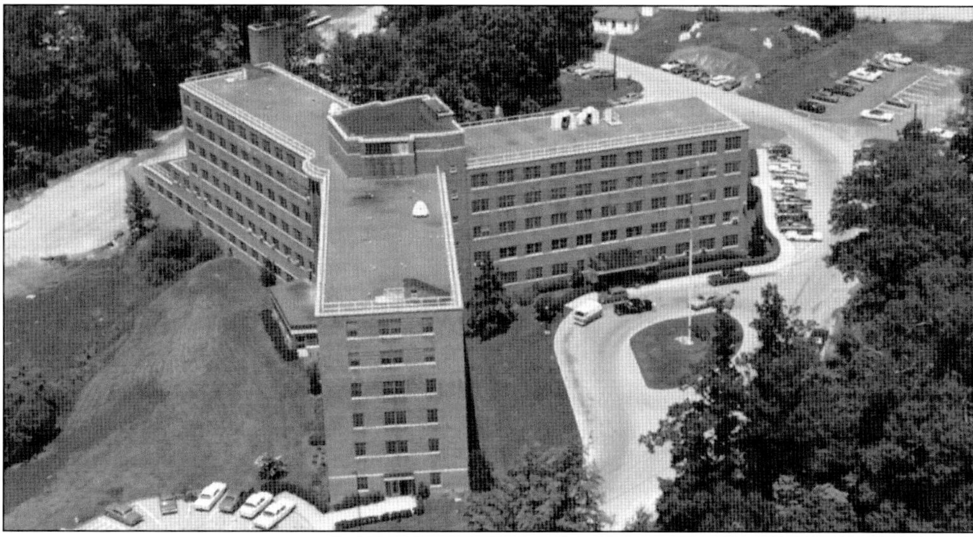

When the Tarrytown Hospital became antiquated, a proposed hospital on the Luke estate was overturned by the building of the Tappan Zee Bridge. Tarrytown and Ossining united to establish a new hospital with land and funds from the James Foundation. Additional donations from the Rockefeller family and local physicians enabled the construction of Phelps Memorial Hospital. It opened in 1956 to serve needs of the growing population, which reached 19,927 by 1960.

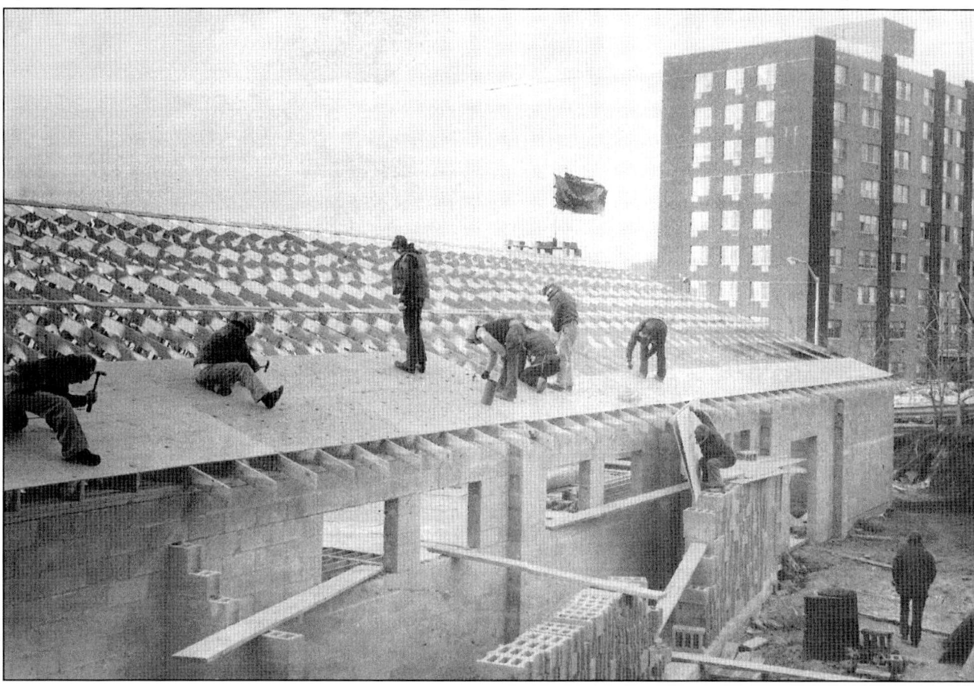

As part of Tarrytown's urban renewal project, land at Franklin and Main Streets became available, and the Portuguese American Citizens Club acquired the property. The club building (shown under construction and completed in 1981) became a vital part of the cultural and social life for 200 local families. After 1980, Hispanic immigrants from several countries moved to the area. The large number of Spanish-speaking children in the public schools reflected the diverse cultures and traditions of the growing population.

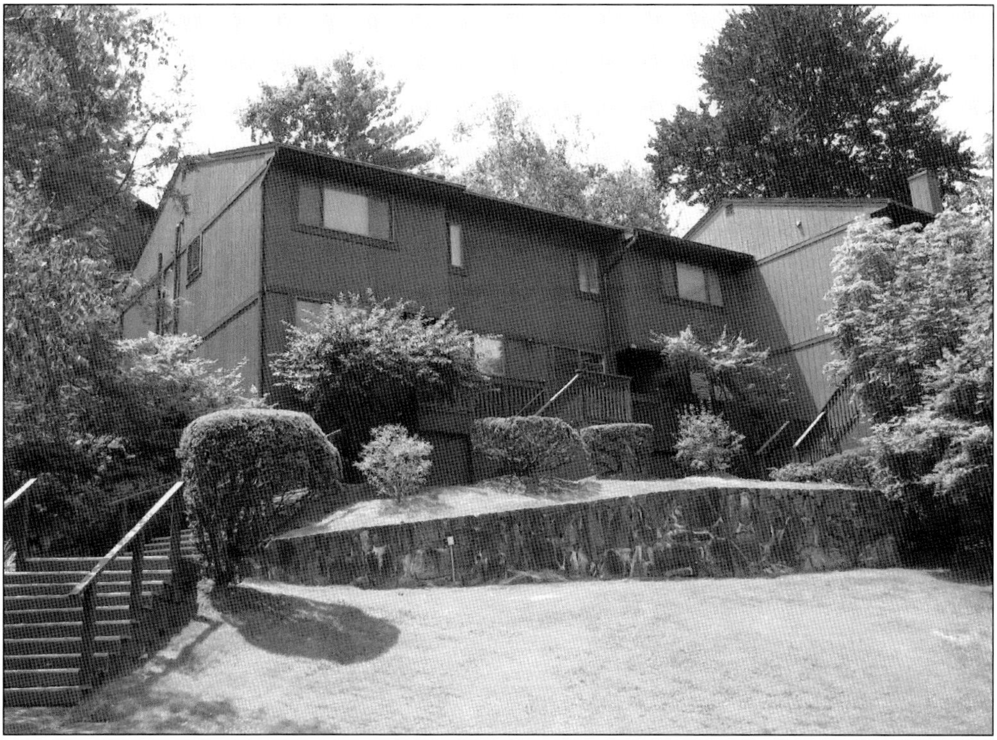

When Julian Detmer lived in Edgemont Castle on Benedict Avenue, the property had nearly 850 varieties of meticulously maintained flowers, trees, and shrubs. Although the population of the villages was not growing as quickly, the property was developed into a 188-unit condominium complex after the castle was destroyed by fire in 1971. Much of the beauty of the landscape remained, with scenic pathways and a variety of plantings throughout the 23-acre site.

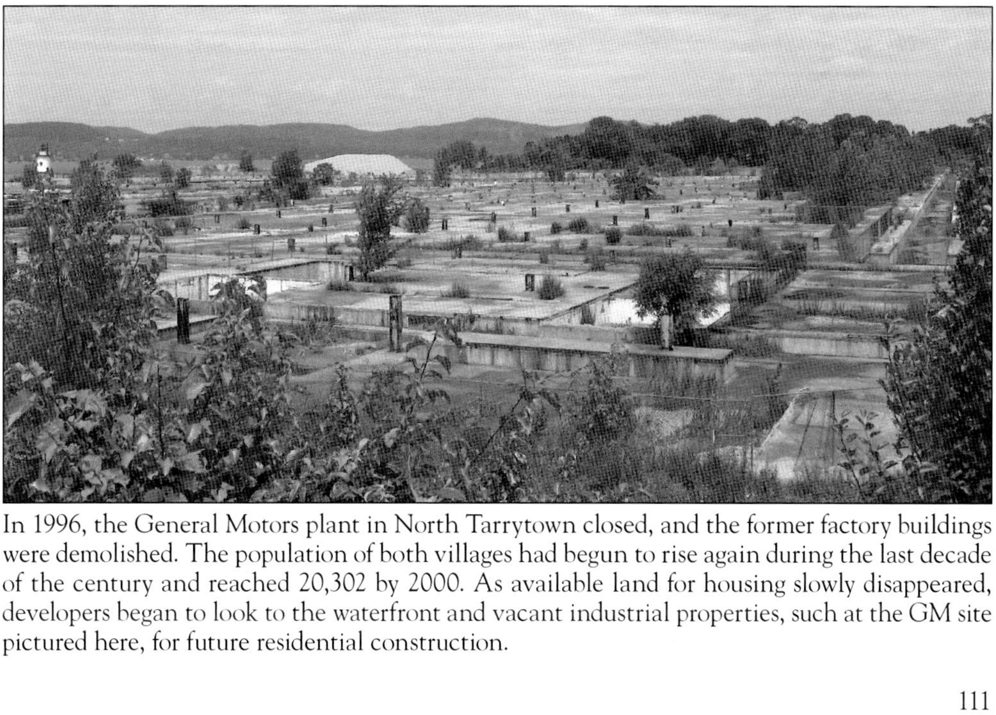

In 1996, the General Motors plant in North Tarrytown closed, and the former factory buildings were demolished. The population of both villages had begun to rise again during the last decade of the century and reached 20,302 by 2000. As available land for housing slowly disappeared, developers began to look to the waterfront and vacant industrial properties, such at the GM site pictured here, for future residential construction.

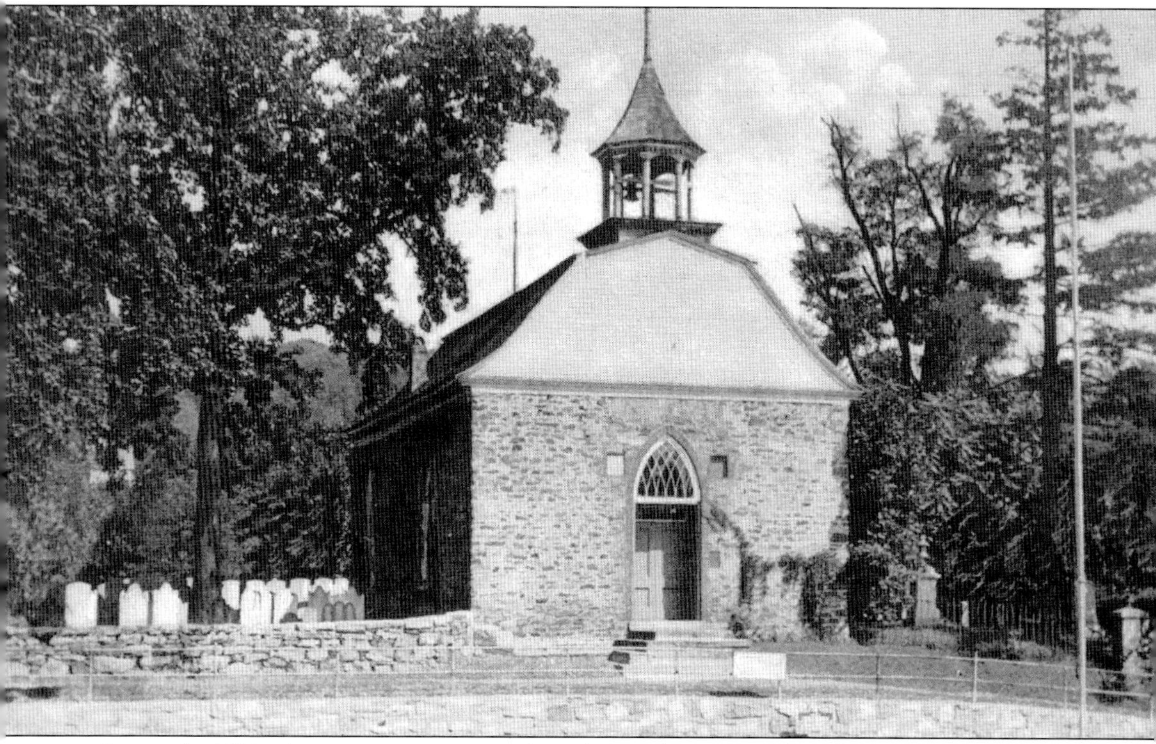

During the 1980s, there were many proposals to change the name of the village of North Tarrytown (incorporated in 1874) to Sleepy Hollow. After two unsuccessful attempts, village residents voted to change the name to Sleepy Hollow in December 1996. Voters expressed many different reasons for supporting the name change, including to celebrate the village's literary connections to Washington Irving's *Legend of Sleepy Hollow* and to distinguish it from neighboring Tarrytown. Following the vote, village and state signs as well as police and fire department vehicles were changed to reflect the new name. Each December, a group of residents gathers at the Old Dutch Church and marks the successful vote with a commemorative ringing of the bell.

# *Ten*

# A Few Favorites

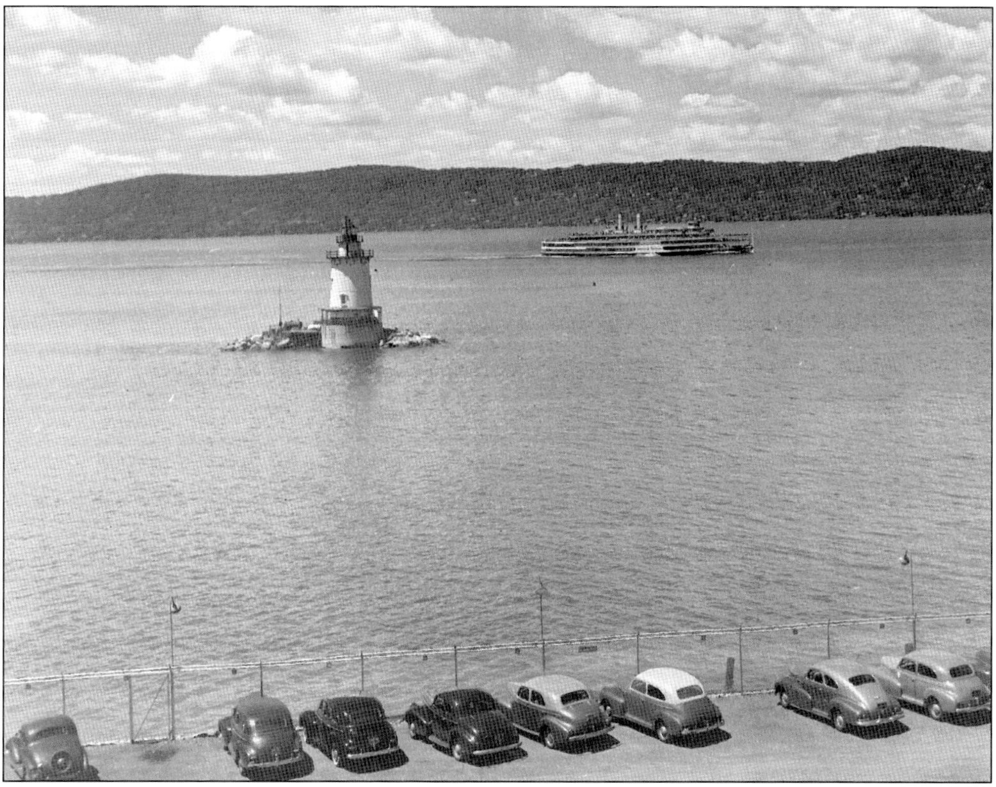

Among the treasured photographs in the archives of the Historical Society, Inc., are numerous images that have become favorites for many visitors. The following pages contain a small sampling of these favorites from the 20th century. This view dates to the late 1940s and shows the lighthouse prior to General Motors landfilling activities. The *Hendrick Hudson* dayliner, scrapped in 1951, is shown in the background transporting tourists on a trip up the Hudson River.

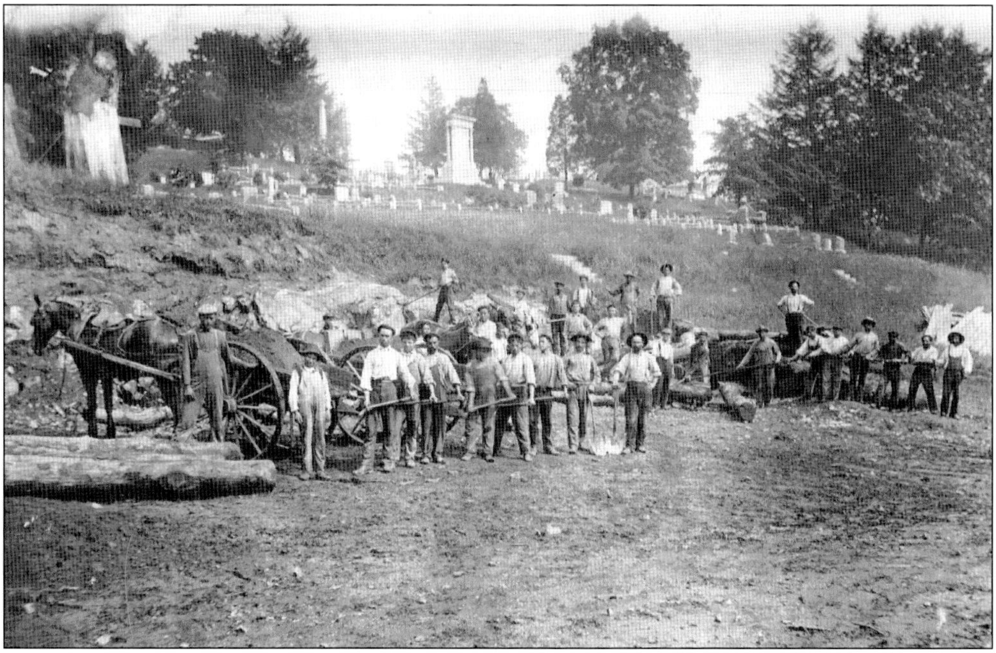

Dating from the first decade of the 20th century, this photograph shows Italian immigrants, who lived on Division Street, working to build the stone wall between North Broadway and Sleepy Hollow Cemetery. The crew is cutting down trees and breaking up the bedrock using only hand tools.

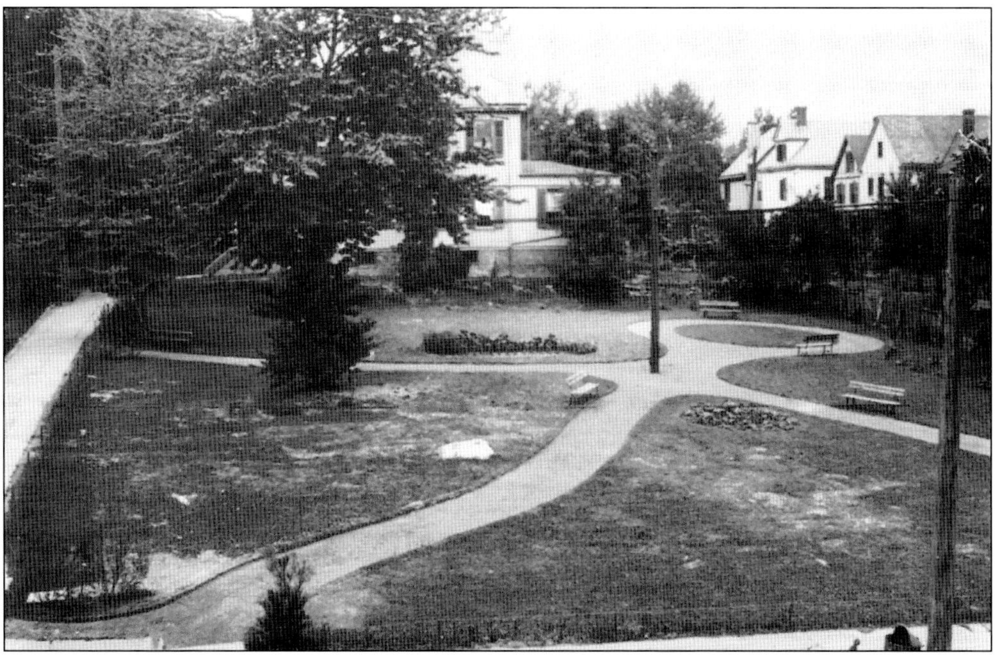

Dean Park was located at the corner of Main Street and Broadway from 1912 to 1923. Newspaperman Edward W. Harden donated the park to the people of Tarrytown after the old Dean Corner Store was demolished. The park was sold to a developer in 1923, and a large commercial building was constructed on the site.

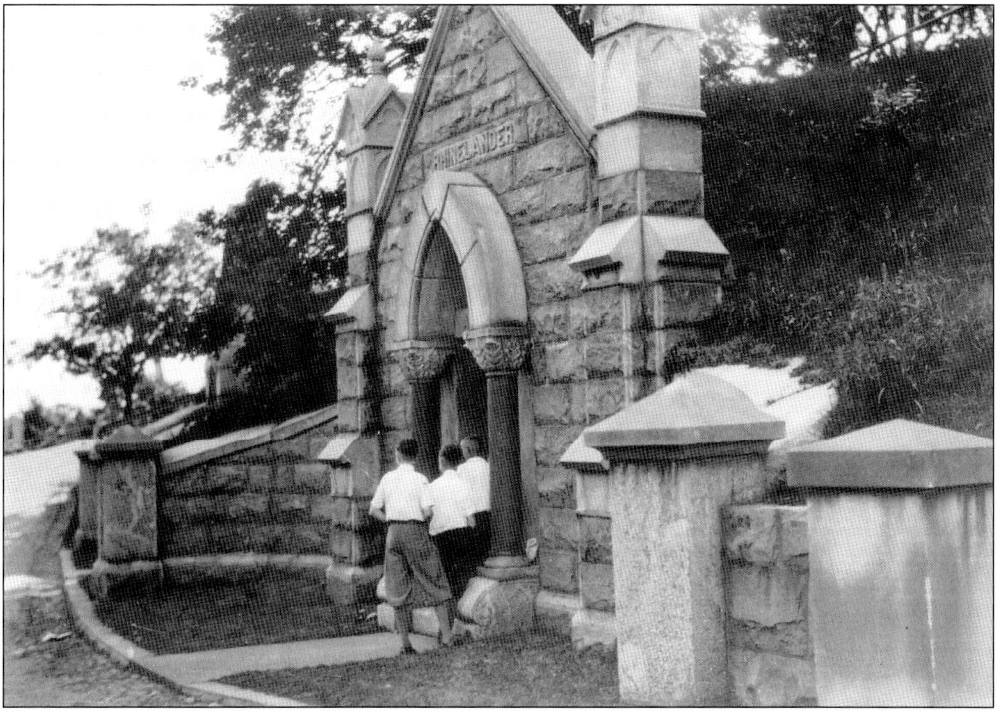


Three young boys in their knickers are shown hiding at the Rhinelander mausoleum in Sleepy Hollow Cemetery. The cemetery offered residents a quiet refuge to walk and visit their ancestors, and children an imaginative location to search for the Headless Horseman.

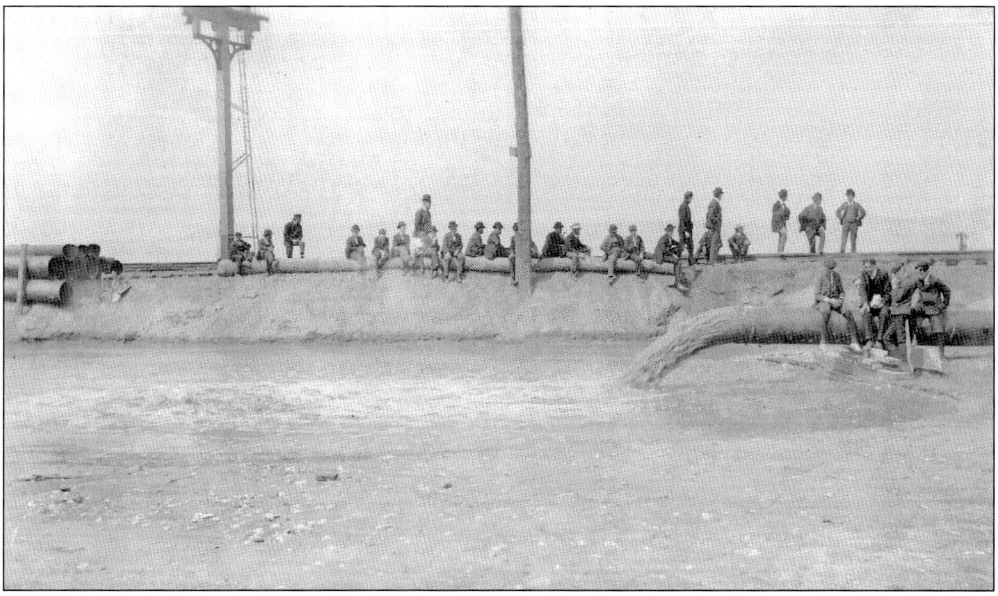

During the early 20th century, Leslie V. Case took several photographs of the landfill activities that took place along the waterfront. This image depicts the large pipes utilized by New York Central to pump sand from the river bottom into the bay for the creation of a freight yard along the waterfront. Residents found the process fascinating and would often watch the progress of the project for hours.

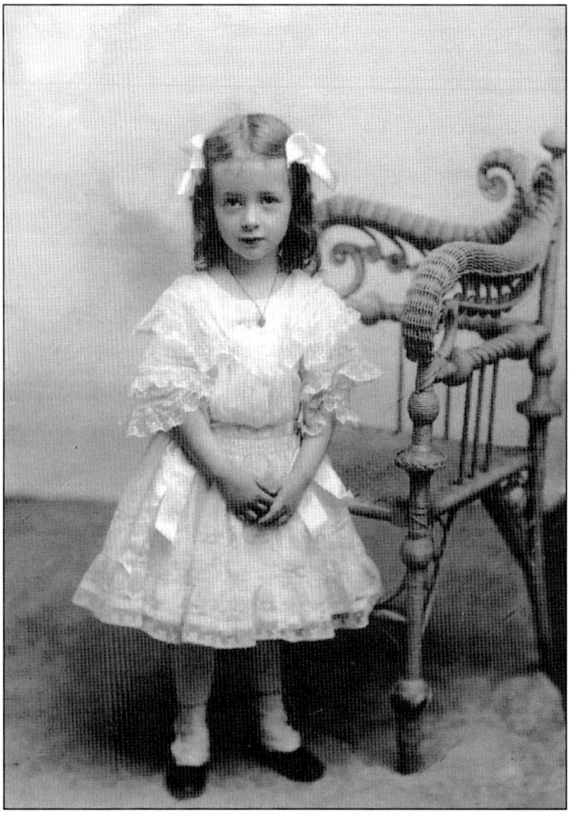

The Historical Society, Inc., has many pictures of children in its archives. This charming and favorite picture from the early part of the century shows Helen Hoar posing in a white dress with bows and ruffles when she was about seven years old. As an adult, she became active as a Girl Scouts leader and participated in other community organizations.

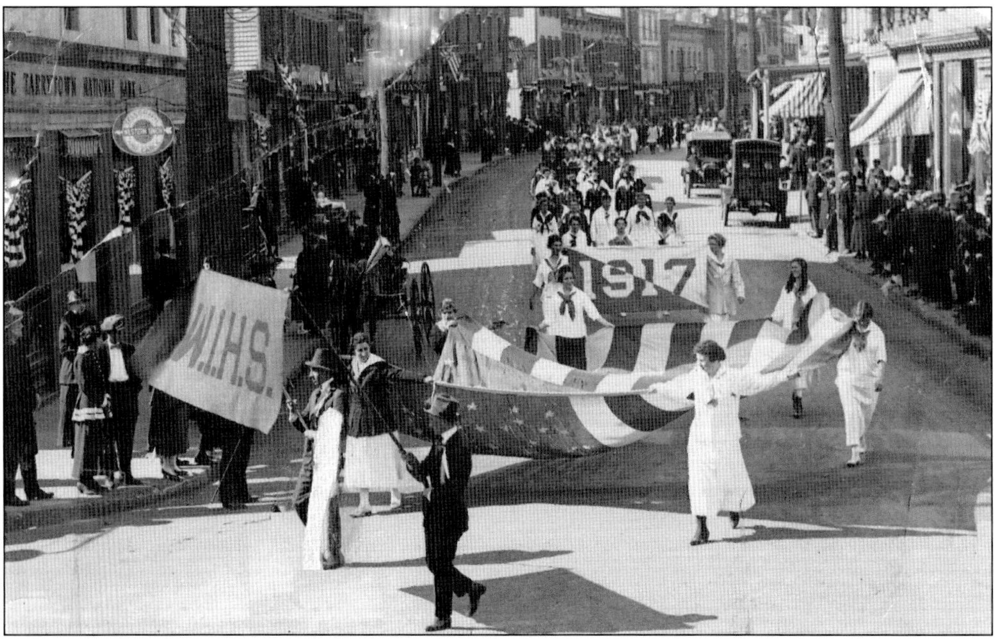


The Washington Irving High School class of 1917 is shown in this photograph marching in a parade on Orchard Street. Class members are carrying a large American flag down the unpaved road as residents watch from the sidewalks.

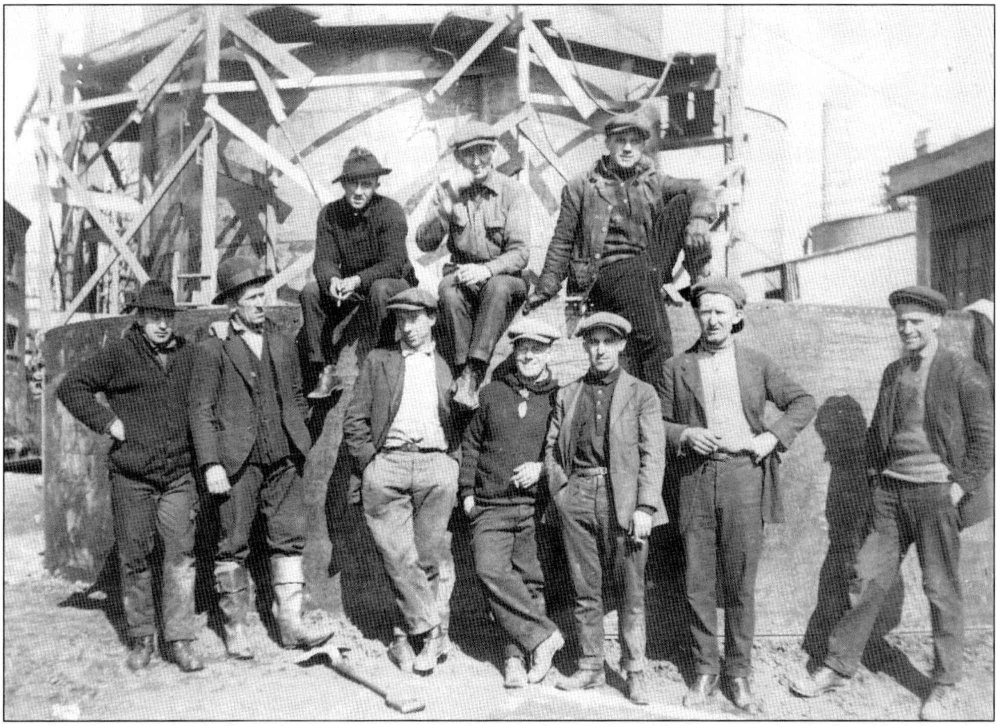

Workers at the Tarrytown and Irvington Union Gas Company are shown taking a break in front of one of the company's large storage tanks.

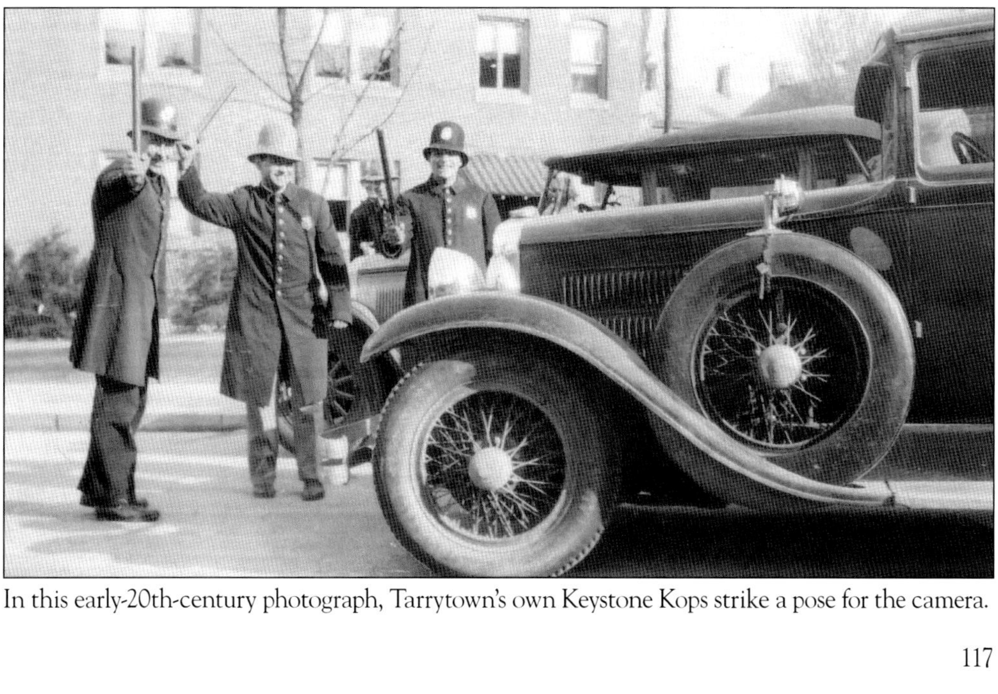

In this early-20th-century photograph, Tarrytown's own Keystone Kops strike a pose for the camera.

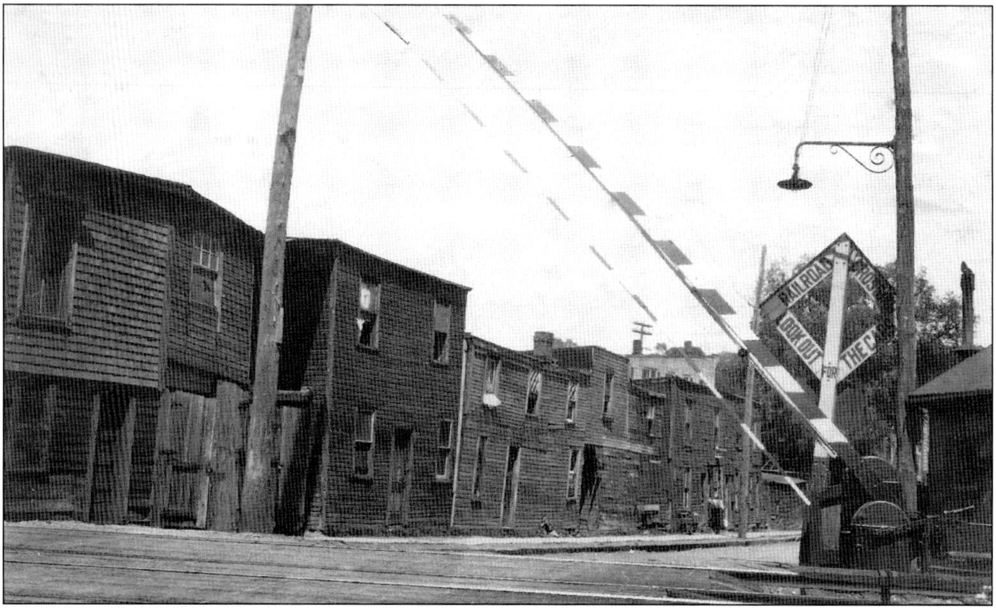


The Peek-a-Boo Flats, shown here around 1911, were located to the east of the railroad tracks on Wildey Street. The Flats were notorious tenements where the local police were summoned almost nightly. During one visit when Tarrytown police chief William Bowles and his men raided the apartments, a female resident tossed a kerosene lamp at the men and set the wooden buildings on fire. The burned-out ruins were subsequently demolished.

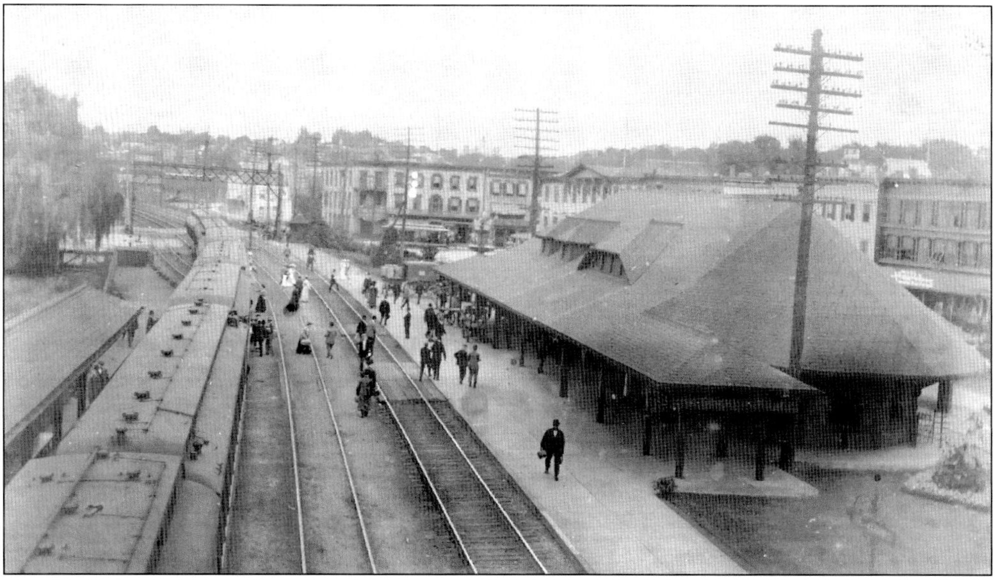

Prior to 1925 and the construction of the H-Bridge, residents had to walk across the tracks to catch a train or to get to the waterfront. This photograph depicts a typical day at the busy railroad station in the early 20th century. The commercial buildings of Depot Plaza, several of which were demolished after a fire in 1907, can be seen behind the station.

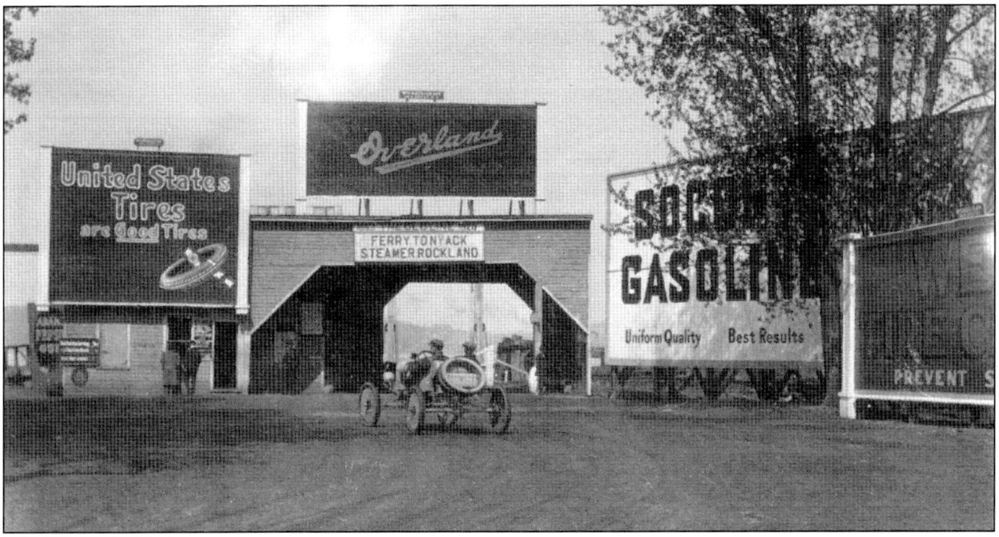


The photograph above shows the old ferry landing on the waterfront in 1920. Several times each day the steamer *Rockland* would shuttle passengers between Tarrytown and Nyack.

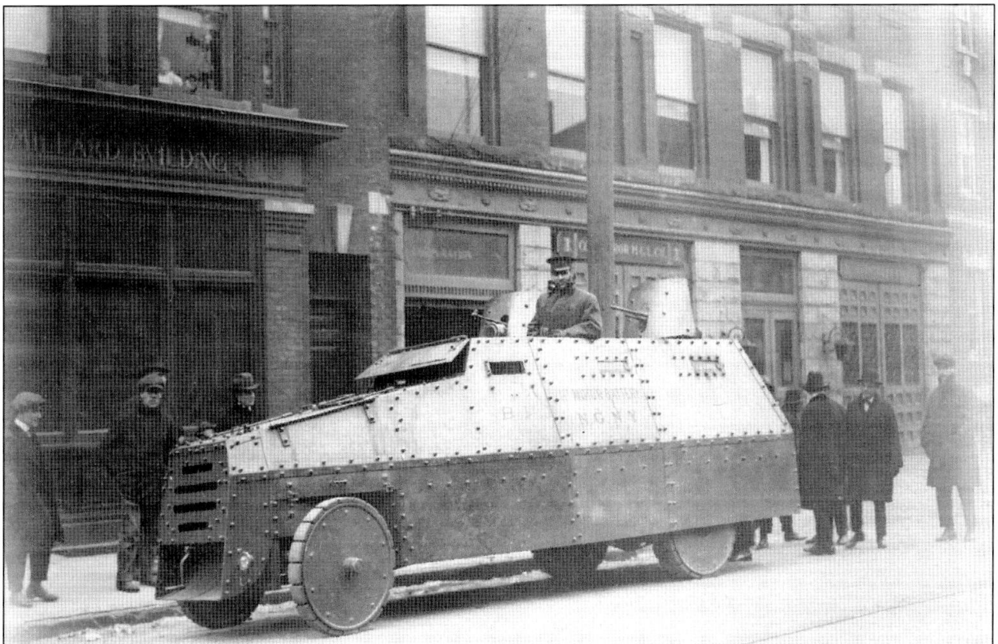


The first armored motor battery of the National Guard New York (NGNY) caused quite a stir when it was parked in front of the Corporation Building on Main Street in the 1920s.

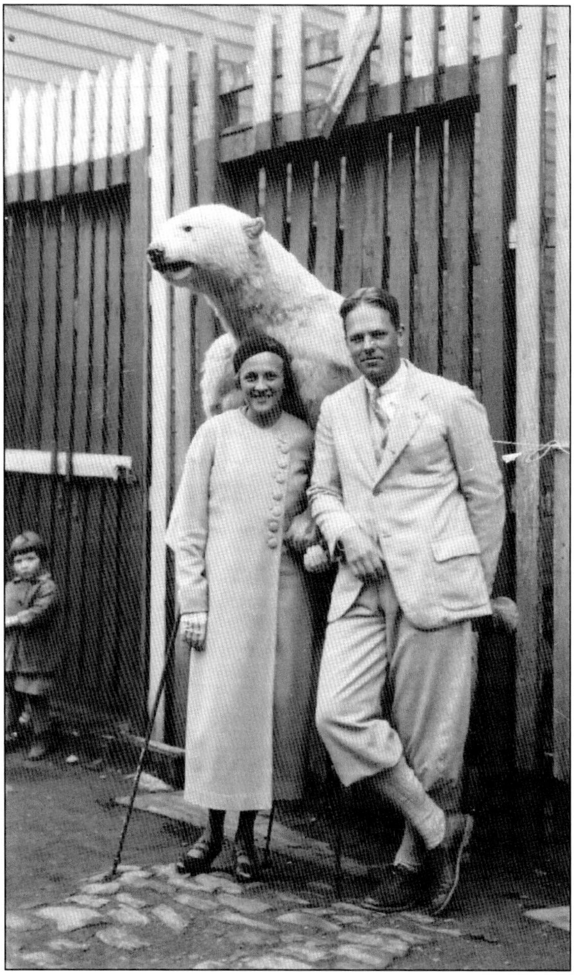

Local socialites, the Detmers are shown during their travels posing with a polar bear. A former navy flyer, Eugene Detmer often participated in air shows during the 1920s and 1930s. Esther Marie Detmer spent a great deal of time at social and charitable events in New York City and Florida.

F. R. Pierson's successful flower and plant business, located in Tarrytown and Scarborough, won many awards at flower shows, including five gold medals for the Mrs. F. R. Pierson Rose, named for his wife. In 1912, he opened a large retail store, where his greenhouses were formerly located, on the corner of McKeel Avenue and Broadway. Villagers are shown gathered in front of the store to celebrate the grand opening.

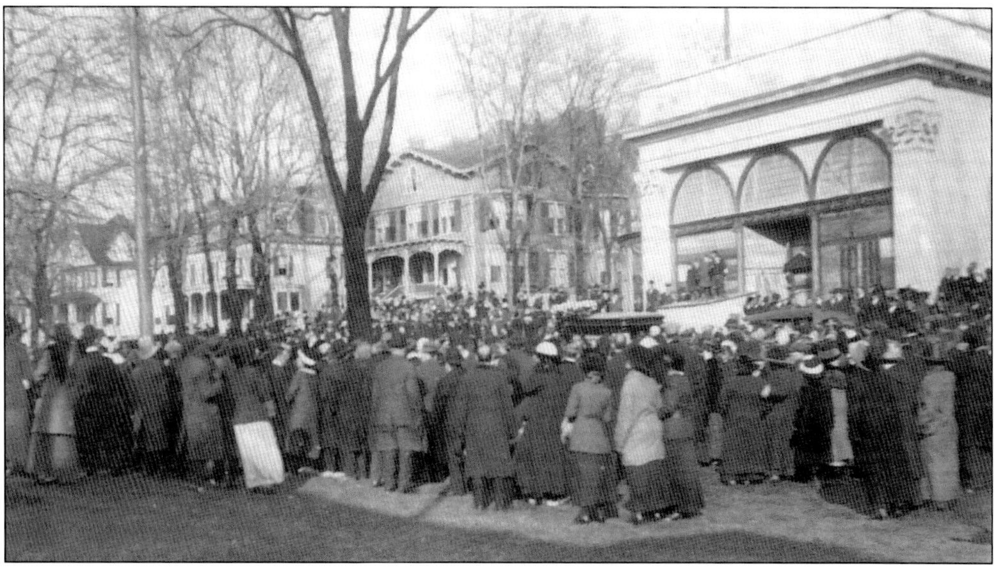

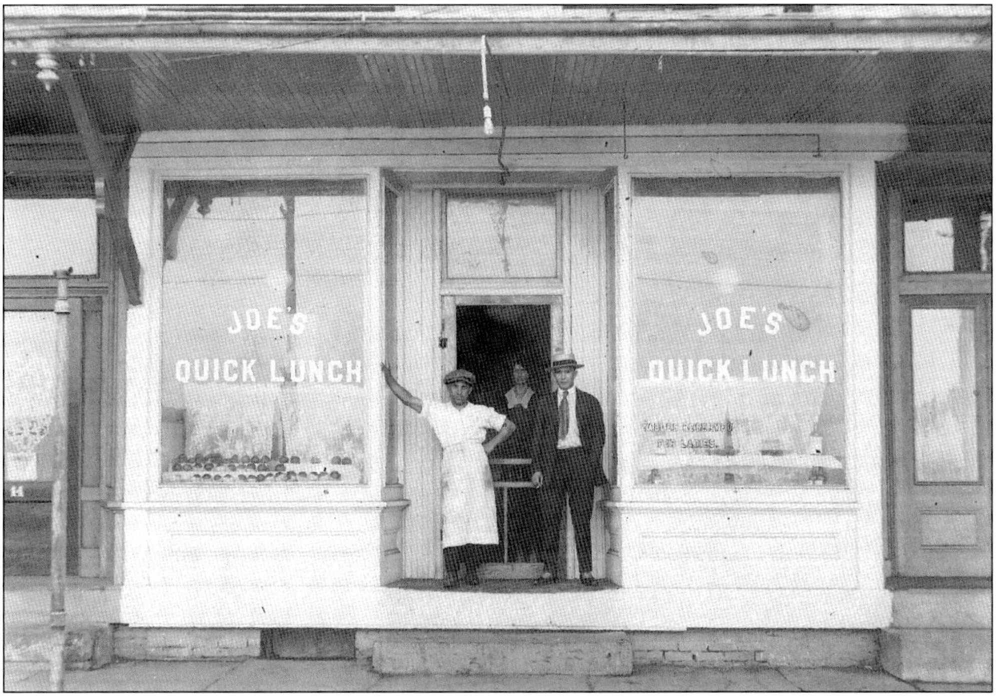


Joe's Quick Lunch was one of many small family-owned businesses that flourished in the early part the 20th century. Serving local laborers and businessmen, it also promoted "tables reserved for ladies."

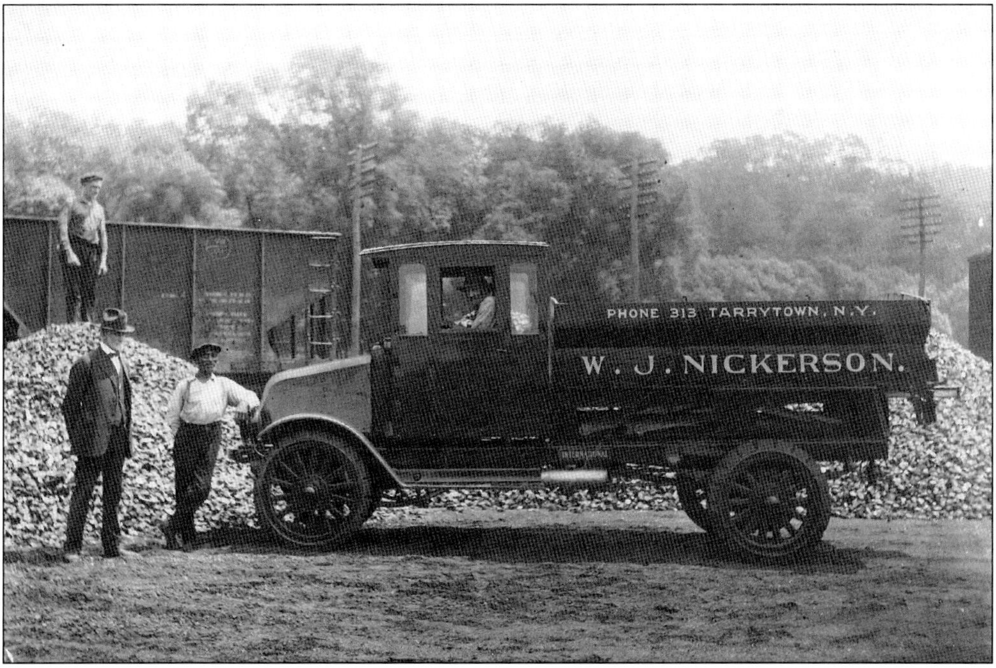


Walter J. Nickerson advertised that he sold the best grades of anthracite coal from his yard located at 202 Main Street. For over 25 years, before most residents stopped using coal to heat their homes, Nickerson kept the houses of Tarrytowners warm.

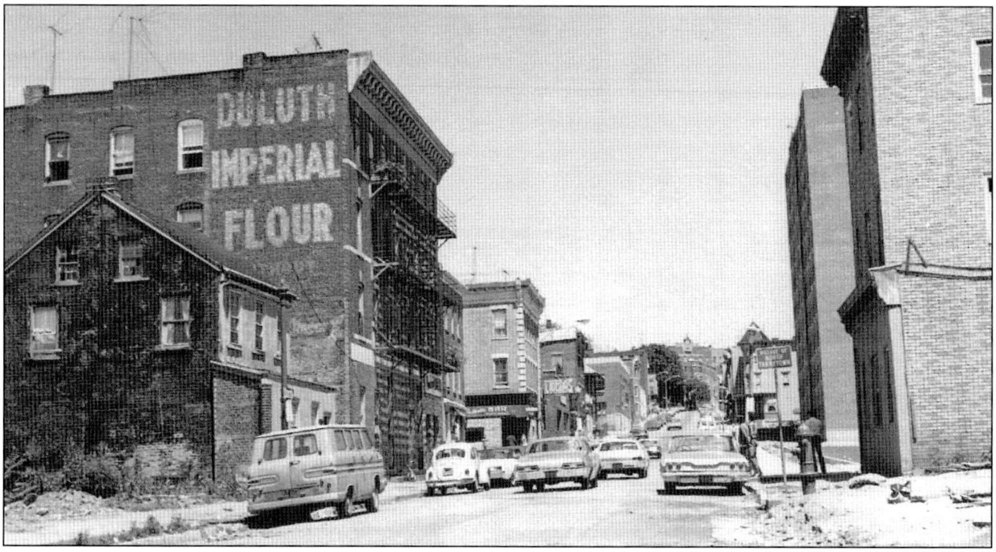


In this 1972 photograph, a familiar advertisement—"Duluth Imperial Flour, Without Rival"—is visible on a Cortlandt Street building. During the early 20th century, many advertising slogans were painted directly on the exterior of brick buildings. The ghosts of these signs remained long after the companies had ceased to exist.

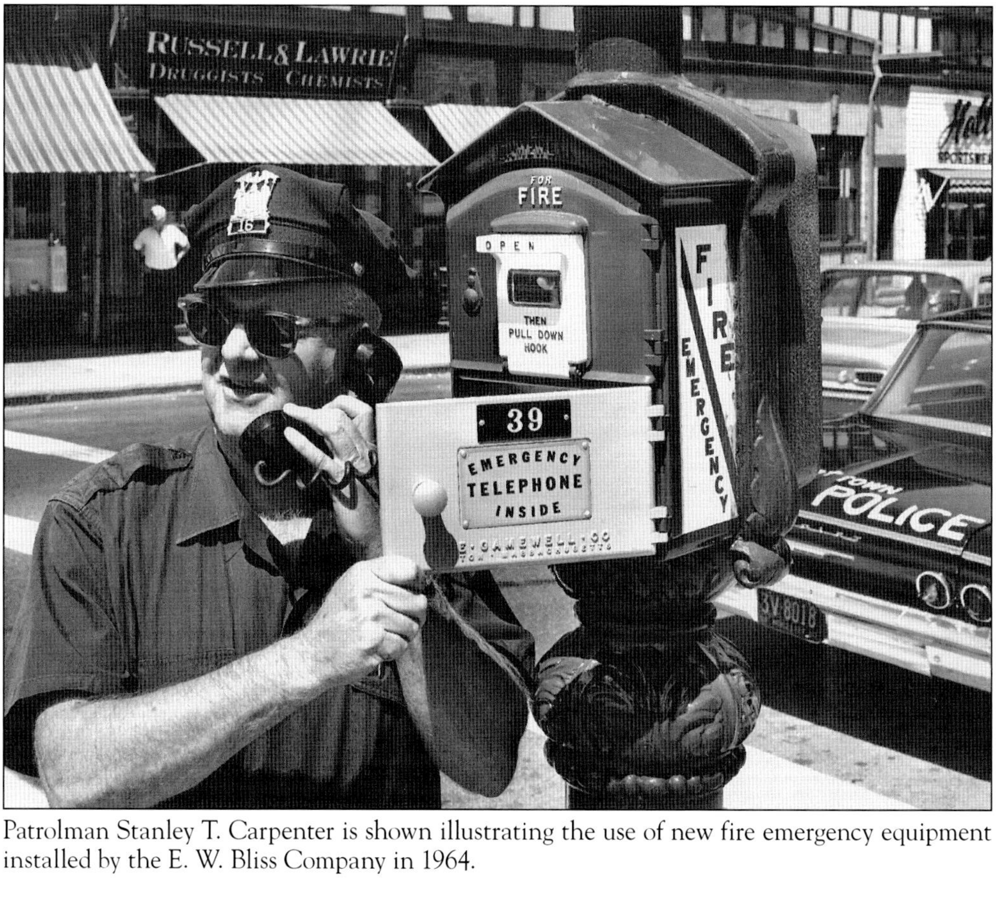


Patrolman Stanley T. Carpenter is shown illustrating the use of new fire emergency equipment installed by the E. W. Bliss Company in 1964.

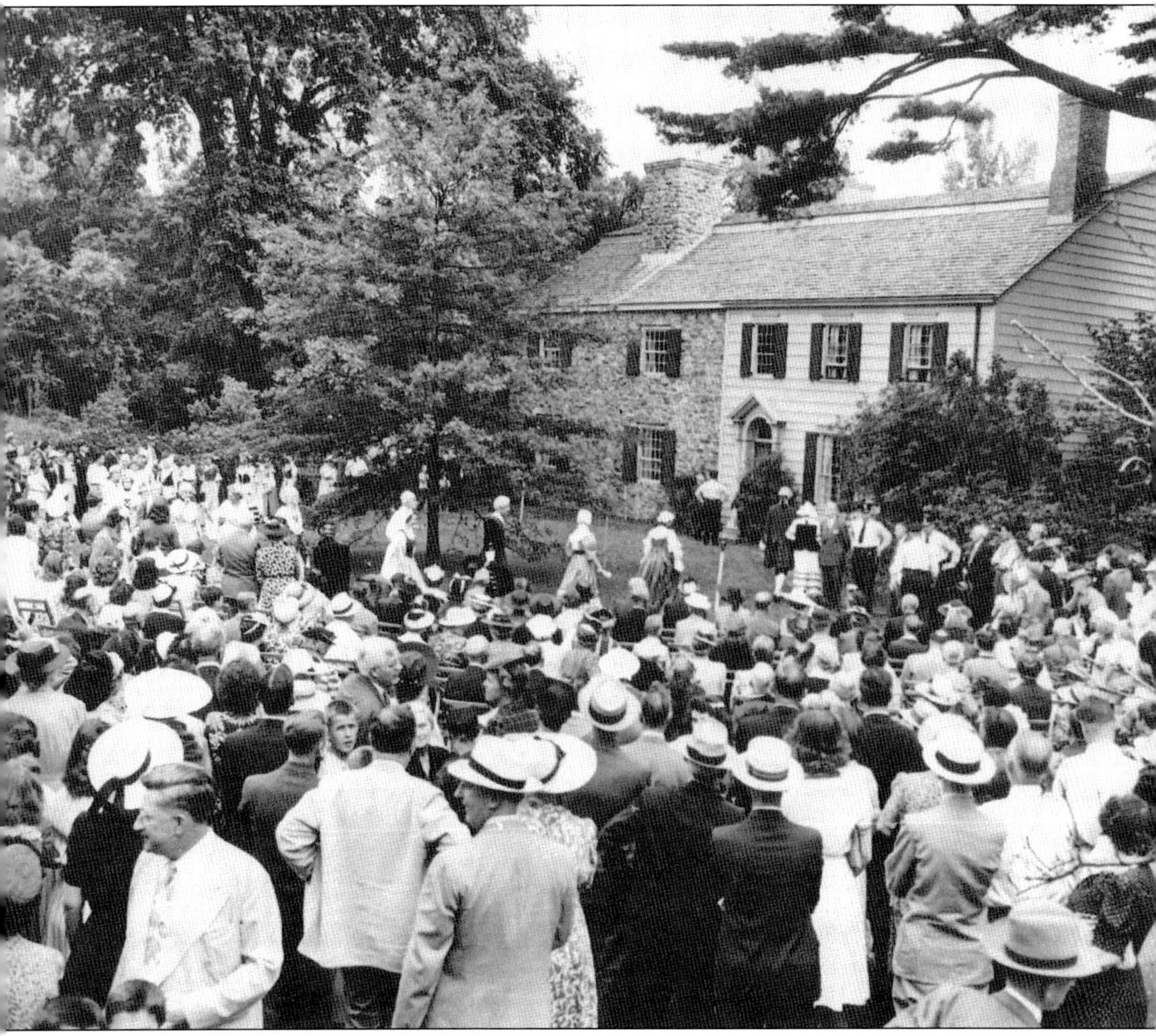

On July 4, 1943, Philipse Castle opened its doors after five years of extensive restoration work. The property consisted of 10 acres of land, the Philipse Manor House (including the wing added by Gerard Beekman), the Old Mill, the Smokehouse, and the foundations of the old stable. The grounds also had picnic areas and a natural amphitheater. The celebration, hosted by the Historical Society, Inc., featured costumed guides and interpreters and was attended by local dignitaries and villagers from Tarrytown, North Tarrytown, and surrounding communities.

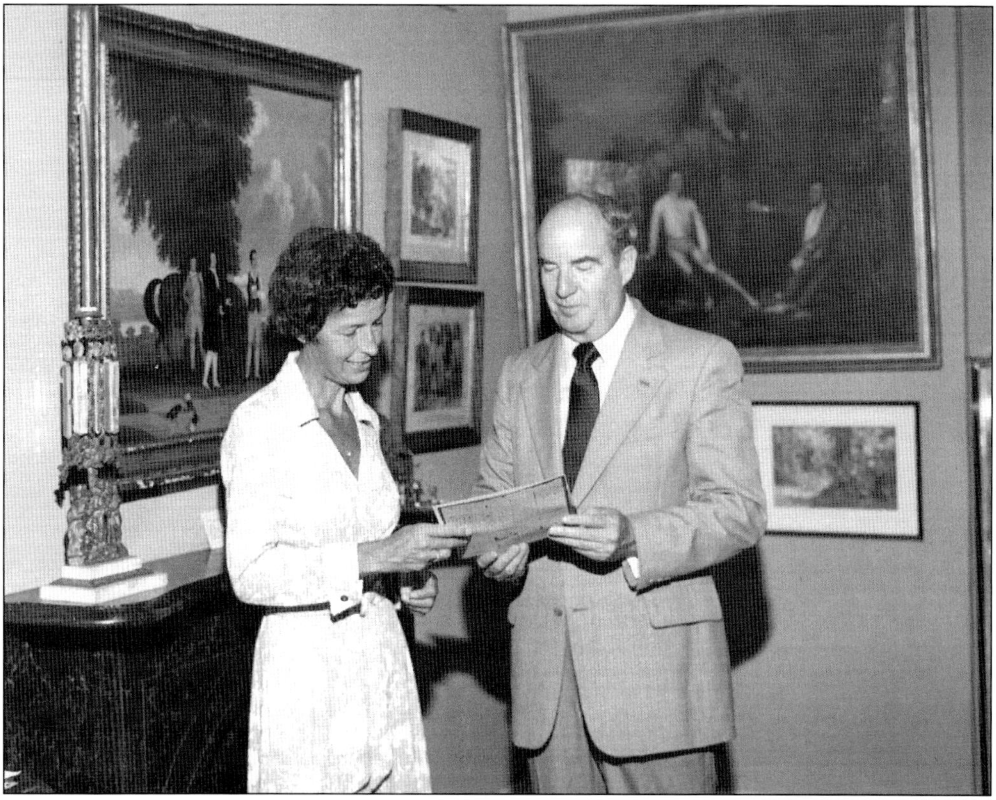

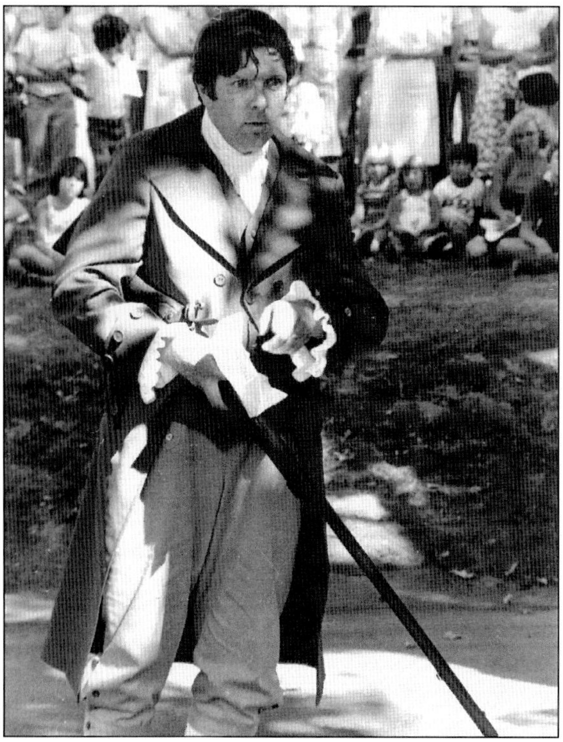

The Historical Society, Inc., located at One Grove Street, owns a collection of artifacts and documents relating to the capture of Maj. John Andre by three local militiamen during the Revolutionary War. Ann Phillips, a member of the society, is showing a visitor replicas of the secret plans Benedict Arnold had given to Andre to pass on to the British command.

David Logan, a lifelong resident of the community, is shown participating in a reenactment of the capture of Major Andre during a commemorative event. The Historical Society, Inc., sponsored such events on significant anniversaries throughout the century.

The Boys Choir of the Tarrytowns was started in 1973 at Christ Church under the direction of Jane Schoener. By 1975, members were singing at various locations throughout the villages. They performed sacred and secular music at Philipsburg Manor, many local churches, Rockefeller Center in New York City, and Tappan Hill Restaurant. Shown at the Goebel Collectors Club in Tarrytown, the boys pose for the cover of their first recording.

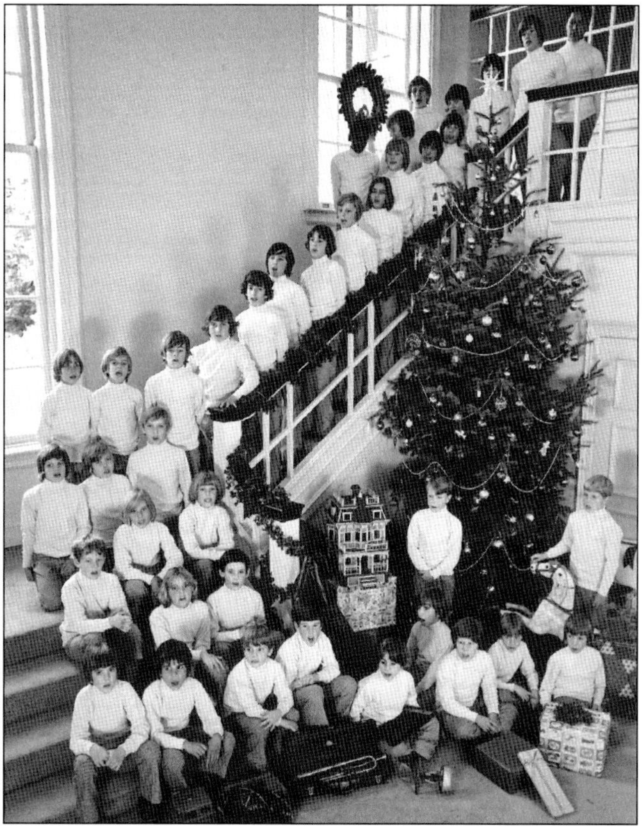

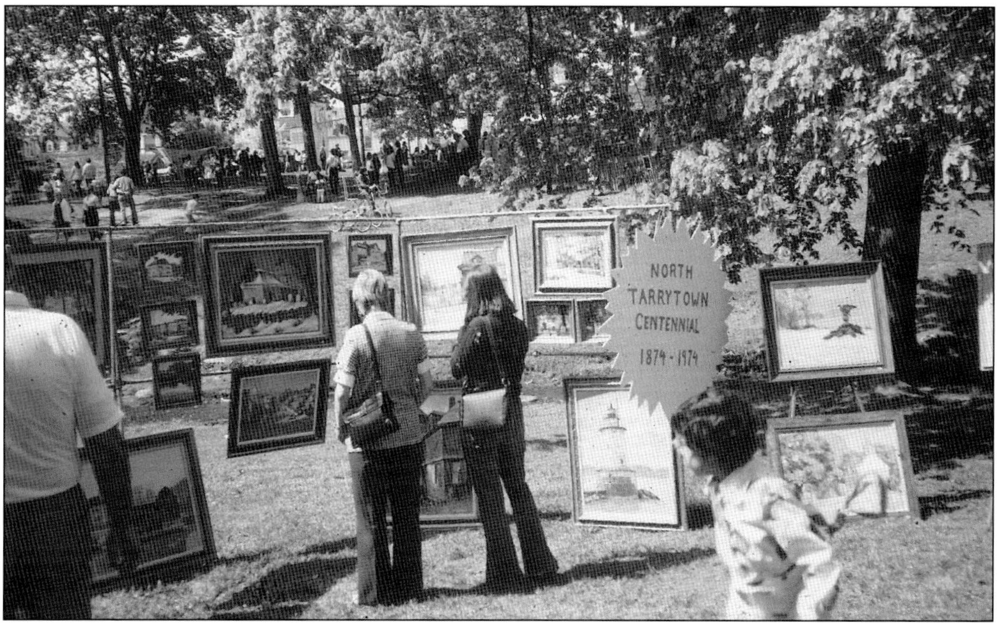


Art in the Park was an annual festival held in Patriots Park beginning in the 1960s. The Friends of the Warner Library started this event, which featured local artists, music, crafts, refreshments, and a book sale. This photograph shows one of the displays in the summer of 1974.

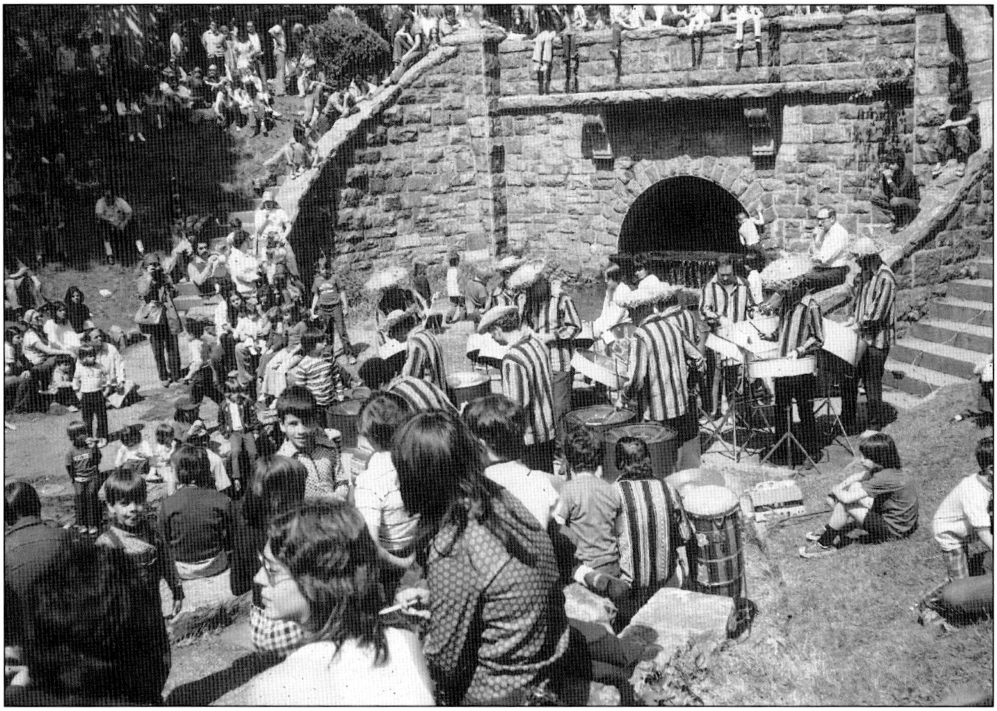

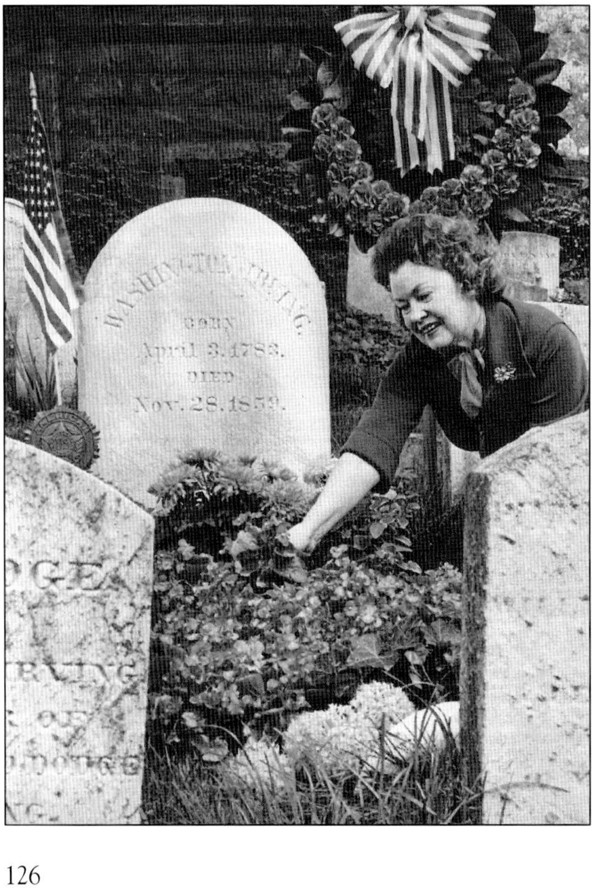


A local steel band is shown playing at an Art in the Park Festival during the 1970s. Residents were treated to a variety of bands during the three days of this annual community event.

Mrs. Jack Dorland (Betty), the national director of the Washington Irving Graveplot Restoration, tends to Irving's grave at Sleepy Hollow Cemetery. After discovering that the Irving family plot had become overgrown and unsightly, Dorland spearheaded the movement to clean and repair the gravestones during the 1970s. She spent the next two decades working with volunteers to ensure that Irving's grave was maintained.

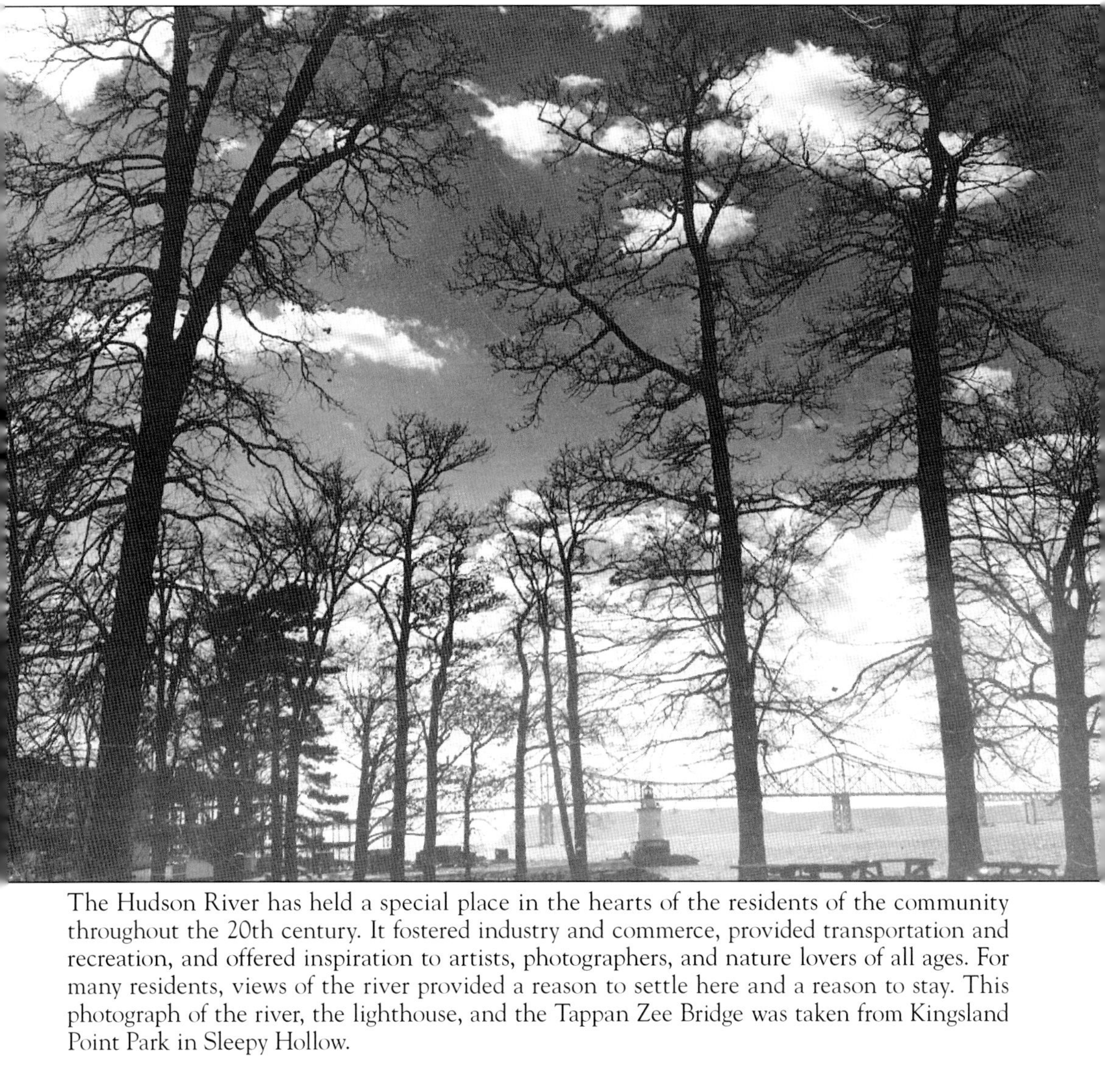

The Hudson River has held a special place in the hearts of the residents of the community throughout the 20th century. It fostered industry and commerce, provided transportation and recreation, and offered inspiration to artists, photographers, and nature lovers of all ages. For many residents, views of the river provided a reason to settle here and a reason to stay. This photograph of the river, the lighthouse, and the Tappan Zee Bridge was taken from Kingsland Point Park in Sleepy Hollow.

Consistent with our mission to preserve history on a local level, this book was printed in South Carolina on American-made paper and manufactured entirely in the United States. Products carrying the accredited Forest Stewardship Council (FSC) label are printed on 100 percent FSC-certified paper.

MADE IN THE USA